KU-825-779

# THE·POLITICS·OF
# HEALTH
## EDUCATION
### RAISING THE ISSUES

—EDITED BY—
## SUE RODMELL & ALISON WATT

E02910

# THE·POLITICS·OF
# HEALTH
## EDUCATION
### RAISING THE ISSUES

—EDITED BY—
## SUE RODMELL & ALISON WATT

ROUTLEDGE & KEGAN PAUL
LONDON

First published in 1986 by
Routledge & Kegan Paul Ltd
11 New Fetter Lane, London EC4P 4EE

Set in 11/13pt Bembo
and printed in Great Britain
by Butler & Tanner Ltd,
Frome, Somerset

©Alison Watt and Sue Rodmell 1986
No part of this book may be reproduced in any form without permission from the publisher
except for the quotation of brief passages
in criticism

British Library Cataloguing in Publication Data
The Politics of health education: raising the issues
1. Health education—Great Britain
I. Rodmell, Sue    II. Watt, Alison
613'.07'041        RA440.3.G7
ISBN 0-7102-0879-0

# CONTENTS

# CONTENTS

# LIST OF CONTRIBUTORS

MARY BOULTON was Research Associate for the Health and Prevention Project in the Department of General Practice, Guy's Hospital Medical School.

MICHAEL CALNAN is Research Fellow in the Health Services Research Unit, University of Kent.

NICKIE CHARLES was Research Fellow in the Department of Sociology, University of York, and now lectures in Sociology in the Department of Sociology and Anthropology, University College of Swansea.

ALAN CRIBB is Research Officer for the Cancer Research Campaign, Education and Child Studies Research Group, University of Manchester.

WENDY FARRANT was Senior Research Officer at the University of London, Institute of Education, and now lectures in Health Education in the Academic Department of Community Medicine, St Mary's Hospital, Paddington.

MARION KERR was Research Fellow in the Department of Sociology, University of York.

GED MORAN was Health Adviser to the London Borough of Greenwich and is now Health Liaison Officer for Leeds City Council.

JENNIE NAIDOO was Research and Projects Officer for the

Health Education Service in Avon, and is now Health Education Officer for Bristol and Weston District Health Authority.

MAGGIE PEARSON was Director of the Centre for Ethnic Minority Health Studies and now lectures in Medical Sociology in the Department of General Practice, University of Liverpool.

SUE RODMELL is District Health Education Officer for Hounslow and Spelthorne Health Authority.

JILL RUSSELL was Research Officer at the University of London, Institute of Education.

ALISON WATT was Development Officer for the Community Health Initiatives Resource Unit, and now lectures in Community Health Education at the University of Bradford.

ANDREW WATTERSON worked for the General, Municipal and Boilermakers Allied Trade Union, and now lectures in Industrial and Health Studies at the University of Southampton.

ANTHONY WILLIAMS is Research Associate for the Health and Prevention Project, in the Department of General Practice, Guy's Hospital Medical School.

# PREFACE

Whilst there is no direct link between the London-based Feminist Health Education Officers Group (founded in 1980 and now a little weary) and this publication, the ideas, insights and angers generated in those meetings were certainly significant in our decision to produce the book. The sense of isolation we all experienced as HEOs attempting to pitch ourselves against conventional wisdom reinforced our assessment that a book of this nature was well due. The meetings of the feminist HEOs, often held after hours in the shabbier end of London's range of alternative venues, acted as a vital source of support in a period when health education departments were undergoing major changes. We recognised then, as now, that we were lucky: there were enough of us to form a group. To those who are still isolated we hope this book will go some way towards creating an acceptance and respect for critical analysis, and that the airing of radical politics in health education will gain as much common currency as that currently enjoyed by the airing of conservative politics.

The sorts of people who tread the politics of health circuit were our imagined audience during the preparation of the book. This helped us to develop consistent criteria in selecting and editing contributions. We expect that the actual audience will be composed of a much wider readership. All students and practitioners of health education will find the book relevant. We hope, however, that people interested and involved in all aspects of health and illness will pursue the text, for two reasons. Firstly, because so much of health work *is* health education, whether it is recognised as such or not. Secondly, we believe that our call for an acknowledgment and understanding of the politics in and of health education is too important for any health worker to ignore.

# ACKNOWLEDGMENTS

Our contributors leapt into action and produced their chapters with very little prodding, and we are grateful to them all for making our task so much smoother than it is for many editors. The number of others who have helped us both through periods of excitement and crises of confidence in the production process are too numerous to list individually, but all are deeply appreciated. We extend special thanks to Janet Harrod for her unfailing reliability and for finding the tedious part of putting the book together interesting. Not surprisingly in a joint venture such as this, we have been most dependent upon each other for inspiration and ongoing support. So this is with thanks from one to the other.

For permission to reproduce illustrations and tables we thank: The Health Education Council for the illustration on p. 169; See Red Women's Workshop for the illustration on p. 168; Penguin Books Ltd for the table on p. 208; The Office of Population and Census Surveys for the table on p. 209.

We should like to point out that the views expressed here are those of the contributors in their personal capacities, and are not intended to represent the views of employing institutions or authorities.

# CHAPTER 1

# CONVENTIONAL HEALTH EDUCATION; PROBLEMS AND POSSIBILITIES

## Sue Rodmell and Alison Watt

One way or another, people have been engaged in health education for a long time. As a concept, its history stretches back as far as that of health care. As a discipline it can be traced from the mid-nineteenth century onwards, via the sanitary reforms, education acts and first attempts at health visiting. Finally, as a semi-profession, health education has been institutionalised within the National Health Service (NHS) for the last twelve years.

Today, depending upon its location, health education can still be conceived as a discipline, an occupation and, in generalist terms, as a profession. Within each of these three modes there are no standardised terms of reference for the philosophy, aims or methods of health education. It is practised at different levels, in different places, by different people. Consequently, the definitional problems involved are considerable. The most cursory inspection of any health education text reveals a heroic variety of attempts to get to grips with this common dilemma.

In a sense, our task has been easier, because we are not so much concerned with defining health education as with what actually happens when it is done. That people define themselves as health educators is sufficient. Our starting point is the politics of health education and our aim is to raise the issues, via radical critique, of much of existing practice. We mean here that practice which is set

1

within the medical model, founded on the principles of behaviourism and individualism, and which we can call conventional health education. In offering a radical critique, the contributors to this volume begin to 'get to the roots of' conventional health education. The subject areas represent as wide a range of issues as is possible in one book and reflect the diversity of health education as it is currently practised. Just as the authors do not speak with one voice about the nature of health education, neither do they exhibit a political consensus. All, however, also take as *their* starting point that the politics in and of health education cannot be ignored.

'The politics of' has become a recognisable strand in many disciplines. It suggests a reasoned excursion into the more radical issues on the political continuum of whichever discipline is under scrutiny. This use of the term 'politics' signifies the attempt to expose the inequitable distribution of, and access to, material resources, power and privileges in any given area. The underlying principle is that this inequity has unacceptable consequences for those who are deprived of a fair share in the allocation, whilst at the same time it allows the dominant social order its continued existence. To confine the term political to only radical analyses is not to suggest that conservative positions and practices are apolitical. On the contrary, the decision to do nothing, to make no change to the status quo, is an intensely political decision. It is, however, in the nature of most of our social order to allow conservative politics an unfair hearing. Applying the term radical to the left of the continuum is our attempt to redress this imbalance.

The extent to which health education is able to challenge inequities in the arena of inequalities in health and illness is the basic subject matter of this book. In this opening chapter we identify a number of problematic issues which recur throughout subsequent chapters: the extent of medical dominance over health education activities; the stereotyping of social groups according to their lifestyle; the notion of choice, and the significance of health promotion strategies for health education. The focus throughout is on formal rather than informal health education, as practised either in the health service by health professionals, or in another public authority by social welfare workers, or in a voluntary organisation. While we focus primarily on formal health education we acknowledge that the bulk of health education does not take place within a formal setting: women constitute the largest group of health educators as they perform their familial caring role (Graham, 1984). Tackling inequalities in people's experience of health and illness requires, however, that the statutory services be scrutinised, and in particular that the medical profession be recognised as a major determinant in the success or otherwise of formal health education.

We are aware that by focusing on the role of the medical profession in health education, we might be criticised for elevating doctors to a position of eminence that may be serving to reproduce the very medical dominance which some health educators find so problematic. It is important, though, to acknowledge that historically the medical profession has determined the ideological imperatives for health education, and continues to attempt to do so. To refer to health education in terms of this relationship with allopathic medicine is, however, at one and the same time to elevate and to demean. Health educators constantly seek affirmation of their activities from medical practitioners who retain the power to confer the necessary status, but at the same time seek to resist the medicalisation which this conferment of status imposes. Those who practise health education, therefore, frequently engage with the medical model and the medical profession with reluctance. So in identifying the medical profession as central to the practice of health education, our authors conclude that there is more to criticise than to congratulate. The positive assessments of health education emerge more in recommendations for change than in celebration of what exists.

Nonetheless we remain committed to the potential value of health education. We do not take issue with the concept of preventing rather than treating illhealth, and we are not discomforted by the recognition that this requires fundamental social change. By the same token, we have not set out to identify cases of ineffective or inappropriate activities as evidence that health education is intrinsically worthless. Rather, we are concerned to

3

show that health educators who continue to practise in ways that are unhelpful and perhaps unhealthy have been unable to shake off the ideological imperatives underpinning such practices.

The perpetuation of ineffective, unhelpful health education practices occurs, we argue, because of entrenched notions about adequacy. An assessment of the extent to which people are physically, mentally and emotionally equipped to deal adequately with their lives is a central task for health professionals. This task has been conventionally undertaken by health educators from within an individualistic behavioural framework which manifests itself through a focus on habits, attitudes and values—on *lifestyles*. One of the discussion points which recurs in this book is that health educators' efforts to change people's lifestyles in order to make them more 'healthy' is ultimately unhelpful. It may be done more or less intrusively, with more or less subtlety, but it is nonetheless a baseline for health education that individuals in many social groups have 'unhealthy lifestyles'. Any critique of health education ideologies must, we suggest, take issue with the promulgation of notions of 'adequacy' and the association of these with particular social groups. This pathologising of typical conduct, the packaging and labelling of social behaviour according to some stereotypical perception of certain ways of life, we refer to as 'lifestylism'. We see lifestylism as unhelpful and unhealthy in its manifestations, because it can lead to a sense of moral failure and emotional inadequacy. Lifestylism is the realisation of the ideology of individualism and as such is significantly resistant to change or adaptation, thus allowing many health professionals uncritically to perpetuate stereotypical notions and subsequently to intervene appropriately. As a case in point, many community physicians consider health education to be solely about 'changing people's lifestyles' (Nutbeam, 1984: 117).

Of course, not all health professionals share this view, and in implying that lifestylism is a health professional's *modus operandi* we may be accused of oversimplifying. It is certainly the case that a number of health education officers hold a *theoretical* critique of a lifestyle approach. The point to be made, however, is that in practice they actually find it difficult to work against the dominant ideology.

Although a critique of lifestylism is central to our discussion, it is important not to reject the concept of lifestyle in itself. A reappraisal of the concept of lifestyle can go some way towards a reworking of conventional health education practices, and will, we hope, inform development of a radical critique. Hitherto, the notion of lifestyle has been conceived and applied to individual patterns of behaviour within the context of shorthand and simplistic notions, usually ones of social class. Typically commentators refer to working-class or middle-class lifestyles, and although there is a common understanding of these labels they can act as ideological devices in the control of individuals and groups. In acknowledging the dangers in the pathologising of typical conduct, we argue for a reconceptualisation of lifestyle in terms which allow for greater complexity. In this understanding of lifestyle, it is accepted that many ways of life may be at odds with the dominant mode. The authenticity and validity of these is recognised, however. Indeed, alternative ways of life are perceived as a creative and adaptable set of responses to the environment. The context within which individuals and groups develop their lifestyles is, therefore, particularly important.

At the same time as acknowledging the creative nature of lifestyle, it is also useful to understand it as representing a set of practices established through time and over which people do not necessarily have control. Thus lifestyle is also a *framework* within which action is situated and which sets to some extent the terms of reference for that action. Lifestyle is a label which refers to the manifestation of this framework in the day-to-day responses of any one person or group. In this way, lifestyle is both the material expression of an ideology—an ideology as it is experienced in day-to-day living—and the framework within which that day-to-day living is structured and patterned.

The relative stability of these patterned sets of actions indicates that individual members of a social group cannot be expected to easily alter their lifestyle in response to the recommendations of professionals. Making 'healthy choices easier choices' (Dennis, *et al.* 1982) is, therefore, likely to require significant transformations of the social conditions under which any choice is made.

On the one hand it is important to postulate that individuals and groups *can* make choices. To do otherwise is to fall into a reductionism in which behaviour is entirely determined by monolithic structures. On the other it is equally important to recognise the limitations within the concept of 'choice'. To argue simplistically that the task of the health educator is to facilitate an 'informed choice' tends to deny these limitations. Some people may be able to exercise choice, in as much as they have a wider range of options, but this 'choice' should not be understood in terms of privilege, nor elevated to a moral principle from which action necessarily follows in a straightforward manner. Choices are decisions made for complex reasons. The decision to change well-established patterns of behaviour cannot be fully anticipated or accurately predicted. So the expectations held by health professionals that once informed, individuals will act in logical and reasonable ways, is frequently inappropriate. Nor do those who subscribe to dominant social mores have a monopoly on what is logical and reasonable in any given context.

Furthermore, this argument allows for the unwitting promulgation of conservative notions of consumer participation in health care. One of the points made by those who propound the rights of the individual to make a 'free choice' about health care is that they are often unable to do so. But this is not, it is argued, because of differential access to services. It is because they do not have enough information on which to make an informed choice. Once that information is given, then people will appreciate the diversity of health care provision within a market economy. They will then, the argument continues, exercise their right to choose the appropriate service. But there is no evidence from countries with fully fledged private health care systems that this is the case. Although there is no space here to enter this debate, we want to make two points about the notion of free choice: firstly, that the giving of knowledge by professionals to clients is not in itself sufficient to facilitate choice. The means to act on that information must be available. Secondly, that the making of a 'free choice' does not necessarily equate with a 'healthy choice' and nor does this necessarily equate with health.

It may be politically expedient to reify the notion of choice but it is not morally acceptable as a rationalisation for health education activity. It is not difficult to envisage a situation in which health education offers nothing other than a glossy, eye-catching but superficial array of products, using the argument that it is up to people to choose whether or not to pick them up, read them, discuss them and act on them.

Of course few would wish to see this level of activity constitute the sum total of health education work. Nonetheless the tendency to reduce the discipline in this way can be seen. Ironically, it is not so much witnessed within conventional health education with its emphasis on the use of established educational methods, even if these are sometimes still didactic. Rather we see this as one possible way in which the emerging health *promotion* strategies may develop.

As a relatively new concept health promotion appears full of promise: with a broader remit than health education it has the potential to overcome some of the failings of conventional health education identified in this book. Over the last two or three years health promotion has put out shoots in three directions, using NHS centred practice as its point of departure. Firstly, health promotion is looking towards the generation of policies, be they locally or centrally governed, which would have a direct bearing on people's health. For example, the food industry, and indeed the entire food chain, is a fertile area for health promoters, as of course are the tobacco and alcohol industries. The broad aim is to stimulate legislation against anti-health processes and activities, and for measures that proactively extend the concept and experience of health. The second shoot is also policy-orientated, but remains within the medical model, and is governed by the rather narrower terms of reference of community medicine. Within this framework health promotion strategies involve the identification of targets for improving the quality of life and longevity. They are defined largely in epidemiological terms, in which for instance a target is set for reducing the number of smokers by 20 per cent over the next fifteen years. Thirdly, there are other promotion strategies which attempt to step beyond the individualistic model to address the full range of activities giving rise to illhealth, and which are therefore based in 'the' community. Such strategies include sport and fitness programmes, safe play campaigns for parents with small children, and mass public awareness campaigning around a particular illness, such as coronary heart disease. These strategies can offer a major challenge for existing patterns of health and illness, particularly if based upon the principles of community development. (See Watt, Chapter 8).

From this range of activities it would appear that health promotion, as a new concept, can potentially look beyond the confines of medical practice. Some reservations are in order here, however.

We are not alone in suspecting that one reason for the ready acceptance of health promotion is that it adds new vitality to the sometimes turgid discipline of health education (Tones, 1984). Whilst this is obviously not in itself contentious, it becomes so if health promotion fails to address the problems responsible for the shortcomings manifest in conventional health education. As yet, most health promotion strategies can offer little evidence of successfully tackling health inequalities at their root. Neither the epidemiologically based health promotion strategies nor the community-based 'health is fun' interventions demand a redistribution of resources for their implementation. They are frequently set within the individualist behavioural framework of the medical model, although they employ sophisticated technological techniques and marketing strategies to encourage behaviour change. For the most part, therefore, health promotion strategies seem to be reproducing some of the inadequate practices of conventional health education. Most health promoters are health educators in thin disguise. Can we be sure that the ideologies which inform health education will be successfully discarded by health promotion professionals?

In our view, health education is not yet ready to be replaced by a newer version that is too close to the original to be sufficiently distinct. We support many of the ideals of health promotion, but we are keen to see health education sort out its own difficult issues. We fear that those who have moved into health promotion may be too absorbed by health being fun, or being about improving mortality rates, to offer to health education the sustained and detailed analysis of practice that is needed for health educators to address health inequalities. Whilst we see the need for health promotion, it must absolutely not be at the expense of health education—at least until health education has strengthened its theoretical base, and has devised effective methods of practice that make a realistic contribution to the challenging of health inequalities. Then health promotion will have a basis for its own proper development. We hope that this publication will go some way towards meeting these ideals.

Let us turn more closely to the content of the book. As our overarching theme is one of tackling the individualism inherent in conventional health education, we found it difficult to ascribe any one other logic to the contents. Inevitably, when issues are raised, more questions are asked than answers found. For our own purposes we found it useful to cluster the questions posed into four broad areas. If individualism is to be adequately challenged, how, when, where and by whom should health education be practised? Each chapter, by focusing on a different issue, makes a number of contributions to each of these questions.

Jenny Naidoo begins the process of scrutinising individualism by arguing, firstly, that it is an ideology, and secondly, it is the predominant ideology informing the practice of health education. By theoretically considering its limitations, Naidoo then poses examples of individualistic health education beside alternative forms, examining and assessing the differences manifest in health education practice when its ideological base changes.

Appreciating the ideological nature of health education may require an examination of complex relationships between conflicting forces. Maggie Pearson takes issues with the perpetuation of racist ideologies in health education campaigns. She exposes the relationship between the individualism of the medical model of illness on the one hand, and the institutional racism embodied in ethnocentric anthropological theories on the other. The latter typically project a view of the lives of black people in terms of exotic and alien practices. This insidious link between medicine and conservative anthropology allows health professionals to intervene with health education campaigns which hold the Asian and Afro-Caribbean community responsible for their own illhealth on the grounds that their alien lifestyles are problematic. This has a particularly detrimental effect on black women who are perceived to be, at one and the same time, the guardians of family welfare and a cause of their illhealth. Regarded as the upholders of outdated restrictive practices (Asian women), or are employing 'loose moral codes' (Afro-Caribbean women), each are defined in terms of their lack of compatibility with the white indigenous population.

Individualism in practice is often termed victim-blaming. The majority of health education is aimed at women, our socially constructed pivot of family health and welfare. As prime targets for health education women experience disproportionate amounts of victim-blaming, often in subtle form. This issue is addressed in relation to the provision of meals within the family, by Nickie Charles and Marion Kerr. Drawing on their own field research, they indicate the central role which the provision of a 'proper meal' plays in symbolic and actual negotiations between men and women. They argue that health education messages about healthy eating and giving the family 'good food' are directed at women by health educators, when in reality women have little control over what gets put on the table. Men's attitudes to food are shown to be problematic: the 'real men don't eat quiche' syndrome is entrenched in many family eating patterns, and governs what all family members eat. Moreover, the production and distribution of food products is also out of the control of women, even though they show a marked awareness of current issues in food production. The significance of this work for health educators is clear. Messages about healthy eating are currently central to the work of health education, yet much of it is being directed inappropriately and ineffectively.

This evident lack of power to control food consumption illustrates the importance of identifying the locus of control when planning health education activities. All the contributions here discuss this in one form or another. It is, therefore, the identification of the locus of control which allows an understanding of the continuation of ideologies which are harmful to health. The issue of masculinity as an ideology which generates hazardous activities is one example. In Andrew Watterson's chapter this is discussed within the broader framework of the process of production in the workplace. He criticises current occupational health education, which relies on a victim-blaming and individualistic approach to health and safety and to work hazards. One of the reasons why a more radical approach to health education at work has not occurred is that workers are not able to exercise control over the production process whilst employers collude with the notion that 'it's a man's job' to be dirty, and to engage in dangerous activities. This absolves managers of responsibility for the provision of safe working environments, and reduces occupational health education to the conventional approach of trying to influence 'bad habits'. Watterson argues that these issues have to be tackled at their roots, both in terms of the production process itself and in terms of the ideologies which allow these to continue. Occupational health education about work hazards should be introduced into school curricula, so that students are made aware of the issues before they enter the labour market. If this is combined with teaching which effectively challenges ideologies of masculinity then a more creative health education in the workplace may ensue.

The nature of health education in schools is the focus of Alan Cribb's chapter. He identifies the disjuncture between the content of school health education and the educational philosophy which underpins most teaching. Conventional health education in schools often takes the form of didactic instruction about hygiene and body maintenance. More recently, innovatory methods and subjects have been introduced in which students are encouraged to take decisions, understand group dynamics and peer-group pressure, learn about community action and self-empowerment, and thus about the nature of social change. Cribb argues that this approach is welcome because it teaches political literacy and should be openly acknowledged as a political activity, rather than perceived merely as a new educational method. Although the content of most school subjects is controlled by a set agenda, health education remains relatively flexible and can, if taught with imagination, act as a catalyst for the creation of a more politically informed student population, one which recognises the detrimental effects of conservative ideologies and practices on patterns of health and illness.

Several chapters discuss the most effective location for health education: the workplace, the school, and the community are all potential and actual sites for health action. Ged Moran analyses the role of the local authority in the promotion of health action. He identifies the problems and the possibilities for local authorities in prioritising health on their political agendas. Exposing the differences and similarities between the bureaucratic structures of District Health Authorities and Metropolitan or County Councils allows us to consider the scope for innovative policies in health education and promotion. Moran suggests that the constitutional structure of local councils allows for greater accountability to the community than that of health authorities, since health authority members are nominated rather than elected. Local councils do not typically give health issues high priority, but they are theoretically able to institute policies and programmes in which innovation and imagination feature. Thus, Moran argues, health education workers should consider working through the channels of local authorities when introducing new ideas and activities.

Recently, with changes introduced into the NHS under the rubric of general management, the extent of accountability to the community has lessened. 'Cost effectiveness' and the 'maximisation of a revenue profile' are current catch phrases, indicating the increasing trend towards the marketing of health as a commodity, and the organisation of the NHS as a business. Increasingly, health authorities are required to set targets and to identify need with only nominal reference to the local population. Such accountability as does exist occurs through the representation of health service users' views through Community Health Councils. The views of groups in the community about *health* issues are becoming more difficult to assess as CHCs endeavour to respond to *illness* issues. Enquiring into individual cases of inadequate treatment in hospital and assessing changes in the quality of care, as well as responding to the steady supply of consultation documents from Regional and District teams, constitutes the bulk of the work of CHCs.

The centrality of community-defined need in the creation of effective and responsive health care is discussed by Alison Watt. She argues for a reprioritising in the needs hierarchy, with a shift away from the prominence of professionally defined need. At the same time, the point is underlined that if community health education fails to take account of the principles of community development, it is destined not to succeed as a progressive method of practice. The romanticism embodied in notions of community is exposed, and the medical interest in the perpetuation of individualism in the community is explored. The chapter concludes with a consideration of how the advent of health promotion may serve further to erode the possibility for a proper implementation of community health education.

That people in the community are interested in health issues is increasingly clear as the number of self-help and community health groups proliferate. Wendy Farrant and Jill Russell draw on their own research into health education publications to discuss the different ways in which health issues are expressed in official and community materials. The extent to which health education officers, working within the NHS, are able or willing to support community-based health initiatives is the main subject of this chapter. The differing views of HEOs as to the role of community-based activities and their political implications are clearly evident. Farrant and Russell raise the questions: How political *can* health educators be? How much political activity can health educators reasonably be expected to take on? How *able* are health educators to work in radical ways if their professional socialisation is grounded in individualism?

Michael Calnan, Mary Boulton and Anthony Williams address these issues in their consideration of general practice as a locus for health education. GPs are the front-line practitioners most frequently encountered by people in their management of health and illness. As such, they have the potential to effect significant change in the way people *do* manage their health and illness. There are doubtful expectations, however, of their ability or willingness to intervene creatively in the doctor–patient relationship. This chapter illustrates the low expectations which both doctors and their patients have of their creative abilities: paternalistic advice about 'healthy lifestyles' is the usual form of health education by a professional group which is constrained by the structure of the one-to-one consultation. Some GPs sadly find health education dull and tedious, whilst others consider it moralistic and intrusive. The work of Calnan *et al.* highlights some of the difficulties encountered by people as patients in identifying and getting their health education needs met.

Although some health professionals see health education practice as intrusive, particularly when it is aimed at individual changes in lifestyle, they are nonetheless propelled into it by the institutional nature of health care delivery. In our final chapter, Sue Rodmell discusses the difficulties encountered by health visitors and other community nurses in their attempts to introduce pre-pregnancy care 'to the community'. Largely because the need for education on issues like prepregnancy care is identified normatively from professional bodies, and passed down through the nursing hierarchy, health visitors attempt to 'do' health education in ways which are inappropriate for the groups they are serving. Inevitably, recourse is made to the easier option of focusing on individual 'bad habits'. This gives rise to feelings of guilt for women who are being encouraged to become 'fit' in order to lessen the chance of having a malformed foetus, but find it difficult, if not impossible, to act on the information received.

These, then, are the issues as we see them. The contributions gathered here are not intended to be exhaustive, and do not necessarily reflect our own views as editors. This is a first collection of papers which we hope will prove stimulating and act as a catalyst for future work. The debate has barely begun, as, in the late 1980s, we enter a challenging new phase in the management of the NHS. The impact of these changes on health education cannot be fully anticipated, but there can be no doubt that it will be significant.

# REFERENCES

Dennis, J. *et al.* (1982), 'Health Promotion in the Reorganised National Health Service', *The Health Services*, 26 November 1982.

Graham, H. (1984), *Women, Health and the Family*, Wheatsheaf Books, London.

Nutbeam, D. (1984), 'Health Education in the National Health Service: the differing perceptions of community physicians and Health Education Officers', *Health Education Journal*: 43.

Tones, K. (1984), *Health Promotion: a new panacea?* Paper presented at the Annual Health Education Officers' seminar, March 1984.

# CHAPTER 2

# LIMITS TO INDIVIDUALISM

## Jennie Naidoo

### INTRODUCTION

The key issue under discussion here is individualism—the dominant ideology underlying modern health education practice. I shall argue that the effectiveness of such practice is severely limited by this ideology, by looking at the extent to which individualism currently provides the theoretical basis for health education. Three examples of individualistic health education practice, incorporating both educational and marketing strategies, will be analysed and compared with two examples of alternative forms of health education. Finally, the pros and cons of health education activities predicated on different ideological assumptions are discussed.

### THE INDIVIDUALISTIC APPROACH TO HEALTH EDUCATION

Individualism is here defined as the ideology which views individual free choice as both an accurate account of the status quo, and as a desirable goal for which to aim. Individualism views health status as a matter over which the individual has control: 'Much of the responsibility for ensuring his [sic] own good health lies with the individual' (DHSS, 1976: 95). This is the ideological cornerstone of government and Department of Health and Social Security (DHSS) attitudes to health education. Modern western diseases 'are related less to a man's outside environment than to his own personal behaviour; what might be termed our lifestyle' (DHSS, 1976: 17). Because individual free choice is also seen as a desirable goal, direct government intervention in health matters is taboo. Instead, a laissez-faire attitude is recommended:

> The role of the health professions and of government is limited to ensuring that the public have access to such knowledge as is available about the importance of personal habit on health and that at the very least no obstacles are placed in the way of those who decide to act on that knowledge (ibid.: 62).

One definition of ideology is that it is a closed system, self-fulfillingly accurate within its own parameters. Individualism implies certain strategies and ways of evaluating outcomes—ones which do not come into conflict with the over-riding aim of individual freedom. Education and persuasion are both seen as appropriate methods, because they do not over-ride individual free choice and responsibility. The health educator may provide persuasive arguments and relevant information, but the responsibility for change lies with the individual. At the end of the health education input people are free to accept or reject the health education message, and, as long as they have understood it correctly, their decision is immaterial. The important factor here is the effective transmission of a message. This bias towards education is continually reaffirmed, even when the problem under review is seen as one of law and order as much as of health. The Advisory Council on the Misuse of Drugs stated that 'our major recommendations in respect of future prevention policy emphasize the role of education' (ACMD, 1984: 62). Again, the government Chief Medical Officer, questioned recently about AIDS (acquired immune deficiency syndrome), stated that the government's role was to educate the public about the true risks of AIDS, as well as perform its monitoring and co-ordinating functions (Acheson, 1985). By contrast, coercive measures are seen as inappropriate.

Examples of coercive measures are legal and fiscal policies which constrain individual choices and behaviour, for example, the legal requirement to wear car seat belts, or to increase the price of products which affect health (such as alcohol and tobacco) through taxation.

Ideology is also reflected in how projects are *evaluated*. Following the premises of individualism, a purely cognitive evaluation may be sufficient, such as measuring increased knowledge of the effects of smoking after a health education input. The ultimate goals of health education campaigns are usually changes in behaviour, such as a decline in the smoking rate, or the increased take-up of vaccination programmes, and these are evaluated whenever it is possible to do so. Behaviour is dependent on many factors including knowledge, attitudes and beliefs. Whilst knowledge is an acceptable target for health education programmes, the extent to which attitudes and beliefs are legitimate targets is less defined. This is because health education must not be seen as propaganda. Propaganda aims to change attitudes, beliefs and behaviour by any available means, including manipulation of emotions. It therefore rides roughshod over the sanctity of the individual. This leads to a tension between the two goals of health education—behaviour change and individual choice. In practice, health education does often aim to change attitudes, beliefs, and health practices, but proceeds in a cautious manner so as to avoid charges of indoctrination. So the extent to which individualism underlies current approaches to health education is manifest not only in the content of contemporary programmes, but also in their methodologies and evaluation.

## A THEORETICAL CRITIQUE OF INDIVIDUALISM

Three major criticisms can be levelled against individualistic health education: first, it denies that health is a social product; second, it assumes free choice exists; third, it is not effective within its own terms of reference.

Individualism states that health is a matter of individual responsibility and individual choice. There is ample evidence that this is not the case. The Black Report on inequalities in health found that social class differentials in health status are becoming more, not less, marked. The working group concluded that '. . . it is difficult to begin to explain the pattern of inequalities except by invoking material deprivation as a key concept' (Townsend and Davidson, 1982: 21). The Black Report's thirty-seven recommendations concentrated on measures designed to improve the material conditions of life of poorer groups, as the most effective means of improving their health. This is in tune with the general consensus—acknowledged by the DHSS (DHSS, 1976)—that epidemiological evidence shows the great medical advances of recent history owe more to direct government intervention in fields such as public health, housing and social welfare than to medical discoveries and treatment.

Contrary to popular mythology, illness is not bad luck, randomly distributed throughout the population, nor is it a thing that some have and some have not. 'Illness is socially structured and patterned, and working class people experience more ill health than middle class people, not through choice but because . . . they are more exposed to a health-damaging environment over which they have little control' (Mitchell, 1984: 98). This is because our society puts a premium on profits and economic expansion, to the detriment of health and well-being. It is not just that illness is a spin-off from some capitalist processes, a regrettable byproduct of economic growth, but that 'the health of the majority of people is not compatible with the present form of organisation of our society' (ibid.: 112). Available evidence and expert opinion strongly support the notion that health is a social product and, as such, is not amenable to individual control. The ideology of individualism thus has as its central theme an assertion which is untenable in the light of what is known about patterns of health in our society.

The second criticism concerns the assumption that free choice is possible, and is relevant to health. The concept of free choice derives from the free market model of the economy. Free choice is the mechanism whereby supply matches demand, and the economy is kept running smoothly. This theoretical model of pure capitalism does not exist in reality. The scale of government economic activities, multi-nationals and monopolies constrain choice in the market place. Applying an economic concept to health, which is not a consumer product, is even more unrealistic. Some individual behaviour (for example, cigarette smoking, or sedentary leisure) is undoubtedly important in the aetiology of much modern disease. But this behaviour is not a matter of free choice. Choices are limited by environmental factors (the provision of sports facilities) and by commercial interests (tobacco promotion). When '... expensive psychological and social science skills are currently devoted to promoting or maintaining personal life-styles which are unhealthy' (Draper et al., 1976), it is unrealistic to talk of free choice. The assumption that free choice exists within a market economy may be challenged, and it is, therefore, illegitimate to extrapolate the concept of free choice to other fields such as health.

The third major criticism of individualism is that traditional health education interventions based on this ideology are ineffective even within their own terms of reference. The individualistic theory of health education seeks to educate people about preventive health measures in the belief that this is sufficient to change behaviour and lead to the adoption of healthier lifestyles. Evaluation studies show that this approach is not very effective in generating behaviour change (Gatherer et al., 1979).

The first two criticisms, that health is a social product, and that free choice is not applicable to health, are prima facie, in that they strike at the theoretical heart of individualism. They are also, as has been shown, supported by sound empirical evidence from the field of public health. The third criticism, that individualistic health education is ineffective within its own frame of reference, is more contingent. I shall examine this last criticism by reference to three recent health education campaigns which are based on an individualistic ideology: Look After Yourself!, Play It Safe! and the Great British Fun Run.

# HEALTH EDUCATION—THE NATIONAL CONTEXT

Health education in Britain is the prime concern of two institutions—the national quango the Health Education Council (HEC), and local health education units which are located within the framework of the National Health Service (NHS). A current estimate of the annual *per capita* expenditure on health education by the HEC is 18 pence (HEC, 1985a). It is possible that this sum is matched by local District Health Authority expenditure, but it is impossible to get accurate figures. Whilst there is strictly no requirement for NHS units to become involved with HEC projects, publicity and support materials are freely available, and thus there is considerable pressure on NHS units to support HEC programmes. Through this process local and national health education inputs can be synchronised to maximise the effect. For example, an extra advertising campaign was mounted by health authorities in the West Midlands to coincide with the national HEC and BBC (British Broadcasting Corporation) campaign 'So you want to stop smoking'. This, it is argued, led to the West Midlands achieving higher than average smoking–cessation figures.

How the HEC sets its priorities is determined by a combination of epidemiology, government pressure, and proven effectiveness. Coronary heart disease, Britain's number one cause of death, is an HEC priority. So too is drug abuse, a topical issue which it is politic to be seen to be tackling. Some HEC priorities are dubbed 'client centred', but this has more to do with the fact that they are directed at 'vulnerable' client groups (young people, the elderly) than that they are actually determined by these client groups.

To look at the influence of individualism, three HEC programmes will be considered: the Look After Yourself! (LAY!) programme, the Play It Safe! campaign, and the Great British Fun Run. Two smaller projects will be looked at as examples of alternative strategies which can be adopted by health education units: the Wessex Positive Health Team, which is a regional initiative, and GASP, the Group Against Smoking in Public, which is a district initiative.

## LOOK AFTER YOURSELF!: INDIVIDUALISM PURE AND SIMPLE

LAY! is a major HEC programme, and was launched in January 1978. LAY! 'articulated the apparently simple notion that small changes in ways of living, especially in youth and middle age, offer the prospect of large improvements in health and well-being . . .' (Health Education Council, 1978: 10). Attempts were made at the inception of LAY! to tailor it to the perceived needs of the client: 'Preparation for the "Look After Yourself" campaign included a survey of what, if anything, people wanted to know about their health in positive terms' (ibid.: 23). This programme is still in operation, with the latest developments being LAY! adult education classes in the community and the workplace, and monitoring and evaluation of LAY! tutor training courses. LAY! is a near-perfect example of individualistic health education in practice. The programme is about healthier lifestyle options, which are presented in a vacuum. The message is that individuals make healthy or unhealthy choices, and the role of LAY! is to act as a catalyst, and encourage the uptake of 'healthy choices'. By conceptualising illhealth as due to individual behavioural choices, it becomes easy to blame people who are ill for inflicting such damage on themselves. This is known as 'victim-blaming'. Victim-blaming is a handy alibi, for any failure can be viewed as the fault of the client, not the health educator. This is how the argument goes: we will not be guilty of over-riding individual free choice, so we will merely advise and educate the public about health and safety. If they choose to ignore our suggestions, then they are feckless and have chosen illhealth. This viewpoint has an inbuilt bias conferring any blame for failure on to the client, or victim of illhealth, and dispels any need for self-criticism on the part of the health educator. Structural constraints affecting choices, and the possibility of collective solutions to such constraints, are ignored.

Strategies used by LAY! are education and persuasion. Evaluation is limited to estimating the numbers of leaflets and posters distributed nationwide, and assessing the take-up of LAY! adult education classes. The initial exploration of LAY! as a client-centred initiative has been abandoned. The possibility of making LAY! an action research project, informed by continuous feedback from the client, hinted at by the HEC's preparations for it, has been lost. The crudity of evaluation by such 'number-crunching' methods as distribution figures is acknowledged by the HEC: 'The Council recognise that mass distribution of pamphlets and provoking displays of enthusiasm by people aware of and often already dedicated to the pursuit of fitness are not in themselves indications of success' (Health Education Council, 1978: 10). The HEC does claim, however, that the positive results of such evaluation imply change in knowledge and attitudes, and so are important prerequisites for behaviour change. This is a big assumption, unsupported by hard evidence. However, it is presumably on the basis of such an assumed link that evaluation of LAY! continues in a similar vein:

> LAY! ... continues to grow and gain popularity. Tutor and trainer numbers have now risen to 1700 and the number of courses organised has increased by 30%. It is estimated that the programme reaches 60,000 people a year through its present network of classes (Health Education Council, 1984: 18).

Although the prevention of major disease is an ultimate aim of LAY!, epidemiological evaluation of the programme is impossible, as there is no way of isolating the effect of LAY! in relation to other factors affecting morbidity and mortality rates.

## PLAY IT SAFE!: INDIVIDUALISM UNDER ATTACK

Play It Safe! was launched in autumn 1981 as a joint HEC and BBC venture. Its primary aim was a reduction in the number of child accidents. Accidents account for 30 per cent of all deaths in children under 14, and there is a significant social class differential in mortality from accidents and violence (Office of Health Economics, 1981). The standardised mortality ratio for accidents and violence to children of unskilled parents is nearly five times that for children of parents in the professions. The Play It Safe! campaign centred around a series of ten short programmes broadcast on BBC, and a supporting booklet produced by the HEC. Regional meetings to stimulate local initiatives were held, and the campaign evaluated. Although the HEC and BBC recognised the social class differential in child accident rates, and directed the campaign at parents in social classes IV and V (semi-skilled and unskilled manual workers), child accidents were paradoxically viewed as preventable by individual parental action.

The focus was the identification of hazards in the child's environment and the encouragement of parental action to remove these hazards. The methods used in this campaign were primarily educative and persuasive.

The ideology underlying this campaign is one of individualism, redefined as adult parental responsibility for the safety of their children. Environmental and structural factors affecting child safety were ignored. For example, the programme and booklet section 'On the roads' covered the green cross code, and stressed that parents should accompany children on the roads and also be conscientious drivers. It said nothing about safety engineering or design, or the creation of safe urban play areas, which are known to lower road traffic accident rates (Williams and Sibert, 1983). The campaign's methodology—education and persuasion—is compatible with an individualistic ideology. The official evaluation, which looked at the 'penetration' of the campaign, and its effects on individual attitudes and behaviour, reinforces this individualistic bias. The creation of local action groups offered potential to broaden the scope of the campaign, but in practice local initiatives tended to back up Play It Safe's central message of individual responsibility rather than seeking to generate any collective or social response (BBC, 1982). No doubt this was partly a response to how the HEC and the BBC disseminated the campaign and to the content of the programme itself. To reinterpret the message of Play It Safe! in terms of a social analysis of accidents would be to discredit the original campaign. It would also involve a different type of health education input, one directed more at the physical and social environment in which children have accidents. This kind of input would rely more on lobbying legislators, manufacturers, architects, engineers and builders for changes in specifications and safety regulations. These two types of input, educational and lobbying, are to some extent incompatible, because their assumptions and analyses of why and how accidents occur are so different. However, the support activity undertaken by the health education department in the Area Health Authority of Kensington, Chelsea and Westminster was exceptional in stressing '. . . the need for people to be made more aware of those aspects of public responsibility—the environmental and social factors which predispose certain children more than others to have accidents' (Kensington, Chelsea and Westminster Health Education Department, 1982: 1). This kind of analysis stresses social rather than parental responsibility for child safety, and places safety on the economic and political agenda, whilst recognising that inbuilt safety features, in houses, roads or equipment, cost money and are, therefore, unlikely to be given high priority.

The Play It Safe! campaign was evaluated in several ways. The official BBC evaluation examined the degree of 'penetration' of the campaign and showed it to be relatively successful, in that some of the programmes were seen by 59 per cent adults, and the accompanying booklet by just over 10 per cent (HEC, 1983b). But behaviour was not significantly altered. A survey found '. . . the campaign had not stimulated action on safety' (HEC, 1983b), and a Welsh study showed no significant difference in the incidence of serious accidents to children before and after the campaign (Williams and Sibert, 1983). An evaluation of Play It Safe! conducted in Bristol also found no discernible behavioural effects. Child presentation rates at hospital accident and emergency departments before and after the Play It Safe! campaign were compared, and no significant differences observed (Naidoo, 1984). By contrast, 'The environmental approach to child accident prevention ... has proven successes, in particular with child resistant containers, bicycle design and flameproof nightdresses' (Williams and Sibert, 1983).

## THE GREAT BRITISH FUN RUN: A MARKETING APPROACH TO HEALTH EDUCATION

The Great British Fun Run, which took place in May and June 1985, was billed as 'Britain's biggest ever health promotion campaign ... Along the route ... will be some 80 health fairs, designed to help millions of people become fitter' (HEC, 1985b). This event was part of the HEC's coronary disease prevention programme, and a primary aim was to persuade people to incorporate some form of regular exercise into their lifestyle. Other factors known to be more closely linked to coronary disease were given a low profile. Smoking, which is 'on the evidence we have, clearly the biggest known risk factor (for coronary disease) (DHSS, 1981: 63), diet, and raised blood pressure, all of which are more powerfully correlated with coronary disease than exercise, took a back row. The exhortation was for individuals to choose one or more forms of physical recreation as a regular exercise activity. The cost involved in using private exercise facilities, and the lack of adequate public provision, was not addressed by this campaign. To do so would have involved a fundamental rethinking of the premises of the campaign. The decision to exercise or not is informed by many factors, of which health beliefs are but one. Convenience, cost and accessibility are other relevant factors, but to tackle these would require the use of different strategies such as lobbying. Instead, two different techniques have found legitimacy under the umbrella concept of health promotion—marketing and sponsorship.

Ideally, 'health promotion represents a mediating strategy between people and their environments, synthesising personal choice and social responsibility in health to create a healthier future' (WHO, 1985: 5). In practice, however, the marketing aspect of health promotion seems to be its most popular manifestation. Marketing health as a consumer good is not traditional health education, but it can be seen as a form of individualism. Marketing involves creating a demand for a product (using advertising to do so), and ensuring a competitive product is delivered to the market place. Health promotion's use of marketing to date has concerned itself more with the advertising side, creating an image and a demand for 'health', than with the service delivery side. This kind of health promotion, relying heavily on mass media advertising, addresses the individual as a consumer whose buying decisions are capable of manipulation by a wide variety of techniques. Advertising works by equating 'X' product with some desirable quality, such as, 'manliness' or 'sociability'. The commodity being advertised acquires, by association, the concrete expression of this desirable quality. Thus, to achieve status, or happiness, all one need do is purchase 'X' product. The product becomes the social signifier of the purchaser—who possesses the desirable attributes portrayed in the advertisement. Advertising may be wildly inappropriate, and impart no information to the consumer. Virginia Slim cigarettes were marketed in Britain under the slogan 'You've come a long way, baby!'. This slogan, directed at women, implied both femininity (baby!) and feminism (you've come a long way), but failed to inform women of the devastating effects on health of cigarette smoking.

Advertising health as a commodity obscures the social construction of health, and it is in this sense that the marketing type of health promotion is individualism in a new guise. The fact that the marketing component of health promotion was the one most eagerly adopted by the HEC is surely no coincidence.

Although education was an important strategy in the Fun Run, this event also stimulated the first tentative use of marketing techniques to 'sell' the concept of positive health. The Fun Run was also the first HEC event to take sponsorship money from a commercial company, Allied Bakeries. This sponsorship gave valuable funding for the event, but also, inevitably, affected the content of the campaign. Thus the educational message to 'eat more fibre' became translated into the selling message 'eat more Allinson's wholemeal and Hi-Bran bread'. Sponsorship affects not only content, but also credibility. It is known that the source of a message is important in determining the credibility of the message (Gatherer *et al.*, 1979) and that whilst health professionals have a very high credibility rating amongst the general public, advertisers do not (Health Education Council, 1983a). It is likely that sponsorship gives professional legitimacy to a product, so that people will think more highly of Allied Bakeries because their product is associated with the HEC. But it is equally likely that some of the HEC's credibility as an impartial adviser on health could be jeopardised by such an association with a commercial company. There is no easy way to balance the losses and gains for health educators in such a sponsorship deal, but it is important that any undesirable side effects, in terms of both message content and credibility, be acknowledged and if possible evaluated. This has not so far happened.

## EDUCATION AND MARKETING: TWO FACES OF INDIVIDUALISM

Education and marketing are both currently reliant on individualism, albeit in different forms. Whilst education seeks to change the knowledge, attitudes and ultimately the behaviour of individuals, marketing seeks behavioural change first and foremost. Educational models of health education address the individual either as an empty vessel requiring knowledge input, or, in a more enlightened fashion, as a knowing person whose decisions are informed, not dictated by that knowledge. Marketing appeals to the consumer as an individual economic unit whose demands are expressed and met in the marketplace.

These two forms of individualism, education and marketing, are to some extent contradictory. Whilst the educational model states that 'If individuals are to accept some responsibility for their own health, a positive self image is vital ...' (Schools Council Health Education Project, 1982: 2), the marketing model may use techniques which abuse self-respect, in order to achieve the desired change of behaviour. In an advertisement produced by health education services in Australia to promote breast self-examination, for example, negative stereotyping reproduced the sexism prevalent in media representations of women (Cowley and Catford, 1983). The advertisement showed an attractive woman in profile, in a shower, exclaiming 'I do it every month in the shower!'. The obvious sexual connotations of this advert were deliberately exploited to beat the advertisers at their own game. It worked, in the sense that the message was well remembered, and led to a 16 per cent increase in breast self-examination rates (Cowley and Catford, 1983). But what this advert was also conveying, via its hidden agenda, was the antithesis of its overt message. On the surface, the message was directed towards women, encouraging them to take preventive screening measures to safeguard their health. But the projection of women as sexual objects, and the use of titillating images (surely designed to appeal more to men than to women) reveals a different, unhealthy message. This hidden message implies that women are valued only in relation to their sexual attractiveness to men. Such objectification of women denies positive self-respect. The overt message is look after yourself, you matter; the covert message is, you matter only as a desirable-to-men sexual object; the outcome is the maintenance of unhealthy and oppressive experiences for women.

These three examples of an individualistic approach to health education, whether they are using educational methods (as in LAY! and Play It Safe!) or marketing strategies (as in the Great British Fun Run), demonstrate the shortcomings of an individualistic ideology, and the mutually antagonistic nature of health education goals. Purely educational campaigns are relatively ineffective in achieving behaviour change, as was clearly shown by evaluations of Play It Safe! Marketing approaches to health education are potentially more effective in achieving changes in behaviour, but at the cost of hindering other goals such as the development of positive self-regard. The two examples which follow give some indication of how health education might develop once individualism is no longer its prime mover and goal.

# THE WAY FORWARD: THE WESSEX HEALTH PROMOTION TEAM

The Wessex Health Promotion Team has adopted a multi-disciplinary approach to health promotion, incorporating health education. This kind of health promotion includes a range of methods, from personal education, mass media advertising, preventive health services and community development, to organisational developments and economic and regulatory activities. The focus is on preventing illness and promoting health by developing strategies and plans at every level. Health promotion is necessarily multi-disciplinary because 'health is affected by many factors other than the Health Service' (Catford, 1983). Evaluation is an integral part of health promotion, and feedback of programme results is used to modify future initiatives. In 1980 the Wessex team reported on '. . . the effect of a substantial programme of integrated health education promoting the use of seat belts (which) showed no major change in rates for occupants of front seats . . .' (Wessex Positive Health Team, 1980: 1477). The team concluded that '. . . health education alone is insufficient to increase significantly the use of car seat belts. Britain should follow its European partners and pass legislation requiring front seat occupants to wear belts' (ibid.). Accordingly, the Wessex team played a significant role in lobbying parliament on this issue, and claim some credit for the seat belt law which came into force on January 31 1983. This was followed by a take-up rate in the wearing of seat belts of 95 per cent (compared to the pre-legislation figure of 40 per cent), and a subsequent 25 per cent reduction in deaths and serious injuries to drivers and front seat passengers (Evening Post, 1983).

Health promotion as practised by the Wessex team is pragmatic and opportunistic in its choice of method. It is also more rigorous than traditional health education practice in its use of epidemiology and research to set objectives and evaluate them. This is an important benefit within the NHS context of health education and the need to compete for scarce resources with other more scientifically respectable specialities. More importantly, this

31

type of health promotion achieves results in terms of desired behaviour change. What, if any, are its drawbacks? When the results are as overwhelming as in the case of seat belt legislation, it seems petty to point out that such activity is a modern form of benevolent paternalism of health experts doing what is best for the public good. Yet, this dilemma has been identified in situations when 'others [are] prescribing what individuals should do for themselves, and how they should behave, which is contrary to the principles of health promotion' (WHO, 1985: 8).

## THE WAY FORWARD: GASP, THE GROUP AGAINST SMOKING IN PUBLIC

An example of local district-based initiative is GASP. GASP was set up in 1981 to campaign for more provision for non-smokers in public places. Its status is that of an autonomous pressure group sponsored by the health education service in Avon. GASP challenges the traditional view that smoking is a matter of individual choice by publicising research which shows that passive smoking—inhaling others' tobacco smoke—is damaging to the health of non-smokers. As a long-term aim, it is hoped that a reversal of social attitudes on smoking in public (substituting disapproval for tolerance) will help smokers cut down or stop, and prevent young people from starting to smoke.

Individualism is not the central theoretical underpinning for GASP. GASP sets out specifically to tackle the social context of smoking, in contrast to the individual context which is the focus of most anti-smoking programmes. GASP therefore reverses the traditional health education approach with its emphasis on the individual smoker, by focusing on the social environment and the rights of the majority of non-smokers.

Three specific factors contributed towards the establishment of GASP. First, new research on the harmful effects of passive smoking was becoming available (Stock, 1980; Trichopoulos et al., 1981; Hirayama, 1981). New research findings tend to have a beneficial effect when they are made available to the general public for the first time (Gatherer *et al.*, 1979). It was thought that GASP could disseminate such information more effectively than the NHS. Second, GASP was a pilot for a community pressure group approach to health issues. It was thought likely that GASP would attract better publicity than more formal health education campaigns. Third, it was felt that the status quo, whereby public provision for non-smokers was minimal and sometimes non-existent, was out of date and no longer reflected public opinion.

GASP uses a wide variety of strategies which are decided by group members at open meetings. These include the use of local surveys to assess people's views, and lobbying for changes in provision for non-smokers. Publicity gimmicks, such as the 'Good Air Garland' for the restaurant offering the best clean-air facilities, have been used to attract favourable media coverage. The production of educational resources such as leaflets and posters, and letter-writing campaigns, are more conservative tactics used by GASP to spread the message. GASP is opportunistic in that it uses any suitable methods to achieve its aims—a shift in public opinion, or changes in actual provision for non-smokers in public places.

Evaluation is usually attempted, either in terms of the amount and type of media coverage achieved (this being used as a surrogate for public opinion), or in changes in provision. Results of different GASP campaigns vary widely. The restaurants' campaign was largely successful, and was followed up with the production of a 'GASP Guide to Bristol', whereas a sustained cinema campaign has led to only one cinema adopting a smoking-restricted policy.

## CONCLUSION: GOING BEYOND INDIVIDUALISM

These five examples of health education practice demonstrate the range of ideologies informing health education in Britain today. Official government and DHSS approaches to health education rely heavily on an individualist ideology, to which national HEC programmes tend to conform more closely than smaller scale local projects. This is not surprising given the greater reliance of the

HEC on DHSS goodwill for future funding. In terms of overall impact, individualism is the most prevalent ideology underlying health education.

However, although individualism informs educational, behavioural and marketing approaches to health education, it has not achieved the position of a hegemonic ideology. Alternatives which adopt a social perspective on health and illness *do* exist and *do* find funding, even though they tend to be scarce, small scale, and innovative rather than mainstream.

The alternatives identified in this chapter, from the Wessex team and GASP, appear to have found a way of resolving some of the problems associated with individualism. The Wessex team and GASP are not guilty of victim-blaming. They recognise and work within a framework which views health as a social product, and health behaviour as determined by factors other than individual choice. But these strategies are not without their own attendant problems: whilst the Wessex team claims notable success in the field of road traffic safety, it may be criticised for adopting a paternalistic approach to health education. GASP, on the other hand, lacks the status and clout necessary to make large-scale changes in provision for non-smokers in public places, despite being more client-centred in reflecting the interests and wishes of non-smokers.

There is no immediate or easy solution to these dilemmas, or to the antagonistic nature of health education goals. However, it is important to debate the seemingly inevitable tensions between educational and behavioural goals, or between relatively effective paternalistic approaches and less effective client-centred methods. As health educators, we must be aware of the implications of adopting different ideologies, methodologies, and goals. It is tempting to opt for expediency, and choose demonstrably effective methods such as marketing and legislation. But it is also important to consider the side effects of techniques chosen for their effectiveness, and to take account of the 'hidden agenda' when selecting strategies. The most effective methods may also have negative spin-off effects, and in the long term may be counter-productive.

So, whilst there is no obvious type of health education which can be identified as being ideal for all situations, there are some guidelines: health education should be effective, client-centred without being victim-blaming, and should focus on the real causes of health and illness. Individualism fails on all these criteria. The dominant ideology of individualism is marred by three fundamental flaws: it ignores health as a social product; it wrongly assumes the existence of free choice; and it is ineffective in preventing illhealth. Indeed, it may well be true that by following an individualistic ideology, health education has limited its potential and ensured its relatively poor performance. To be effective in prevention, health education must concentrate more on the social and environmental determinants of health. To do this requires going beyond an individualistic framework.

## REFERENCES

Acheson, D. (1985), Interviewed on 'World at One', Radio 4, 27 August 1985.

Advisory Council on the Misuse of Drugs (1984), *Prevention*, London.

BBC (1982), Seminar on the *Evaluation of Play It Safe!*, London.

Catford, D. (1983), 'Developing A Strategy For Health Promotion', unpublished seminar paper.

Cowley, J. and Catford, J. (1983), 'Developing A Strategy For Health Promotion', *Health Education Journal*, 43.

DHSS (1976), *Prevention and Health: Everybody's Business*, London.

DHSS (1981), *Prevention and Health: Avoiding Heart Attacks*, London.

Draper, P., Best, G. and Dennis, J. (1976), *Health, Money and the National Health Service*, Unit for the Study of Health Policy, Guy's Hospital, London.

Evening Post (1983), *Seat Belt Saves Lives*: 50, 8 July 1983, Bristol.

Gatherer, A., Parfit, J., Porter, E. and Vessey, M. (1979), *Is Health Education Effective?*, London, HEC.

Health Education Council (1978), *Annual Report, 1977/78*, London, HEC.

Health Education Council (1983a), *Programmes for 1983–4*, London, HEC.

Health Education Council (1983b), *Health Education News*, January/February 1983, London.

Health Education Council (1984), *Annual Report, 1983–4*, London, HEC.

Health Education Council (1985a), Personal communication.

Health Education Council (1985b), *Health Education Council launches Biggest Health Promotion Campaign*, Press Release, London, HEC.

Hirayama, T. (1981), 'Non-smoking Wives of Heavy Smokers Have a Higher Risk of Lung Cancer', *British Medical Journal*, 282: 183–5, 17 January 1981.

Kensington, Chelsea and Westminster Health Education Department (1982), unpublished paper given at the BBC, 'Evaluation of Play It Safe!', seminar, London.

Mitchell, J. (1984), *What is to be Done about Illness and Health?* Harmondsworth: Penguin.

Naidoo, J. (1984), 'Evaluation of Play It Safe! in Bristol', unpublished paper.

Office of Health Economics (1981), *Accidents in Childhood*, Briefing No. 17, London, OHE.

Player, D. (1984), *Health Promotion—Reality or Illusion?* Paper given at a conference organised by the Regional Health Promotion Group, South East Thames Regional Health Authority.

Schools Council Health Education Project (1982), *Health Education 13–18*, Introductory Handbook, London, Forbes.

Stock, S. (1980), 'The Perils of Second-Hand Smoking', *New Scientist*, 10–13, 2 October 1980.

Townsend, P. and Davidson, N. (1982), *Inequalities in Health: The Black Report*, Harmondsworth: Penguin.

Trichopoulos, D. *et al.* (1981), 'Lung Cancer and Passive Smoking', *Int. J. Cancer*, 27(1): 1–4.

Wessex Positive Health Team (1980), 'Promoting the Use of Seat Belts', *British Medical Journal*, 281: 1477.

Williams, H. and Sibert, J. R. (1983), 'Medicine and the Steering Column', *British Medical Journal*, 286: 1893.

World Health Organisation (1985), 'Health Promotion', *Journal of the Institute of Health Education*, 23, no. 1.

# CHAPTER 3

# RACIST NOTIONS OF ETHNICITY AND CULTURE IN HEALTH EDUCATION

## Maggie Pearson

### A NOTE ON TERMINOLOGY

Throughout this paper, the terms 'black', 'ethnic minorities' and 'Asian' are used. Sometimes they are interchangeable and sometimes they are not. *None* of these terms is meant to imply that the people to whom they refer are not British. The word 'ethnic' is used intentionally, but not approvingly, for it is precisely within the culturalist framework that data on black people's health have largely been researched and collected.

*Black* refers in the political sense to those whose skin colour is not white, and whose common experience of racism is not differentiated by culture, language or tradition.

*Ethnic minorities* refers to people who may not see themselves as black, but nevertheless experience discrimination and inequality on account of their way of life, language or religion.

*Asian* refers to people whose ancestors originated in the Indian subcontinent.

### INTRODUCTION—THE 'PROBLEM' OF BLACK PEOPLE'S HEALTH

Ever since British citizens from colonies in the Indian subcontinent, Africa and the Caribbean migrated to Britain for employment during the domestic labour shortage after World War II, there have been policies specifically on the health of black people and ethnic minorities. Early approaches in the 1950s and 1960s addressed themselves to the health problems of then 'immigrant' populations (Donovan, 1984), emphasising imported, exotic diseases which were seen as a potential threat to the health of the indigenous white population. Often, a medical officer was given responsibility for 'immigrant health'.

This early approach was the precursor of a currently growing interest in 'ethnic' differences in morbidity and mortality, which have been the subject of several recent initiatives, policies and professional conferences in the health service. The Rickets Campaign launched in 1981 was directed at the 'Asian' community, and was followed by an Asian Mother and Baby Campaign launched by the DHSS in June 1984. Some health authorities vaccinate all babies of mothers of Asian origin with *Bacillus Calmet Guerin* (BCG), as a protection against tuberculosis to which they are assumed to be at higher risk of exposure and some also screen Asian and Far Eastern women for Hepatitis B virus when pregnant. A distinction is also made when screening for genetic disorders. In Brent Health Authority, for example, genetic screening services are widely available to the white population, but in addition counselling and screening services for those genetically inherited disorders which occur more frequently amongst black people have been set up.

The majority of these 'special' initiatives have met with fierce criticisms and charges of racism from some of those whom they purport to help. The objections are that the campaigns and the policies and research which inform them are racist, because they focus exclusively on the culture of people from black and ethnic minority communities—a culture which is seen as somehow deficient—and do not tackle the racism which determines black people's health and their experiences of the health service.

This emphasis on black people's clinical pathology is reproduced in health education practice, and in the ideological framework of a particular tradition of 'ethnic relations' sociology (Lawrence, 1982). These medical and 'ethnic relations' ideologies converge and reinforce each other to produce a particular approach to black people's health in which their ways of life are seen as pathological and pathogenic, resistant to the change deemed necessary for health. Health education campaigns have attempted to rectify these perceived cultural deficits, by emphasising the need for minorities to 'adapt' to English ways of life in order to achieve improved health.

This chapter reviews several health education policies and campaigns aimed at black people and ethnic minorities in Britain, setting them in the context of the particular history of racism in the National Health Service. The central theme is that *medical* ideologies which blame individuals and their cultures for their illhealth reinforce *racist* ideologies which view minority lifestyles as pathogenic and deviant. The result is an approach to health education which is depoliticised, diverting attention away from the social causes of black people's illhealth, and stressing instead their deficient culture, 'ignorance' and unwillingness to change.

## RACISM AND THE HEALTH SERVICE—SECOND-CLASS IMAGES OF BLACK PEOPLE

Black people and ethnic minorities have always had a second-class image in the health service, firstly as migrant workers recruited to do the less-prestigious medical, nursing and ancillary work which the indigenous white British population would not do, and secondly as patients whose different diets, languages, lifestyles and religion are seen as causing problems for the established service.

In the early 1950s, manual labour was in short supply in post-war Britain. Ancillary workers and trainee nurses were actively recruited from British colonies, particularly the Caribbean, to staff the rapidly expanding new National Health Service and other public services such as London Transport (Doyal *et al.*, 1980). Migrant workers were more willing to accept the low rates of pay and poor working conditions in hospital wards, laundries and kitchens. Many overseas nurses were recruited to the 'Cinderella' psychiatric, geriatric and mental handicap services, and were often recruited to the lower tier of training as State Enrolled Nurses, even though this qualification was often not recognised in their home country.

The recruitment of cheap manual labour from the Caribbean was followed by similar active recruitment of doctors from the Indian subcontinent during the 1960s, when British medical schools were producing too few graduates for the rapidly expanding number of medical posts, and British doctors were emigrating to North America for higher salaries. Migrant doctors were appointed to the unattractive posts in less-prestigious peripheral non-teaching districts which did not have university medical schools with professorial research units (Smith, 1980; DHSS, 1981). Post-graduate medical training was also inferiorly resourced or non-existent in these districts, and staffing ratios were lower than in the central and prestigious districts. There were, therefore, fewer senior staff from whom these junior doctors could learn.

The medical profession itself has traditionally purveyed its own racist ideologies, embodied in spurious biological notions of 'race' which categorise people like plants and other organisms on the basis of physical characteristics (Montagu, 1964; Banton and Harwood, 1975). Racial categories have persisted as a valid concept in medicine, despite the arguments of geneticists that there is no evidence to support such a taxonomy, since the variation in genes *within* groups defined by any one characteristic (for example, skin colour) is greater than any variation *between* such groups (Glass, 1943; Lewontin, 1972). These spurious 'scientific' theories have been the basis of a current approach which focuses on 'ethnic differences' in morbidity and mortality and takes 'ethnic group', however defined, as the explanatory, independent variable to which illhealth is attributed. In this approach social class is rarely considered as a component of the samples.

The approach to 'immigrant health' in the 1960s, which explicitly defined black people as an infective hazard, has died hard (Gordon, 1983). The medical emphasis is often on diseases such as tuberculosis or hepatitis which are not necessarily the priorities for black people themselves, because they experience the same illhealth as other people in their socio-economic situation

(Webb, 1982). For example, several health authorities screen Asian women for hookworm, but do not ask white women whether they have had holidays abroad in places known to have a higher incidence of gastro-intestinal parasites.

The most recent manifestation of racism in the medical profession has been the profession's active involvement in virginity and paternity tests on black women and children coming to Britain from abroad, to join their relatives (Gordon, 1983). The medical profession's silence on the potential effect of NHS Charges for Overseas Visitors in deterring presentation for treatment is also a subtle manifestation of this collusion with racism.

Despite challenges by community health groups and the women's health movement, medical ideology still has hegemony over professional thinking *within* the health service. Consequently, these aspects of medical collusion and reproduction of racism are fundamental to an understanding of the politics of current health education campaigns directed at black people in Britain.


## 'ETHNIC RELATIONS' SOCIOLOGY

An explicit focus and implied definition of black people and ethnic minorities as 'the problem' in race relations is the nub of extensive controversy and criticism of race/ethnic relations studies (Jenkins, 1971). There are perspectives which take *culture* as their focus (e.g. Khan, 1979) and others which address the *political* sphere, seeing racism as an integral part of contemporary power relations (Centre for Contemporary Cultural Studies, 1982).

The dominant approach has been within a framework of cultural pluralism and ethnic diversity, in which a society and its ideologies are essentially unproblematic (Ben-Tovim and Gabriel, 1982). The relationship between 'culturally distinct' minorities and a majority white society are seen exclusively in terms of culture, apparently autonomous yet interacting with other social processes. 'Problems' are therefore the result of mismatches between minority and majority cultures which, according to the pluralistic view, meet on equal terms. The assumption that both sides in the ethnic relations equation are subject to the same forces means that tinkering with the cultural differences until there are equal components on each side will get the balance right. The potential for adequate reforms within the status quo are taken for granted, denying a major political dimension. Culture is the problem, and the outcome is to focus on minority culture, which deviates from the supposedly uniform 'norm'. It is then a small and almost imperceptible step to locate the cause of the mismatch and problems in black people and ethnic minorities themselves, and in their culture which is so pathologically different from the 'norm' (Lawrence, 1981).

This is the whole nub of the problem: that the 'classic' and dominant ethnic relations school, which has been popularised by health and other professionals, mislocates race relations entirely in the realms of culture, outside the political arena (Black, 1985; Rack, 1982). Such an approach effectively divides what the white majority see as different minorities, ignoring the fundamental entity of their united experience as an oppressed black minority. It obscures and denies the historical and contemporary power relations of race which have created an imbalance between white and black 'culturally distinct' groups. This perspective fudges the issue, serving as a powerful decoy. It is not just that it lets white society off the hook. It categorically excludes the experience of people as *black* people in a white society. In failing to address the issue of racism, this approach does not address black people's experience, and fails to provide an adequate response to their illhealth.

## DIFFERENT CULTURES: ALIEN, DEVIANT AND PATHOLOGICAL

There is an inherent and subtle contradiction in this emphasis on culture. While acting as a powerful decoy from racism, it nevertheless reflects its very nature, by emphasising 'difference' as alien, deviant, abnormal and pathological (Parmar, 1981). We need to take a closer look at what is often meant by 'different culture'.

It is around the issue of *difference* that there is a complex and often contradictory discussion. On the one hand descriptions of the particular differences peculiar to each group are an integral part of the culturalist approach, whilst 'common alienness' is also an issue. Minorities are alien first and distinct from each other (ethnic) second. To ignore differences is seen by some as egalitarian, treating all people the same, but by others as evidence of colour blindness. To emphasise difference within racist ideology is to reinforce and emphasise notions of alienness, whilst within an anti-racist perspective, recognition of difference is a prerequisite for a positive and sensitive awareness, a welcome departure from ethnocentrism.

Cultural differences of 'alien' origin are imbued with pejorative connotations when an uncritical view is held of white society as the accepted healthy norm. The 'generation conflicts' between young Asian girls/women (Ballard, 1979) and their parents are somehow seen as being of a different order from the long known 'generation gap' in English society (Parmar, 1981). Rather than being acknowledged as universal, problems between parents and children in families of Asian origin in Britain are used as evidence that the 'traditional Asian family' is firstly paramount in Asian communities in Britain, and secondly, inflexible and inappropriate (alien) to life in Britain and problematic (pathological) for the children. Clearly black people and ethnic minority families are unable to win, for whilst the Asian family is seen as an oppressive monolith on the one hand, the 'typical' West Indian family is seen as lax and undisciplined on the other (Lawrence, 1981; Black, 1985) and as the cause of an apparently poor performance amongst children at school.

## PROFESSIONAL HEALTH IDEOLOGIES: THEMES OF DEVIANCE AND UNIFORMITY

Health education has developed within a medical ideology, the methodology and concepts of which are rooted in the mechanistic view of life which gained supremacy in the nineteenth century

(Jewson, 1976). This simplistic biological analysis ignored the socio-economic context of health and illness, and paved the way for the depersonalisation of illness, which was seen as biological deviance from the 'normal' workings of the body. The biological agents of disease were seen simply as causes, which could be avoided by healthy living. In consequence, the major determinants of such deviance are located in the personal sphere of habits and hygiene, and the individual careless enough to become ill is held morally responsible for the misdemeanour. Having apparently abdicated responsibility for his/her own health, the ill person yields and submits to the medical profession who expropriate decisions and control over treatment and, therefore, health (Figlio, 1971).

This view has maintained its dominance, despite well-documented evidence of the role of socio-economic factors in determining health and illness (Townsend and Davidson, 1982). The strong association of social inequality and deprivation has not resulted in the success of a public health movement campaigning vigorously for the abolition of such pathogenic social conditions. The major thrust of preventive medicine and conventional health education has, instead, been to educate the 'ignorant' into healthy habits. The feasibility and relevance of such measures in chronically damp living conditions, high unemployment and increasing poverty for those particularly at risk of illhealth are rarely at issue. This situation has major implications for black people in a racist society in which they are seen as inferior. They are particularly vulnerable as victims of discrimination to unhealthy social and material circumstances (Brown, 1984). Their culture and lifestyles are blamed for their illhealth or underuse of health services, and social risk factors are minimised if not ignored altogether.

Management and treatment in the health service are the unquestioned domain of senior, highly trained professionals, against whom the patient and general public are relatively powerless. Entry to these elite ranks is rigidly controlled, and black people and ethnic minorities constitute a tiny minority. It is generally assumed that needs are similar everywhere, and that established policies and priorities are equally appropriate for everyone.

Whilst such a commitment to uniformity may appear egalitarian, it by no means embodies any meaningful concept of equality in a diverse multi-racial society. The obviously 'different' minority experiences or needs which are difficult for those in senior positions to imagine, understand or approve, are often interpreted as awkwardness, intransigence or ignorance. The black person is defined as a problem needing 'special' attention, or having special needs (Rack and Rowell, 1979). This is a misnomer in a service established to meet the needs of all its users, and reflects the view that minorities are alien and cause problems. Various voluntary projects have provided important bridges between homogeneous statutory services for the black and ethnic minority communities for whom they may be inappropriate or insensitive (Ahmed and Pearson, 1985; Pearson, 1985), but their implications are rarely taken on in the mainstream NHS services.

## THE CONVERGENCE OF MEDICAL IDEOLOGY AND ETHNIC RELATIONS: RACIST HEALTH EDUCATION POLICIES AND CAMPAIGNS

There are conceptual themes which are common to the dominant schools of thought in ethnicity studies and medicine, and which reinforce each other in policies on race and health. In both fields there is an uncritical assumption that a healthy 'norm' applies uniformly, and is an entity to which minorities should strive to assimilate. As a result of this emphasis in both ideologies, deviations are interpreted as pathological and pathogenic. The victim-blaming ideology of western medicine is mirrored by a culture-blaming ethos of most approaches to ethnic relations. It is therefore individuals and their alien culture which are believed to cause health problems in Britain.

The major effect of these themes in both ideologies is the value judgment and relative 'weight' attributed to individuals' habits and culture, at the expense of other socio-economic and political-structural factors. The focus and cultural distinctiveness or racial difference as an explanatory factor *per se* has led to some misleading and simplistic conclusions and definitions of 'problems'.

The mutually converging and reinforcing ideologies of western medicine and dominant culture-based ethnic relations ideologies have produced a particular strain of culture- and victim-blaming health education policies and campaigns. The aim has been to change black people's and ethnic minorities' lifestyles, habits, and attendance for treatment to 'norms' defined by professionals as healthy. This has often involved unintentional and subtle racist strategies and approaches which take white, middle-class patterns of behaviour and culture for granted as 'normal' and healthy, and indulge in stereotypes of black and ethnic minority cultures. Rarely has health education critically assessed the relevance of its conventional methods or content to the lives and experiences of those whose health it aims to promote, or sought to avoid the dangers of implicitly assuming that the lifestyles and values of black people and ethnic minorities need changing. An examination of recent health education projects and campaigns directed at the Asian community illustrates the practical impact of this convergence of ideologies.

## LEAD IN COSMETICS

One of the most obvious examples of culturally racist health education was the campaign in the late 1970s against the use of surma. Surma is a fine black powder applied to the conjunctival margins of some Asian infants and children. Most surma is imported from the Indian subcontinent, and in some preparations lead sulphide in the form of galena has become the major component. Other preparations contain charcoal or a mixture of galena, plant juices and ashes (Green *et al.*, 1979). High blood lead levels, and in some cases toxicity, were detected amongst Asian children in Bradford, in whom surma was believed to be the only source of lead. These and other similar findings of high lead levels in Asian children led to the banning of imported surma. There was an extensive campaign criticising the practice of applying surma, rather than education about the dangers of the galena-specific preparations.

As awareness has increased of the many sources of lead in the urban environment, house paint and lead water pipes in old terraced housing have been shown to be significant sources. This is precisely the type of housing in which many Asian families live. Residual lead in decaying inner city areas constitutes a social risk factor which is becoming recognised. Some local councils now give grants for the elimination of lead paint and pipes from houses, and for their replacement with less toxic materials.

Recently, there has been a welcome change in emphasis in health education warning of the potential dangers of some surma compounds. The Department of Trade has produced translated leaflets and posters entitled 'Surma—is your child at risk?' which warn that lead levels may be high in *some but not all* surma preparations. It also shows how to test for lead in surma, by dropping a small amount into a glass of water to see if it sinks, before applying it to a child's eyes. The change in emphasis from criticising a traditional practice of religious significance, to education about the hazards of some preparations, was the result of community pressure and complaints.

## THE RICKETS CAMPAIGN

Low blood levels of Vitamin D are the major factor associated with rickets and osteomalacia, of which bowed legs and bone pain are symptoms. Dietary deficiencies and lack of sunshine are thought to be the major causes of Vitamin D deficiency. A campaign to eradicate rickets in Britain in the 1950s encouraged the use of foods such as margarine, dried milk and cereals which were fortified with Vitamin D and others naturally rich in Vitamin D such as cod liver oil. Rickets re-emerged in the 1960s in children in poor families in Glasgow, including some Asians (Goel *et al.*, 1976). By the end of the 1970s, rickets was identified by the DHSS as an Asian problem. No single factor has been found to account for the higher incidence amongst British Asians (Sheiham and Quick, 1982) but the explanation adopted by the DHSS Rickets Campaign was the maladaptation of 'them' to our climate and way of life. For reasons which are still debated and unclear, the DHSS decided not to fortify chapati flour in the way that margarine and cereals had been fortified for the white community twenty years before. Instead, a change in Asian diet to those foods which had been fortified years before was encouraged, and more Asian women were extolled to expose themselves and their children to sunlight (DHSS, 1980).

The root causes of Vitamin D deficiency in poverty and deprivation were not mentioned. The lack of sunshine to which rickets and adult osteomalacia amongst women were attributed was seen as an obvious, avoidable by-product of insistence on living an 'Asian way of life' in Britain. Reluctance to go outdoors was seen as a manifestation of how Asian culture locks women away, rather than the by-product of fear of racist attacks. Exposure to sunshine was seen as a possibility, despite the fact that the majority of British Asians were forced to live in damp, inner city housing with little space in which to bask in the sun. Poverty and the financial constraints on trying to produce a balanced diet on low incomes or supplementary benefit, particularly when information on nutrition and health is not available in a relevant medium, language or appropriate background, were never encountered as possible. For example, one film entitled *New Ways* was produced by Ealing, Hammersmith and Hounslow Area Health Authority in 1979, and awarded a British Medical Association silver medal. With soundtracks in different Asian languages *New Ways* actively promoted 'integration' (assimilation, anglicisation), including eating cornflakes, as a strategy for achieving a health status which was perceived to be hampered by an Asian lifestyle in Britain. The points that the white British diet was sufficient in Vitamin D only because of fortification, and that there is no single homogeneous 'Asian culture', were missed by the Rickets Campaign. The outcome was that Asian people were perceived to have an inherently unhealthy diet, because of their 'ignorance' about nutrition. The solution to rickets was simple: 'the long term answer lies in health education and change towards a western diet and lifestyle' (Goel *et al.*, 1981: 405).

## THE ASIAN MOTHER AND BABY CAMPAIGN

The Asian Mother and Baby Campaign was well nicknamed 'son of rickets' at the DHSS. The same culture-blaming ideology was the basis of the campaign launched in September 1984 to improve the health of the Asian mother and her child. By the end of 1985 the campaign had been launched in eight health districts after consultation with local health professionals. Local Asian organisations were involved only at a very late stage, and were not always part of local steering groups or interview panels. For a campaign which claims to be aiming to help 'health professionals gain the co-operation of Asian families', such a top-down approach is regrettable. Already, the pejorative connotations creep in: Asian families are unco-operative with the NHS, resulting in late bookings for antenatal care, and higher perinatal mortality rates. It is 'their' intransigence which is to blame.

The campaign publicity identified 'language and cultural barriers' as problems which 'prevent them making full use of the service'. The onus slips once more on to those who do not speak the English uniformly required by the health service, or who may wish to see a female doctor. One of the video films shows a female doctor saying to a patient who does not speak English that she hopes she will be able to speak more English by the time the baby arrives. The problematic realm of 'their' culture creeps in once more. The barriers erected by institutionalised and personal racism which black and ethnic minority women encounter in the NHS, as anywhere else, are not acknowledged. The health hazards of living on supplementary benefit in down-town houses are not mentioned. The overall problem of poverty in all ethnic groups being associated with perinatal mortality is side-stepped. The solution is to cajole the dilatory, deficient Asian mother to avail herself of the all-welcoming NHS.

Asian link workers have been recruited by health authorities to work with health professionals, encouraging Asian women to attend for antenatal care. But experience has shown that the most successful link worker schemes are those in which there is a clear base and accountability to the community (Ahmed and Pearson, 1985; Pearson, 1985). It is only in these situations that the deficiencies of the service can be discussed with professionals, and rectified. Asian link workers responsible directly to health professionals, have a clear structural allegiance to the health service. In many cases they may have little scope for anything other than interpreting the midwife or health visitor's instructions.

## GENERAL DIETARY EDUCATION

There is a prevailing ethos amongst health professionals that different, alien diets cause health problems amongst black and ethnic minorities because 'their foods' are not available here and because their diets are somehow inherently unhealthy. Health visitors and health education officers seem unable to provide appropriate dietary advice, since 'their' foods are so different, even though many of them may call at an Asian greengrocer on the way home to buy vegetables for themselves. The problem of professionals' ignorance of black people's diets is compounded by a lack of appropriate health education material. The Health Education Council has begun to make a welcome departure by producing leaflets on nutrition which are translated, illustrated with photographs rather than poor drawings, showing Asian foods such as lentils and chapatis alongside English foods such as potatoes.

The pitfalls of vegetarianism have tended to be overemphasised at the expense of the positive benefits of eating pulses, wholemeal chapati flour, or cooking vegetables without draining the juices off. It is automatically assumed that dietary deficiencies are *inherently* part of pathogenic 'Asian' or Rastafarian vegan diets, and are the causes of iron-deficiency anaemia and other nutritional deficiencies, including rickets and osteomalacia. The constraints of poverty on choice of available food is rarely mentioned. To some extent, these attitudes reflect a generally carnivorous bias to dietary health education, but they also reflect a racist assumption that all Asians and Rastafarians are vegetarian. The implication once more is that the alien culture is unhealthy.

## PLAY AND CHILD DEVELOPMENT

It is possibly in the area of play and child development that conventional health education displays its most racist assumptions about black people's cultures and lifestyles. There are various issues involved. Firstly, methods of assessment and socialisation milestones are culture bound and take middle-class norms as their starting point in, for example, the ability to stack building bricks. Many of these milestones assume that the child has had access to toys and the undivided attention of a parent. Literature abounds with discussion of how the apparently ubiquitous 'West Indian' matriarchal, single-parent family results in an unstimulated child who has been farmed out to unregistered childminders and subsequently underachieves at school (Black, 1985; Pollock, 1982). The implicit blame is upon the single parent for using unregistered childminders, rather than pressure being brought to bear on local authorities to provide enough nurseries for children who need them.

While the stereotypical Afro-Caribbean 'problem' is perceived as lack of parental involvement in the home, the Asian family once again offends by its supposed excessive authority and control. The lack of toys for young Asian children to play with is often bemoaned as resulting in understimulated children who spend their day in the company of unstimulating parents. For some reason, playing with siblings is not seen as adequate, although this would be an important early socialising factor for white families. Many health education units have produced translated leaflets emphasising the importance of toys, but many families may not be able to afford them. More recently the Health Education Council has produced a more helpful leaflet showing children playing with boxes, tins and paper bags which may be more easily available, without incurring great cost. This leaflet also reflects multi-racial Britain, including photographs of children of all ethnic groups.

Many black and ethnic minority families live in high-rise flats or inner city housing where play space is woefully scarce. Concern is often expressed about the high number of road traffic accidents amongst Asian children in big cities, resulting in the production of many leaflets on road safety. Unfortunately, many children have nowhere to play other than the street, in areas where traffic may not be restricted, although the streets are narrow. On the one hand, play outside in the sunshine is encouraged, but on the other it is blamed for a higher incidence of accidents. Play schemes and traffic restrictions in the terraced streets, built for families when road traffic was sparse, would contribute far more to the health, safety and stimulation of black and ethnic minority children than exhorting parents to buy toys which they can ill afford.

## CONCLUSIONS

It is argued here that a conventional, uniform and victim-blaming approach to health education sees black and ethnic minority cultures as alien and pathological. This results in campaigns and approaches which hold 'different' minority experience, lifestyles and culture responsible for patterns of illhealth. Both the cause and solution to black people's health problems are located *outside* the political sphere, in the apparently depoliticised sphere of culture, integration and assimilation. Potted guides to culture (e.g. Henley, 1979), rarely written by minorities themselves, have become a vital source of instant 'expertise' on these cultures which are thought to cause so many health problems.

Only when health care and health education become de-professionalised, and have a multi-racial staff at all levels, will damaging stereotypes of people from black and ethnic minority communities be dismantled. When white staff work as equals with black people who have traditionally been in 'second-class' positions in the health service, so the inferior image should evaporate. With a direct input from black and ethnic minority communities and health service staff, health education strategies and policies will be more likely to address the most pressing issues and include those which are the priorities of the black communities themselves. This approach would also allow more scope for greater sensitivity in portraying and reflecting more accurately the social and material situation of black and ethnic minority communities, rather than depending on *ill*-informed and often racist stereotypes of other white health professionals.

## REFERENCES

Ahmed, A. and Pearson, M. (1985), *Directory of Maternity Initiatives for Black and Ethnic Minority Women*, Maternity Alliance, London.

Ballard, C. (1979), 'Conflict, Continuity and Change' in V. S. Khan (ed.), *Minority Families in Britain: Support and Stress*, Macmillan, London.

Banton, M. and Harwood, J. (1975), *The Race Concept*, David & Charles, Newton Abbot.

Ben-Tovim, G. and Gabriel, J. (1982), 'The Sociology of Race—Time to Change Course?' in Ohri, A. *et al.*, *Community Work and Racism*, Routledge & Kegan Paul, London.

Black, J. (1985), 'Child Health in Ethnic Minorities: the Difficulties of Living in Britain', *British Medical Journal*, 290: 579–654.

Brown, C. (1984), *Black and White Britain*, Heinemann, London.

Centre for Contemporary Cultural Studies (1982), *The Empire Strikes Back*, Hutchinson, London.

DHSS (1980), *Rickets and Osteomalacia*, Report of a Working Party on Fortification of Food with Vitamin D, Committee on Medical Aspects of Food Policy, HMSO, London.

DHSS (1981), *Civilian Doctor Statistics*, HMSO, London.

Donovan, J. (1984), 'Ethnicity and Health: A Review', *Social Science and Medicine*, 19(7): 663–70.

Doyal, L. *et al.* (1980), *Migrant Workers in the National Health Service*, A Report to the SSRC, Department of Sociology, Polytechnic of North London.

Figlio, K. (1971), 'The Historiography of Scientific Medicine: An Invitation to the Human Sciences', *Comparative Studies in Society and History*, 19: 262–86.

Glass, B. (1943), *Genes and the Man*, Columbia University Press, New York.

Goel, K. M. *et al.* (1976), 'Florid and Subclinical Rickets among Immigrant Children in Glasgow', *Lancet*, i: 1141–5.

Goel, K. M. *et al.* (1981), 'Reduced Prevalance of Rickets in Asian Children in Glasgow', *Lancet*, ii: 405–7.

Gordon, P. (1983), 'Medicine, Racism and Immigration Control', *Critical Social Policy*, 7: 6–20.

Green, S. D. R. *et al.* (1979), 'Surma and blood lead concentrations', *Publ. Hlth. Lond.*, 93: 371–6.

Henley, A. (1979), *Asian Patients at Hospital and at Home*, Pitman Medical Library, London.

Jenkins, R. (1971), *The Production of Knowledge at the Institute of Race Relations*, Independent Labour Party Publications.

Jewson, N. (1976), 'The Disappearance of the Sick Man from Medical Cosmology 1778–1870', *Sociology*, 10: 225–44.

Khan, V. S. (ed.) (1979), *Minority Families in Britain: Support and Stress*, Macmillan, London.

Lawrence, E. (1981), 'White Sociology, Black Struggle', *Multiracial Education*, 9: 3–17.

Lawrence, E. (1982), 'In the Abundance of Water the Fool is Thirsty', in Centre for Contemporary Cultural Studies, *The Empire Strikes Back*, Hutchinson, London.

Lewontin, R. C. (1972), 'Apportionment of Human Diversity', *Evol. Biol.* 6: 381–98.

Montagu, A. (ed.) (1964), *The Concept of Race*, Collier-Macmillan, Toronto.

Parmar, P. (1981), 'Young Asian Women: Critique of the Pathological Approach', *Multiracial Education*, 9: 9–29.

Pearson, M. (ed.) (1985), *Racial Equality and Good Practice— Maternity Care*, National Extension College, Cambridge.

Pollock, M. (1982), 'The Care of Immigrant Children' in C. Hart, *Child Care in General Practice*, 2nd edn, Churchill Livingstone, London.

Rack, P. (1982), *Race, Culture and Mental Disorder*, Tavistock, London.

Rack, P. and Rowell, V. R. (1979), 'Health Education Needs of a Minority Ethnic Group', *Jnl. Inst. of Health Educn.*, 17(4): 3–18.

Sheiham, H. and Quick, A. (1982), *The Rickets Report*, Haringey CHC and CRC, London.

Smith, D. (1980), *Overseas Doctors in the National Health Service*, Heinemann, London.

Townsend, P. and Davidson, N. (1982), *Inequalities in Health: The Black Report*, Penguin, Harmondsworth.

Webb, P. (1982), 'Ethnic Health Project 1979/1980', *Royal Soc. of Health Jnl*, 1: 29–34.

# CHAPTER 4

# ISSUES OF RESPONSIBILITY AND CONTROL IN THE FEEDING OF FAMILIES

## Nickie Charles and Marion Kerr

Current nutritional thinking links coronary heart disease, constipation, bowel cancer, tooth decay, diabetes and a host of other ills to the modern western tendency to consume over-refined foods high in fat and sugar content. The solution to these problems, so the story goes, lies in individuals changing their diets. We must eat wholemeal bread, lean meat, drink skimmed milk and give up sweets and sugar. But such a transformation is not as easy as it seems; white sliced bread is cheap, lean meat is expensive, the milkman delivers full-fat milk to the doorstep and children (not to mention adults) love sweets. If we have a limited amount of money to spend on food, no transport to get to an 'enlightened' supermarket and two or three toddlers to drag around the shops with us, we will continue to buy the foods that are easy to get and 'bad' for us, but in addition to all our other problems we will feel guilty. Clearly, it is not enough simply to persuade individuals that a certain foodstuff is not good for them. If they do not have the power to act on this knowledge, then all that will be achieved is the creation of an enormous burden of guilt and frustration; a recipe for deterioration in health rather than anything else. It is the question of power in relation to food choice which is the principal focus of our discussion here.

In the case of diet and nutrition, exhortations to eat more

healthy food are often directed towards women as they, suppos-edly, determine the family's diet. Indeed women as wives and mothers are expected to be responsible not only for the feeding of their husbands and children but for their health in general (Graham, 1979). In the course of this paper we shall demonstrate that although women are largely responsible for cooking within families, control over which foods find their way to the table lies elsewhere. Within the family itself men are powerful, and, external to the family, power is exercised by the food industry in the interest of profit rather than health. Women, although burdened with responsibility for family food provision, do not enjoy the power which would allow them meaningfully to control their own and their families' food intake.

In what follows we draw upon the experiences of 200 women, mothers of young children, who shared with us their thoughts and feelings on feeding their families during the course of our research.[1] We concentrate, initially, on food practices within the family and discuss their implications for changes in eating habits. We then move to a consideration of the constraints placed on families' food provision by the food industry and, finally, look at the implications of our findings for nutrition education.

## PLEASING MEN: FOOD CONSUMPTION WITHIN THE FAMILY

The women we interviewed came from a wide range of social backgrounds,[2] but almost all lived within families characterised by a traditional division of labour. The men were away from home for at least 8 hours a day in full-time, paid employment while the women were busy feeding children, cleaning children, playing with children, shopping, cleaning and cooking proper meals; all unpaid. After a day's unpaid work in the house, or sometimes before it, many of them went out to a low-paid, part-time job, often a repetition of the tasks they carried out during the rest of the day but now outside rather than inside their homes. Men's involvement in domestic labour tended to be episodic and, in the case of shopping and cooking, often non-existent.[3]

A central feature of women's food preparation consisted of cooking a 'proper meal' ready for their husbands' return from work. This meal consisted of 'meat and two veg', and its regular provision and consumption made the women feel that they were feeding their families 'properly'. By this they meant that they were eating foods that were healthy in the form that was appropriate to the family (Murcott, 1982; Charles and Kerr, 1984). Most women felt it was extremely important that their husbands and children ate proper meals on a daily basis. One woman told us:

'As long as they have one good meal down them a day and their breakfast then I don't worry. . . . I think that as long as you get a good square dinner in front of them every day they can't go far wrong.'

And men, in particular, were thought to 'deserve' proper meals.

'I still think myself that when it comes down to it a woman runs a house and has children—I've never changed my views. . . . If you're at home all day then naturally your (husband) expects to come home to a cooked meal.'

The proper meal, and its consumption together by mother, father and children, in a fundamental way symbolises the family. It has a strong social significance as well as providing the conceptual framework through which women assess the nutritional adequacy of their own and their families' diets. Proper meal consumption structures families' diets and its provision is not only something that women feel is important for men, but also something which men themselves feel that they deserve. Foods such as salad were not an acceptable substitute; beans and pulses would probably be even less so.

'Fresh meat, vegetables, potatoes, fresh greens, just a meal. Unless I do a meal like that he won't class it as a meal, if I do a salad it's not a meal to him. . . . My husband won't come home from work after a long day and have a salad, he'd fly. He expects a hot meal and I think he deserves it.'

Men's need for a 'proper meal' affects the diet of the whole family. Women do not feel it appropriate to provide them with other foods; indeed they would not be fulfilling their role as homemaker if they departed from tradition in this way. However, when men were away from home practices might alter.

'If Greg's been away I've not bothered to cook proper meals— proper meals in as much as a cooked meal. I probably wouldn't go to the trouble of cooking myself meat, vegetables and potatoes.'

The preference of many men for a traditional meal of meat and two veg, and the views expressed by the women that men deserved a proper meal, are not the only factors determining what food women cook. A second and equally important consideration is that women cook *for* men, they cook to please men and to show their affection for men. The old saying that the way to a man's heart is through his stomach is not dead. It lives in the daily practice of women in families up and down the country. Their own likes and those of their children are set aside in order to ensure that those of their husbands are catered for.

When talking to the women, we asked them what were the sorts of things they took into account when considering which food to buy. Time and again men's likes and dislikes headed the list, time and again women's own likes and dislikes were not mentioned until they were specifically asked. In fact many women told us they did not have any strong likes and dislikes.

'I like to please my family more, I mean it doesn't matter to me, I can eat anything.'

Clearly men's and, to a lesser extent, children's food preferences have more of an impact on the family's diet than those of women. We would argue that this stems directly from the fact that it is women who prepare and cook the food and they aim to please those for whom they are cooking. When women spoke about their experiences during the early stages of their marriages this became particularly clear.

'To start with I used to try lots of things on him and if he liked them I'd make them again and if he didn't I'd know not to do them again.'

Pleasing a man through cooking is often regarded as a fundamental part of the marital relationship and much support was evident for the belief that 'the way to a man's heart is through his stomach'.

'Well I think ... I mean as much as I sort of dislike role playing and, you know, women being expected to be the "little wife", cooking and looking after the children and staying at home and baking and being there with a pinny on, slippers—I hate it—it is still there, you know, you can't ignore that it is there. I think it is very much there and I think—if a fella likes you, I mean before you are married, if he likes you and you invite him round for a meal and you impress him with your cooking he likes you even more. If you served him a boiled egg he dislikes you, he goes off you a bit, yes I do think so, yes.'

Preparing meals with care and trying to please the person for whom you are cooking is regarded as an expression of love, a demonstration that women are looking after their partners as they 'ought' to be.

This desire to please men and, indeed, retain their affection and loyalty through cooking meals that they enjoy, inevitably leads to adapting the family diet to men's preferences. Thus men do not need to refuse food for its absence from the family diet to be ensured; most women tailor the meals they prepare to their partner's preferences as a matter of course. It is a sign of their affection.

'He ain't faddy, he eats anything put in front of him. But if I find there's something he particularly likes like steak or gammon I try and do it again a bit sooner than the time I did it before.'

The sexual division of labour within the family, of which women's role as provider of food is an important part, is fundamentally a relation of power. For most of the women we spoke to these power relations were apparent in the way they subordinated their own food preferences to those of their partners and in the views they expressed on these issues. However, in some families the power of men over women was expressed much more directly. This most often happens through the sanction of refusal of food, a hurtful event which many women had experienced, particularly at the beginning of their marriages.

The interchange between husband, wife and interviewer reported here illustrates the power enjoyed by men which some clearly regard as their right.

Hus: There was once when you made something I didn't like— I remember that.

Wife: Oh yes I forgot about that.

Hus: Yeah. But apart from a broken plate and a rather dirty wall there was no other damage.

Wife: I forgot about that altogether.

Hus: Yeah, I threw it at you didn't I? Do you remember?

Int: Did you?

Hus: Yeah. Oh dear me I think I said something like shove that fucking muck—oh, sorry, the tape's on, isn't it, I don't want to be rude. That was when we'd just got married, wasn't it, and you thought that was an acceptable standard of nourishment.

Wife: I thought it was nice, it tasted nice.

Int: That was right at the beginning of your marriage?

Hus: That's right, yeah. She's never given me any of that rubbish again so that's all right.

Most men did not need to react so violently;[4] simple refusal of food that they did not wish to eat was enough to ensure that their wives did not provide it again.

The desire on the part of women to please men with their cooking, coupled with the centrality of the notion of the 'proper meal' to the structure of family eating, means that it is often difficult for women to change the family's diet even if they want to. In response to current nutritional guidelines, several women had tried to change from white to wholemeal bread but had given up in the face of opposition from their partners. One woman recounted her experience.

'My husband won't have wholemeal bread all the time but he will eat small amounts of it. I've tried to cut white bread out, but that just doesn't work, so I buy the white bread to keep the peace.'

On the other hand, in families where men take a liking to wholemeal bread then women are able to change the whole family over onto this type of bread.

'The kids prefer white but I never get it for them. . . . Mike doesn't like the texture of white bread, thinks it's a bit pappy.'

One woman who had recently separated from her husband felt liberated from the tyranny of his preferences for fried, fatty foods. Previously his demands had totally determined the family's diet.

'He was a fry up, always fried foods, all the time, greasy foods, always the same things and if I put in front of him what we have now, "What's this rubbish, take that away, I don't want that, that's not going to fill me up". . . . He liked solid food on his plate. He wouldn't have salad and none of this noodles. That's not good enough for a working man.'

Worries about the fat content of men's diets were fairly often expressed but, as these comments indicate, women's concern over health issues does not necessarily lead to changes in diet.

'I used to worry a bit about my husband's eating a lot of fried things . . . but I would never, I don't think I would ever be able to change my husband's eating habits so I'm not even bothering trying. Sometimes I think, I look at him and I think he shouldn't really be eating all that fat but I wouldn't be able to alter him so I don't really actually worry about it. . . . He'll just sail on through fatty things no matter what anybody says . . . so I'm not going to make his life a misery nagging and mine a misery worrying about it. My philosophy is to change the things I can change and accept the things I can't.'

Women also told us that they were unable to buy food which they thought would be healthier precisely because partners and children would not eat it.

'I would prefer to eat food that hasn't got a lot of things added but to do that you have to go to a health food shop and my husband wouldn't eat that type of food and I'm sure the kiddies wouldn't.'

The *control* exerted by men over the family diet is graphically illustrated by the experience of one of the women. She was married for the second time and now ate very differently from the way she had eaten during her first marriage. This she described as follows:

'He ate a lot of chips and fried things, I used to cook loads and loads of fried things and loads of horrible, fatty, starchy things, white bread, he was completely different.'

Her second husband 'changed her over' and now her diet is quite different. She described the change.

'When I first started living with Simon we both decided not to fry so many things and I recognised food values more . . . he ate better than me, you see, so when we started living together I just went on to what he liked.'

This family's diet contained wholemeal bread, brown rice, relatively high amounts of fresh fruit and raw vegetables; pulses and pasta were also included. These foods are typically part of middle-class diets and indicate the radical change that has occurred in her and her children's food intake since she began to live with her second husband.[5] Men, although they do not stir the cooking pot, control to a significant extent what goes into it.

The cost of food is another factor that women have to consider. For most women in low-income families cost has over-riding importance in determining the food they can buy and where they can buy it. If women have little money to pay for public transport and no car to drive to large supermarkets, they are bound to rely on the local shops. These are not, necessarily, more expensive than larger supermarkets but the range of products they stock is much smaller, and the likelihood of their stocking skimmed milk and wholemeal bread is practically non-existent. They *do*, however, stock a wide range of tinned, packeted and frozen foods—precisely the sorts of foods which typify the over-refined, high-fat, salt and sugar diet that we are being told we must avoid.

Women in higher-income families may be able to go to the large supermarkets and afford to buy expensive 'healthful' foods. However, even then there is no guarantee that their expensive wholemeal loaf contains no pesticide residues and that the fruit in the additive-free jam was grown organically.


## 'HOUSEWIVES' CHOICE? FOOD PRODUCTION AND THE CONSUMER

Women as individuals are powerless when faced with the organised strength of the food industry. And the women we spoke to were far from happy about this situation. This is important because it is often assumed that the 'average British housewife' is not greatly concerned about the content and properties of the food she buys and that many have swallowed the myth of consumer sovereignty in the marketplace. Such assumptions are made both by manufacturers and retailers—who work hard at the process of convincing us that we do have a real and unrestricted choice—and their critics (Turner and Gray, 1982; Wright, 1981). We have found, however, that underlying apparent consumer apathy and lack of concern are significant feelings of impotence. The women we spoke with expressed dissatisfaction and unease about issues such as pesticide spraying, the injection of meat and the addition of preservatives, colouring, sugar and salt to the food they buy and consume. But they feel there is little they can do to alter these worrying practices and exclude possibly dangerous, certainly unhealthful substances from their diet.

The notion of consumer choice rests very uneasily with the comments made to us by the women we interviewed. At the most basic level, they often pointed out that what appeared to be variety was often actually many different brands of the same product.

'I wouldn't say supermarkets always stock a good choice ... you can buy a lot of things that are the same but maybe different brands, instead of widening their scope of foods more.'

'You can go to all sorts of different shops but they all sell the same sort of thing, there's not a lot of variety. I don't know what sort of things I'd like to see but when you see supermarkets in America on the television there seem to be all sorts of different things which we don't get ...'

Some women openly doubted the myth of consumer sovereignty and this was especially apparent to those who tried to formulate their food-purchasing habits around health concerns. A woman who had adopted a wholefood diet, for example, said:

'I know that I'm in a minority as far as eating habits are concerned so I don't expect to be very well catered for. I think most consumers *are* catered for but I'm not sure how much their tastes are manufacturers determining what you eat by putting them in the shops, for example, horrible junk pot noodles. People buy it 'cos it's on the market.'

And another woman commented:

'If you go to buy snack foods or something small to eat then you have to fall back on a bar of chocolate because it's so difficult to get anything. .... I mean they're all sugar and starch, you know, there's nothing tasty or wholesome and healthy that you can buy like that.'

Furthermore, if we delve deeper into the women's comments we find that even those who stated themselves to be satisfied with the range of products available to them do not feel they exercise control over what food goes into shops or the content and composition of it.

Let us take as an example the case of food additives. A range of substances are added to processed foods not only in order to preserve them but also to enhance their flavour and colour in order, so the manufacturers maintain, to make them more acceptable to the consumer. These practices were recognised by the women although they were by no means always appreciative of the cosmetic treatment food received. As one woman said:

'I mean all the colourings and artificial flavourings and things that are added; if they weren't added I'm sure people would still eat the same sort of things without all the added colouring. Manufacturers think they have got to make things look attractive in order to sell them.'

And there was evidence that women felt such processes should be more tightly regulated.

'Like monosodium glutamate they know knocks off brain cells and yet it's still permitted to be used in food as a flavour enhancer. I think that's absolutely ludicrous. I mean when you're cooking a meal like shepherd's pie with potatoes and mince you don't have a little bottle of monosodium glutamate that you sprinkle on food. I mean if it isn't necessary in your kitchen why is it necessary to put it into processed food and I think that the fact it's allowed is very wrong.'

Disquiet was frequently expressed about food additives and they were clearly linked in many women's minds with forms of illness and allergy, in particular, hyperactivity, cancer, arthritis and heart disease.

'Hasn't a lot of research been done into cancer and they've found that additives can—I know they haven't found a cure or a reason why people get it but additives could have a lot to do with it. They think they've found this in hyperactive children haven't they? Things like saccharin and things that are added. And with arthritis as well, I mean that's a horrible thing that a lot of people fear getting in old age and they've found marvellous diets that can stop it. They are not marvellous diets they are just stopping people eating a lot of things with additives, it's just common sense really.'

'Monosodium glutamate ... that's supposed to clog you up, clog up your arteries and things, isn't it, I don't know, give you high blood pressure.... I think so, it's salty stuff, isn't it? I don't really know specifically, I've never—I should know more about it I suppose, but just the preservatives and things that you read in the paper every so often that they cause cancer in fish or something.'

However, women were uncertain about the strategy that they should adopt in the face of such concerns. Selecting food on the basis of excluding additives was felt to be a difficult if not impossible undertaking. For one thing, labelling was felt to be inadequate and often incomprehensible.

'We don't know in straight English layman's terms what they are. Monosodium glutamate—when you really think about it, it sounds horrible, doesn't it? And all these other things you read. They put additives on tins but I would prefer to know what they actually are and what they do to you.'

'I would like to know proper ingredients because half the stuff they put on packets you don't know what on earth it is. You just look and you're no wiser so you accept it.'

Small wonder, then, that few women reported assiduous attention to food labelling when buying food. The time taken in such research might be considerable; as one woman said 'I'd never get round the supermarket if I did that.'

However, the women's comments also strongly indicate that if we take the trouble to search for relatively pure and unadulterated foods we are likely to be disappointed.

'I had a thing at one time when I wouldn't buy anything with monosodium glutamate in it but there again, if you look, you haven't really got a choice, you've got to have some things like that in it ... even crisps have got anti-oxidants in them. It's amazing ... I often spend quite a while looking at tins and checking what they have in and putting some back down again and saying "No, I'm not having that brand." '

'I look at everything that I buy. I find it difficult to buy anything that's ... especially with tinned soup—I don't mind having tinned soup once in a while but I can't find one that doesn't have anything in it, even the H—— has mostly sugar and monosodium glutamate.... And jams, I bought a jar of marmalade the other day, I had to pay 70p compared with say 20 or 30 just to get one that didn't have anything else but sugar and fruit in it.... I find it really difficult, it's a problem buying anything without colouring and things.'

Furthermore, foods with fewer additives were usually found to be more expensive, as the comment above makes clear, and this state of affairs was also observed as operating in relation to more healthful foods in general.

'Wholemeal flour, it's one of the flours that's supposed to be better for you. On the other hand if I do change over, it's a whole lot dearer. Where you're limited to one make—is it Allinson's, the brown one?—if you're limited to their make so they can ask a particular price—is it 43p or 45p for a good self-raising flour, and ordinary flour you've probably got three or four choices.'

Despite their unease about food content, women frequently thought they had to accept the status quo. In these terms the ingestion of food additives was the inevitable price to be paid for the availability of quick and convenient foods. The only means of avoiding such additives was to prepare everything yourself from fresh ingredients.

'I wouldn't say I worry about them but if something's got artificial colouring, artificial sweetening, then I think, ugh. But I wouldn't say it's something that I worry about because it's something I haven't got that much control over. I mean obviously you can buy fresh things but if you want a quicker meal then you have to buy what's available.'

This clearly does not constitute the expression of free choice or control on the part of women themselves. Furthermore the problem did not end here. It was often pointed out that even the consumption of fresh food did not guarantee an uncontaminated diet. One woman expressed the typical consumer conundrum thus:

'The fact that they have to give a list of what's in doesn't mean a thing to me because even if it's written on the packet or whatever—I mean I don't really know what it is. I'm not all that happy about it but, you know, I suppose you just have to trust that there's nothing awful going on. . . . You sort of take it or leave it, don't you? I would say you either cooked all your own food and prepare all your own . . . but there again the vegetables that you buy have probably been sprayed with something or other . . .'

In these circumstances, assailed by potential health hazards no matter what buying strategy was employed, many women under-standably affected to ignore the issue of health as a primary factor in the selection of foodstuffs. After all, we have already seen they have other more obviously pressing considerations to take into account. But, in fact, the women's comments suggest that their apparent lack of concern over food content can, in many cases, be interpreted as an expression of their impotence, neatly summed up in the words of one woman, 'It's pointless to worry about what you're not going to alter.' Worrying, in these terms, was anxiety without hope of relief, lending further credence to the view that acceptance was the best strategy, as this woman graphically describes:

'I mean there's pollution in the air all the time and I mean what can you do. I mean food gets polluted anyway as it's been grown. If I thought about everything we just wouldn't eat. I'd have all the air being purified and we'd all walk round with masks on and you can't do that so I don't see any point in getting uptight really. There's a lot of things that I do think are worth changing but there's nowt I can do about it all no matter how hard you fight so there's no use me getting uptight about it cos I'd make my life a misery and I'd make their life a misery.'

# CONCLUSIONS

The point that came across time and again in our interviews with women was that they lack the power to change their families' diets. Because food plays such an important role in the marital relationship, and regular provision of proper meals for men is a fundamental part of being a proper wife and mother, women are constrained by their partner's preferences. They undoubtedly have the responsibility for food provision at this stage in the family's lifecycle, but the power to control the content of the family's diet is more than likely to lie with their partners. Similarly, their voicing of anxiety about food manufacture and agricultural practices demonstrates that here again individual women feel powerless to change their families' diets for the better. Power over the food we eat lies largely with the food manufacturers and agribusiness, not with women struggling to feed their families on ever-shrinking wage packets.

Examination of these issues highlights the fact that current exhortations to take personal responsibility for our health and, in the case of women as wives and mothers, the health of other family members, is an insufficient, if not inappropriate, response to the problems of dietary change. Furthermore, mere advocacy by health educators implies that information-giving alone can provide a solution. Thus it performs the ideological function of masking the structural determinants of, in this case, a nutritionally unsound diet. The need to effect changes at the level of food production, manufacture and retail has been recognised in recent nutritional reports (NACNE, 1983; DHSS, 1984). Their recommendations include changes in current governmental and EEC regulations governing the grading, content, labelling and pricing of food products. Nevertheless, primary emphasis is still being placed on health education as a means of encouraging an informed choice of appropriate food stuffs; the question of who determines the choice of food within families has not been addressed at all.

Given what we have said about women's effective control over family diets, there is obviously a need for nutrition education which is provided through media and in venues accessible to men as well as women. Antenatal clinics and child health clinics, where most formal education for adults takes place, are rarely frequented by men nor, as we have seen, are food shops, where further developments in communicating information about diet are likely to take place. Yet the message is clear that targeting women alone with health education will only serve to increase their burden of guilt rather than lead to a transformation of family eating habits. Ensuring equal access to nutrition education in schools for both boys and girls is obviously of importance and will hopefully yield valuable results in the future. But there is a need to think creatively about influencing the fathers as well as the mothers of these children if eating habits currently practised in the home are to be changed.

The issues raised here, however, point to more far-reaching changes in the theory and practice of health education. Clearly health educators have much to learn from those they seek to teach; about what information is useful and relevant to their everyday lives and about what action is possible. Here we would emphasise the need for health educators to encourage the pooling of knowledge and concerns rather than assuming expert status for themselves. Furthermore, if health education is to be a genuine force for change, the issue of who has power over the food we eat must be confronted, and this points to the need for organisation as well as information at the level of the community and the workplace. Providing opportunities for women to meet and share their worries over food, for example, would not only help to assuage the significant amount of guilt they currently feel but could also be productive of consumer pressure for changes in food manufacture and retail practices. Similarly, health educators could usefully encourage the placing of health concerns on the agenda of trade unions within the agricultural and food industries. There is also a need to bring collective pressure to bear to change the current practices of many workplaces, hospitals and schools rather than directing attention solely towards home consumption.[6] Such measures would address the question of power which, we have tried to show, is central to any successful attempt to change people's eating habits. Indeed we have tried to illustrate that in the absence of such collective organisation and concerted action, health education can only continue to require individuals to exercise responsibility for a nutritionally sound diet without commensurate control over the processes which largely determine this important contribution to our health.

## NOTES

1 This research was carried out in the city of York and its surrounding villages. Two hundred women with pre-school age children were interviewed during 1982 and 1983. The interview covered all major aspects of family food provision and consumption, including household budgeting, the sexual division of labour within the home, the role of food in family relationships as well as women's concepts of health and diet and their major sources of advice and information. We are indebted to the Health Education Council for funding this research. However, the views expressed here are the authors' own and should not be seen as necessarily reflecting those of the HEC.

2 The social class distribution of our sample is provided in table form below. The Registrar General's classification of occupations forms the basis of these definitions and attributions of class were made according to current or last full-time work outside the home in the case of women as well as their partners.

|  | Women's social class | Men's social class |
|---|---|---|
| Social class | No. of women | No. of women |
| I/II | 42 (21%) | 60 (30%) |
| IIIN | 104 (52%) | 28 (14%) |
| IIIM | 29 (15%) | 78 (39%) |
| IV/V | 18 (9%) | 21 (11%) |
| Student/not given | 7 (4%) | 3 (2%) |
| No partner | – | 10 (5%) |

While women from all social classes were represented amongst our sample, only one woman belonged to an ethnic minority. This reflects the fact that the area in which we carried out our research has a very small black population. Thus we are unfortunately unable to comment on the specific problems which may be faced by women of colour.

3   In 92 families (46%) women alone did the shopping and in only 21 families (10.5%) was shopping shared equally by the marital partners. Women always prepared meals in 121 families (60.5%) and in only 2 families was cooking shared equally. Thirty-three men (17.5%) had never cooked a meal since the couple began living together.

4   Studies of domestic violence have shown that food and its provision can often spark off a violent incident. See Dobash and Dobash, 1980; Ellis, 1983.

5   There are definitely class-related patterns in eating, and changes in diet often follow upon social mobility, as, for example, in the case of women from working families who by virtue of higher education move into middle-class professions. However, it is important to point out that men's conservative eating habits and their expectation of a 'proper meal' were as commonly reported by middle-class women as by their working-class sisters.

6   See, for example, various publications from London Food Commission, PO Box 291, London N5 1DU.

## REFERENCES

Charles, N. and Kerr, M. (1984), *Attitudes towards the Feeding and Nutrition of Young Children*, Report to the Health Education Council, London.

DHSS (1984), *Diet and Cardiovascular Disease*, Report of the Committee on Medical Aspects of Food Policy (COMA), London.

Dobash, R. and Dobash, R. (1980), *Violence Against Wives*, Open Books, London.

Ellis, R. (1983), 'The Way to a Man's Heart: Food in the Violent Home' in Murcott, A. (ed.), *The Sociology of Food and Eating*, Gower, London.

Graham, H. (1979), 'Prevention and Health: Every Mother's Business, A Comment on Child Health Policies in the 1970s' in *The Sociology of the Family*, Sociological Review Monograph, 28, University of Keele.

Murcott, A. (1982), 'On the Social Significance of the "Cooked Dinner" in South Wales', *Social Science Information*, 21, 4/5: 677–96.

National Advisory Committee on Nutrition Education (1983), *A Discussion Paper on Proposals for Nutritional Guidelines for Health Education in Britain*, HEC, London.

Turner, M. and Gray, J. (eds) (1982), *Implementation of Dietary Guidelines: Obstacles and Opportunities*, British Nutrition Foundation, London.

Wright, H. (1981), *Swallow It Whole*, New Statesman Report, 4.

# CHAPTER 5

# OCCUPATIONAL HEALTH AND ILLNESS: THE POLITICS OF HAZARD EDUCATION

Andrew Watterson

## INTRODUCTION

Traditional occupational health and safety education for employees in Britain rests on shaky and highly political foundations. Paid work is presented as a generally healthy and safe activity for all classes in our society. Inequalities in occupational health are rarely mentioned. Those in medical and government circles, who set workplace health and safety standards, portray themselves and their policies as neutral and scientific, entirely separate from the economic and political influences around them. Employers, too, assume a façade of objectivity when hazards at work are examined and occupational health education schemes are proposed. These myths are deeply rooted and widely accepted in our society. There is an urgent need now to analyse how this has happened and what can be done to rectify the position. The solutions will not be found in endless descriptions of hazards but in a close scrutiny of those factors which historically have influenced occupational health education. Once the political causes of hazards at work have been identified, the process of formulating appropriate changes in occupational health education can begin.

For the purposes of this chapter occupational health education refers specifically to worker education on occupational health and safety: it does not cover conventional health education on subjects like alcohol, food, exercise and tobacco, although the two new approaches are linked. Traditional health educators are usually paid professionals, such as occupational health nurses or safety officers. However, trade union activists, community workers and members of tenants' associations may also be involved in workplace health education.


## THE PROTECTIVE CONTINUUM OF WORK HAZARDS

Any attempt to root occupational health education in the generation of work hazards confronts what can be termed 'the protective continuum'. Within this continuum views are held and generally accepted which 'explain' work hazards in various ways. At one end there is the view that work hazards do not exist, thus workers do not need protection from them; at the other, it is argued that hazards exist because of workers' irresponsibility, and thus that they should take measures to protect themselves. These views, limited and simplistic as they are, are reproduced both by management and more traditional health educators in their endeavour to protect the productive process.

I shall illustrate three points in this protection continuum by drawing stereotypical statements which summarise the ideologies being propounded. These will serve to highlight the crux of the problem for the would-be radical occupational health worker. I shall then suggest alternative ways in which the protection continuum may be challenged.

*Firstly:* 'Britain's health and safety at work record is excellent. We have few accidents and even fewer diseases.'
*Secondly:* 'Jobs are crucial to the economy and if we want employment, we must risk a few accidents and illnesses at work. The risks anyway are lower at work than crossing the road. Smoking and alcohol kill far more workers than any British industry.'
*Thirdly:* 'Where accidents do occur at work, careless and stupid workers are to blame.'

These statements are linked together by a certain, sometimes contradictory, view of the world and explain much of past and present thinking on worker hazard education.

## Ignoring occupational hazards

The first statement, claiming that few accidents and fewer diseases occur in the workplace, provides arguments for a very limited occupational health programme: this is what we now have and so represents the 'status quo'. What evidence is there to support the statement? Any set of statistics will produce controversy, especially in medicine, yet official reports have produced occupational disease and injury statistics which seem difficult to ignore and which are widely acknowledged to be underestimates.[1] In 1980 officially recorded non-fatal accidents reported to the Health and Safety Commission totalled 274,800; each year between 1980 and 1984, approximately 630,000 working days were lost to industry due to occupational skin diseases; 1,000 people became eligible to claim benefit for occupational asthma; 764,000 working days were lost in the NHS because of back pain amongst nurses. An estimated 2,000 people each year will die from asbestos-induced diseases and Richard Peto estimates 50,000 such deaths will occur between 1982 and 2012 (Peto, 1982). American scientists have suggested that 30 per cent of all diseases in that country could have occupationally related causes (HSC, 1984: 3). British occupationally related cancer deaths probably account for at least 6,500 deaths each year (Gill, 1985: 400). Whichever ways the figures are interpreted, each year hundreds of workers are killed in Britain by accidents, hundreds of thousands are injured and thousands die from occupationally linked diseases. The pain, suffering and economic damage experienced through occupational health and safety problems is enormous and shameful.

One explanation for the low priority and scant attention given to occupational illhealth by employers, government and health educators now and in the past must lie in the restricted nature of official health and safety statistics. Often no information has been made available to employees; sometimes misinformation on hazard effects has occurred. Under capitalism (and indeed in some other types of industrial society), the production and service workers and their families often bear the costs of occupational illhealth and accidents both physically and economically. It is axiomatic that employers, who consider profitability and high and consistent production levels to be their principal aims, will not give the same importance to health and safety and will try to unload the costs of diseases and accidents on to the employees and the state. This has been done very successfully in the past in the asbestos, construction, agriculture, shipbuilding and chemical industries. The length of time between exposure to hazardous substances and the development of industrial diseases (sometimes four decades or more later) makes it very difficult for employees to connect the events, gain recognition of the disease aetiology and then obtain compensation. With diseases like pneumoconiosis, occupational deafness, asthma and dermatitis, the difficulties of getting a diagnosis from the medical profession are considerable and the civil and statutory legal claims process is then a lengthy, uncertain and often expensive process.

The social, economic and legal obstacles in the way of better accident and disease reporting, recording and publicity provide a solid political explanation for traditional health education inertia on work hazards. Any health educator who wished to help workers identify, firstly, the hazardous nature of their work and consequent injury and disease, and, secondly, how to remove and reduce hazards and claim compensation for past ill-effects, would not be welcomed by most employers. Traditional health education in workplaces has, therefore, become a peripheral activity to many employees. Health educators have ignored or sidestepped the issue of hazardous health conditions and concentrated on the 'individual' problems of workers' bad habits—smoking, drinking, etc.: this approach is acceptable to employers but is marginal and indeed sometimes offensive to the employee whose own experiences at work relate to major hazards not personal habits. 'Habits' are vital for the classic victim-blaming approach but are irrelevant to the political and economic causes of occupational hazards. In a noisy, dusty, fume-filled factory, office or farm, the conditions are created not by the employee but by the owner of the place. Failure or refusal to recognise this fact by health educators explains why trade unions and pressure groups have contributed most to the developments of theory and practice in education on occupational health.

## Justifying occupational hazards

The second statement—jobs are crucial to the economy and if we want employment we must risk a few accidents and illnesses at work—has retained acceptability because of subtle cultural influences which have gone unchallenged by traditional health educators. Employers encourage these conservative attitudes. In some senses, very extensive non-formal education does occur at the workplace and it is devoted to the establishment and maintenance of the 'status quo'. In induction courses, apprentice training, general conversation, posters, leaflets and safety manuals, this view will be explicitly and implicitly put and in this sense the time and resources spent on 'negative' health education is considerable. The socialisation of children and young workers in the family, schools and technical colleges is also very important when any assessment is made of the 'educational' influences which operate to adjust workers to low-risk/acceptable-risk arguments in the workplace. Indeed, in some industries and some parts of the country, the risks of work have historically been emphasised as an attraction of the job: this is the 'machismo' view of dangerous industries. Where mining, fishing, heavy iron and steel and shipbuilding industries existed—and where frequently there was little alternative work and no job choice for working-class children— jobs were made more appealing by associating them with 'manly' virtues. It was 'a man's job' on trawlers and men had to be tough to work in dangerous, exciting steel mills and damp and dustfilled pits. What happened if a fishing hawser took off a limb or a worker fell into molten metal or contracted pneumoconiosis was not emphasised. The older workers were often aware of these health and safety hazards, but recognised that there was little alternative to work in these traditional 'men's industries' and so accepted the accidents and diseases as an inevitable part of 'working for a living'.

With the decline of many traditional industries there is some resistance on the part of workers to accept poor working conditions as inevitable, although in the face of limited job prospects resistance weakens. In the electronics industry, for example, women are frequently recruited into hazardous low-paid jobs because no alternative employment is available and any job may be better than no job. Youth unemployment is now so high that some companies like Pilkingtons in the north west are worried that young people in the future will not adjust to working conditions in factories because expectations have changed and potential workers will never have experienced 'factory discipline'.[2] The hazards of unemployment and the health education response to the phenomenon is an important subject beyond the scope of this chapter but already there are signs that the individualistic approach to this problem is emerging, with initiatives such as exercise classes for the unemployed or ways to keep healthy on the dole.

Nevertheless, for many people in work or hoping to obtain work, their experience of the job as inevitably dirty, dangerous, tedious and hard will be the norm. Physical labour has been presented to young males as a source of independence from the type of work and authority experienced at school. The means by which working-class children still go into working-class jobs has been called an 'irreversible process'; it is only when children get jobs that they realise the shopfloor is just as much a prison as school seemed to be (Willis, 1977: 104, 107).

One solution to this process is to teach school students about work hazards, but as yet very little education about occupational health has occurred in schools. Indeed, as Cribb argues in Chapter 6, not only should health education be central to the school agenda, but the political nature of all education should be recognised. Such education would have to confront major economic and political questions which relate to who creates hazards, who profits from hazards and whether work hazards are inevitable in the 1980s. Workers themselves have begun, albeit in a very limited fashion, to pick up the issue themselves. Trades councils in many cities send speakers to schools to talk about what trade unions do and there is discussion on the health and safety role of the unions in this educational context. Shop stewards and safety representatives in some parts of the country have also devised their own educational strategies to combat the employers' view that work hazards are minimal and inevitable. In a north eastern asbestos factory, for example, a convener took younger workers—who had been offered bonuses and overtime payments to work in a dusty area against union advice—to visit older workers in hospital suffering from asbestos-related diseases. This experience rapidly increased the awareness of the risk of asbestos and the methods open to the workforce to control those risks.

The role of the medical profession in general, and full-time and part-time occupational physicians in particular, has been crucial in the education process about hazards. The social background, education and work experiences of medical staff tends to produce an outlook sympathetic to established economic institutions, and the historical hierarchical nature of medicine tends to mean that doctors dominate or try to dominate the other groups involved in occupational health. The pre-occupation with illness rather than prevention is also an important factor in occupational medicine at the workplace. The obstacles preventing a positive preventative approach by doctors to occupational health in Britain have been widely documented (Watterson, 1984: 41–5). In other sectors of medicine, the profession often proclaims the great importance of its work, the essential tasks it performs, the need for greater funding and so on. Occupational physicians, however, can be remarkably self-effacing: in conversation they are quick to point out that really there are few occupational accidents and diseases and these are often exaggerated by unscientific, emotional and politically motivated workers; there is, therefore, no need to spend more on resources in industry. Yet occupational physicians are paid directly by industry and they often have a lower status in relation to medicine than their colleagues. Furthermore, occupational health nurses occupy a lower position in the employer/ medical hierarchy than occupational physicians and so are even more vulnerable to pressure when they attempt to adopt radical policies and health education techniques to deal with major hazards (Silverstone and Williams, 1982: 58–61).

## Shifting the responsibility

The third statement—where accidents do occur, careless and stupid workers are to blame—follows the first and second, and epitomises the attitudes of many employers and their safety officers. It is an easier and politically safer option to blame individual workers for accidents rather than spend time and possibly the employer's money in identifying and removing the source of hazards. Safety too lends itself to the victim-blaming approach in a way occupational health does not. A worker can, at first sight, be blamed for the removal of a guard on a machine and placing a hand in moving parts: the hazard and the result of 'unsafe' practices are also more obviously connected. Employers can and frequently do argue that accidents happen to foolish, careless, inefficient and lazy workers. Historically, the British Safety First Association and the Institute of Industrial Psychology concentrated on the individual and accidents in British industry and often incorporated the unions into this victim-blaming approach (Djang, 1942). Even today, many health education schemes concentrate on the identification and avoidance of hazards by instructing workers not to be foolish or careless. Employers frequently avoid the removal of the hazard at source, the redesign of machinery or the introduction of fail-safe guarding. This occurs despite research findings which now show that the solution to accidents at work is primarily to be found in the creation of a safe workplace not a safe worker (Booth, 1983: 543–65). The cultural, social, economic and political pressure on workers, whether in offices or factories, to accept that they cause their own accidents is enormous: common accident causes like the demands of productivity, profitability, poor engineering design and maintenance and bonus incentives can then be disguised or ignored (Armstrong and Nichols, 1973: 1–31). It is far less easy, however, to convince workers that occupational illhealth is their fault than it is to attribute blame to them in the case of safety incidents. If a job requires workers to use a glue which can cause dermatitis or a metal which can cause lung damage or a solvent which can cause cancer, the workers cannot be blamed for the resulting illness unless employers (and occasionally traditional health educators) argue that they should have worn what is often very ineffective personal protective equipment.

## CONVENTIONAL HEALTH EDUCATION PRACTICES, PAST AND PRESENT

A brief look at the history of health and safety issues in the workplace show that there are very few examples of good practice in the nineteenth and early twentieth centuries on which to draw. Certainly there were few doctors involved in industrial medicine in this period and even fewer who identified the causes of occupational illhealth and proposed effective solutions for all the reasons mentioned earlier. Sir Thomas Legge was exceptional and two of his precepts on industrial medicine remain unfulfilled models for health education action in the 1980s:

> Unless and until the employer has done everything—and everything means a good deal—the workman can do next to nothing to protect himself, although he is naturally willing to do his share. . . .
> All the workmen should be told something of the danger of the material with which they come into contact and not be left to find out for themselves—sometimes at the cost of their lives (Legge, 1934: 3).

Perhaps the one truly pioneering organisation still relevant to us in the 1980s was the Industrial Health Education Society which aimed to educate 'the industrial workers on the diseases and sicknesses to which they are liable with a view to their mitigation and prevention by means of lectures, meetings, research and information'.[3] This body, established in Glasgow in 1924, brought together doctors, trade unionists and some enlightened employers—though most employers preferred the accident-orientated victim-blaming approach—in a programme of work with trades councils and union branches which reached thousands of workers throughout the country. However, this approach inevitably posed the questions of who created the hazards, who permitted them to continue, who benefited from them, if anyone? All these questions begged profoundly political answers relating to health and safety of employees, and profits and production for employers. Perhaps it is no surprise that the Society became moribund in the late 1930s and vanished before the Second World War.

In the nineteenth and early twentieth centuries it was especially difficult for workers to organise and to get information about hazards at work. Many workers lacked the power to protect their jobs never mind their health but it would be quite wrong to assume that the trade union movement ignored those hazards they did identify—nor did they lack success: on occasions they achieved improvements in working conditions beyond anything company doctors contemplated. Attempts to improve health and safety challenged, and continue to challenge, management assumptions about their 'right' to manage their workplaces in the interests of the employers and shareholders.

## THE CONSTRAINTS ON PRACTISING EFFECTIVE OCCUPATIONAL HEALTH EDUCATION

In this sense, Health and Safety at work did, and still does, continue to raise real issues of industrial democracy in the workplace and offer scope for trade unionists and occupational health staff to work together. Many health educators, however, do not challenge the employer by locating the causes of accidents in the structure of the work process. Not surprisingly, they are accepted, if not welcomed, by the employer. If the worker is the problem, then apparently cheap solutions geared to training the worker to behave more safely will be readily accepted. Campaigns to get workers to wear ear muffs and respirators in noisy and fume-filled factories are still widespread as are efforts to start 'no smoking' campaigns which ignore the lung damage done by dusty environments. Worker education programmes which identify the primary hazards and then relate their activities to a removal of those hazards have been rare. Only when these issues have been raised will wider campaigns on the hazards of smoking, alcohol and food seem credible and relevant to many workers. These workers have low expectations about their working conditions and even lower expectations of 'professional' middle-class health educators. Health educators require re-education themselves if they are to confront these problems and responses in a constructive manner, because education on occupational health cannot be anything but political (McEwan, 1982: 384).[4]

The potential for positive developments in education on health and safety came from the 1974 *Health and Safety At Work, Etc. Act*. This Act has had an impact on occupational health education not through the enforcement of its provisions or the government structure established to administer it, but largely through the way the trade union movement responded to it. S.2.2.(c) of the 1974 Act requires employers 'so far as is reasonably practicable to train, inform, instruct and supervise employees' to protect their health and safety. There is little evidence available nationally on the extent or effectiveness of this training under the Act (Hale, 1983: 31). Bodies like the Aston University Department of Safety and Hygiene which research these areas have been dismantled in the economic recession. There are certainly very few prosecutions of employers who breach these provisions (HSE *Manufacturing Industry Reports*, 1977: 5–83). If this section of the Act were to produce a clear and properly funded policy from the Health and Safety Executive, then an effective health education programme could emerge along the lines of similar work in Sweden and America.[5] Instead, the British Chief Inspector of Factories was forced to express considerable concern in 1984 about 'the drastically reduced expenditure on [health and safety] training in

Britain as a result of the economic recession' (Crawford, 1984: 59).

The state has played a limited role in occupational health education, but what of other organisations? Those which have been government-funded have faced recent cash crises and in some cases have been dismantled. Industrial Training Boards, suffering swingeing cut-backs in numbers recently, have in a few instances developed effective and imaginative approaches to health and safety training, but most, like employers' in-service training, are concerned with production training which runs counter to much Health and Safety education.[6] Some industries do have better training than others but generally they concentrate on safety and ignore health. Employers may tell employees about asbestos problems, radiation or cyanide poisoning but very little is done to educate workers on the causes and cures for widespread workplace noise, dust, fumes, stress and strain hazards; to carry out such education would entail the expenditure of time and money.

Safety officers are in many senses the focal point for health and safety work in factories and offices and in recent years their professional body, the Institution of Occupational Safety and Health, has greatly improved the training of its members and their involvement in health and safety policy issues. However, many safety officers only work part-time on safety and have numerous other and sometimes conflicting functions including security, welfare and even quality control and production. For most, the resources and skills needed to introduce effective occupational health education are unavailable.

Occupational physicians have higher status and a longer training than safety officers and the Faculty of Occupational Medicine has a syllabus for its membership exams which refers to health education and communication with workers as important functions for its physicians. Yet there are few full-time occupational physicians and for most employers hazard education by their medical staff is not a high priority. There would also appear to be a considerable gulf between theory and practice in occupational medicine. Leading figures in occupational medicine have stressed that the workers 'should be given the fullest information on potential risks and some responsibility for his [sic] own health and safety' (Schilling and Hall, 1973: 147). How this advice is to be translated into health education practice is unclear. There are competent company doctors who do not know the names of the trade unions in the workplace. There are other physicians, certainly in the south of England, who profess to know less about the toxicology and epidemiology of their workplaces than safety representatives. This may simply be that they do not wish to discuss with and educate the workforce on the hazards and potential hazards of their workplaces. Occupational health nurses may well come into more frequent and more informal contact with employees than doctors, and their professional bodies have identified a positive health education function for them. However, any advocacy of an education programme to remove hazards at source would create tensions and serious problems for nurses with their 'superiors' and employers.

Professional bodies which may or could have a progressive health education function are, therefore, fettered by their employers and by their class, education and status. Just as employers fear employees challenging their 'right to manage', so occupational physicians are sensitive to any challenge to their status when assessing the medical/scientific nature of actual and potential hazards, even though it is the workers and not the doctors who face these on the shopfloor. So conventional health education is acceptable to employers and government alike because it reflects rather than critically examines current occupational health education in theory and practice. It thus falls far short of creating and realising a radical approach to work hazards.

## THE ALTERNATIVES

Critical education on worker occupational health has not been abandoned since the Health and Safety At Work Act was introduced twelve years ago: on the contrary, it has flourished. Unlike conventional health education in the same field, it has contained debates about both theory and practice. For the economic and political reasons already mentioned, an 'independent' form of workplace education has sprung up which in a number of ways has taken on board and sometimes pre-empted the principles, methods and philosophies now advocated by radical health educators. Some might argue cynically that the absence of conventional professional health education interest in the subject has helped to facilitate these developments and responses which would otherwise have been stifled by the 'professionals' tied to the 'status quo' and 'victim-blaming' philosophies.

The TUC and affiliated unions have, since the early 1970s, trained and educated tens of thousands of safety representatives (who are like shop stewards—and who often are also shop stewards—concerned with health and safety and with legal rights and functions under the 1978 Safety Representative and Safety Committee regulations). The total number of safety representatives trained on the 10-week one-day-a-week, day release courses by 1982 was in excess of 80,000; these courses are more extensive than most in the health education field. Though compared with those of American trade unions British resources on health and safety are meagre, nevertheless the TUC has several staff working on health and safety policy and publicity issues and some of its education staff working on the development of education material for lay officials and members. Unions like Society of Graphical and Allied Trades (SOGAT), General Municipal and Boilermakers Allied Trade Union (GMBATU), Association of Scientific Managerial and Technical Staffs (ASTMS) and the Bakers and Food Workers, all have full-time Health and Safety officers and several others have part-time officers.

The education and research undertaken by the unions is in most instances based firmly on a radical view of occupational accidents and illhealth. This view acknowledges that control policies should have the following type and order of priorities:

firstly, remove the hazard at source;
secondly, if impossible, substitute with safer materials or processes;
thirdly, isolate hazardous processes, control hazardous processes mechanically with guarding or exhaust ventilation;

fourthly, only as a last resort and as a temporary measure, ask workers to wear protective clothing and equipment.

This approach recognises that employers, not employees, own workplaces and so are legally, economically and socially responsible for the working conditions in them; and it encompasses the idea, now technically accepted, of the 'safe workplace' rather than the 'safe worker in a dangerous workplace'. Employers often reverse the process and start with the fourth priority because this is cheap, easy to implement and easy to use to blame the individual worker.

Trade unions are autonomous in theory and have relatively independent resources; this facilitates a more far-reaching and radical analysis of illness in Britain than many other institutions with health and health education functions. Trade union training on hazards at work contains the following crucial elements:

1 an emphasis on workplace solidarity and organisations involving members;

2 a policy of collective action to solve problems;

3 a teaching approach built on group work and the experiences of course members which is student- not tutor-centred;

4 materials and analysis based on the real problems of the workplace but located in a wider economic, political and educational framework;

5 the development of skills to organise, communicate and negotiate within the workplace.

These elements are the antithesis of the schools of thought in which 'expert' professional is counterposed to the 'uninformed' group.

Trade unions, and in particular the TUC bureaucracy, have been prodded into the adoption of radical health education policies, sometimes willingly and sometimes with great reluctance. Well into the 1970s, much of the trade union education material was founded on the belief that the typical trade unionist was a white, male, middle-aged skilled factory worker. Such a belief was and is manifestly incorrect and since 1974 the educational approach of the trade unions has increased in breadth and flexibility. The change has come partly from the economic developments in Britain with the changing patterns of employment— fewer factory workers, more women and black workers, fewer 'skilled' jobs, more new technology, more YTS jobs—and partly from pressures exerted by a miscellany of groups not traditionally recognised for their influence on trade unions.

The women's movement has had a considerable effect on many aspects of trade unionism, albeit without visibly changing the nature of the trade union structure. Women have been far more aware of health problems and health requirements at the workplace than their male counterparts. The movement's concern about women's well-being and its capacity to challenge the indifference and hostility of the medical profession towards women's health problems at home and at work, has greatly increased awareness of health issues generally in male-dominated trade unions. The campaigns to obtain improved cervical and breast cancer screening have had implications for health and safety education in the workplace. Some unions with a generally poor record on occupational health have remarkably effective women campaigners on subjects like reproductive health hazards (Greenwood, 1984: 1–9) and health education. The hazards of office work would probably still be little recognised if it had not been for the work of the Women and Work Hazards group which has highlighted a whole range of hitherto neglected topics for educators in workplace hazards (Craig, 1981). The first major guides on work hazards came from two women working with the Oil, Chemical and Atomic Workers in America (Stellman and Daum, 1973: 1–27) and significantly enough, although still grossly under-represented in trade union full-time officer ranks, there are more women who are Health and Safety officers at a regional and national level than in most other trade union jobs.

The British Society For Social Responsibility in Science (BSSRS) Work Hazards Group—a collection of radical scientists and trade unionists—has also had a substantial effect on British health and safety education with its affiliated local hazards groups and with trade union-based local health and safety groups. The Women and Work Hazards Group too is affiliated to BSSRS. BSSRS produces *Hazards*, a bulletin which is aimed at shop stewards and safety representatives and presented in a readable, relevant and straightforward style. The BSSRS Work Hazards Group has a radical analysis of the nature of conventional science and medicine in the health and safety context and challenges the 'expert' view. Many BSSRS members now work for trade unions, resource centres, colleges and adult education institutions involved in the supply of health and safety information and the provision of health and safety courses for workers. Their approach, although not homogeneous, has been an important influence on the practice of the trade union health and safety officers and TUC education department. The emphasis on group work, collective action, membership education and worker experiences has led in some instances to safety representatives and shop stewards adopting new educational methods and running health and safety courses themselves in their own workplaces. The London Hazards Centre, formerly funded by the GLC, has a similar approach which places a high priority on using education and information to campaign effectively against the causes of hazards, rather than the dissipation of effort through individual, isolated actions.

'Education' on occupational health is recognised by trade unions and hazards groups to be an expansive term: for instance, courses for workers on health and safety might involve the establishment of a course members' committee to run the course in a democratic manner—this would be recognised as educationally relevant to workplace health and safety committees. Other course members might draw up pamphlets, leaflets and posters for use back at work: again this would contain an educational/information/ awareness function which would be relevant to the experiences and needs of workers in their workplace. The trade union health and safety campaigns have contained readable material, well-presented and supported by short courses run by the unions themselves.[7]

These examples of successful trade union and pressure group

activities should not disguise the very real problems which still exist for those concerned with health education at the workplace: problems of numbers, access, facilities and philosophy. The trade union movement now organises less than half the British work-force: its resources and staff cannot meet the health and safety demands placed on it by its own members. There are major obstacles in the way of trade union progress because of the recession: choices are often presented starkly to workers in terms of pay rises, job security or improvements in health and safety. These choices are often not honestly or accurately presented by employers but health and safety educators need to tackle them nevertheless. Racism is also a major problem in many workplaces in Britain and, like sexism, easily divides workers on health and safety problems. Unions in Yorkshire and Lancashire have produced health and safety materials and teaching packs in several Asian languages. This will help to increase hazard awareness but how the trade union movement responds generally to prejudice against women, blacks and ethnic minorities will determine the success of many of their health education initiatives. What of educational provision on health and safety for the majority of workers *not* in trade unions? What about the problems of sweat-shop workers, disabled people, non-literate people, the Youth Training Scheme trainees in the workplace? Very little is done for these groups at present.

If governments accepted health policy as a legitimate health education category and devoted more resources to policy issues (Draper, Griffiths, Dennis and Popay, 1980: 493), then progress could be made. This appears extremely unlikely, however. The HSE is a victim of severe cuts, and even when better funded few of its staff pursued a positive, coherent policy on health hazard education. Some HSE Industrial Advisory Committees have pro-duced information on hazards and one or two staff, primarily nurses, have looked at the effectiveness of HSE literature on workers (Foster, 1983, personal communication) but generally the HSE has had little effect on, and even less interest in, occupational health education.

Action should come from the health education services located within health authorities and occasionally elsewhere; certainly individual health educators throughout the country are familiar with the hazards groups and trade union methods on health and safety education. However, they may find it easier and more effective to work with trade unionists outside their factories, offices and shops rather than inside workplaces where they will either be constrained by employers or refused entry on 'ideological' grounds. The paradox for those concerned about health education in the general sense is that health educators will not gain credibility with workers unless they address the primary health and pollution issues facing workers (factory and office dust, fumes, accidents and noise, before factory food and individual smoking, alcohol and exercise habits): if they do address the causes of those hazards they must almost invariably antagonise employers. By contrast, trade unions are beginning to pick up the general health education issues within the context of the politics of health and are making progress to place these issues with work hazards in a wider politics of health framework.

The lack of resources, rigour and experiment in workplace health education is fundamentally a consequence of British political attitudes to health. One body which has attempted to analyse the totality of workplace health education including hazard education in the 1980s has been the Health Education Council (HEC).[8] Indeed a former employee of the HEC appears to be the only physician in Britain who has written at any length on the subject and who acknowledges the contributions of the trade unions to hazard education. Few radical health educators would argue with him that currently 'health education in the workplace consists largely of "ad hoc" initiatives resulting from individual enthusiasm, but they are poorly supported, unrelated to need, use inappropriate methods and have made little impact' (McEwan, 1984: 211). The exception to this would be trade union work specifically on hazard education.

## CONCLUSIONS

Trade unionists and individual health educators have produced an analysis of hazards at work which eschews the traditional superficial victim-blaming, careless worker, accident approach. Their analysis of the politics of occupational health education has led on to the adoption of relatively successful methods of adult education which emphasise that courses should be democratically controlled, experience-based and group-centred, and connect with the workers' own organisations and institutions. This has in turn produced the means for highlighting far-reaching critiques of our economic, educational and medical institutions in a factory, office or community setting. Workers are increasingly willing and able to challenge the medical experts who advise employers. The Sheffield Occupational Health project epitomises this approach and has led to trade unionists and general practitioners working together not only in health centre surgeries but also in the clubs and pubs in the city, talking to people about their working conditions and the diseases related to those conditions. The project grew out of the local trade union safety committee and has as its foundation the belief that 'health workers were meant to be accountable to users—the patients'.[9] Here education, information, communication and organisation are combined.

Several years ago, two radical health educators begged the question: 'Health Education—can the reformers be reformed?' They noted that in:

a drive for professional status and authority, health education has ... become a conservative agent in the very arena in which it claims expertise and leadership as an agent of progressive social change (Brown and Margo, 1978: 3).

They argue that health educators:

should cease the search for expertise, status, authority and leadership: instead they should work with and for those groups who recognise that society not individuals make many people sick, and help people to examine the social bases of their work and lives for unhealthful conditions (ibid.: 14).

The worker and trade union approach to hazard education in its theory and practice provides a democratic way for health educators to forge new links in workplaces and the community, to gain greater credibility in their work and to change a society in which health is not regarded as a political subject and illhealth is taken for granted.

## NOTES

1   Workplace Health and Safety Statistics are available in a number of official publications which include *Health and Safety Statistics, 1980* (HMSO, 1982: 8) and *HSE Manufacturing and Service Industries, 1983* (HMSO, 1984). Unfortunately the accident notification procedures altered in 1980 and in 1983 the HSE accident information from the DHSS was drastically reduced. This means that the under-reporting of accidents which occurred pre-1980 has probably worsened. In the 1970s, HSE officials gave estimates of 75 per cent under-reporting in office, shops and railways premises accidents and 50 per cent under-reporting in general manufacturing accidents. The occupational asthma and skin diseases statistics from Government reports can be found in A. Watterson 'Occupational Medicine and Medical Ethics', *J. Soc. Occup. Med.* (1984), 34: 41–5.

2   The Society of Industrial Tutors' Conference, Holyroode College, Manchester, 1981.

3   The IHES gained support from eminent physicians and leading trade unionists. *British Medical Journal*, January–June, 1925, 1: 46.

4   The history of trade union health and safety developments which are germane to current health education issues has not yet been written. However, useful insights into the subject are given in Williams, J. L. (1960), *Accidents and Ill-health at Work*, Staples Press, London.

5   The American National Institute of Occupational Safety and

Health has produced a framework for health protection/health promotion which includes worker observations and worker participations on occupational health, programmes on dissemination and education of occupational health materials to workers (personal communication, 1984) and DHEW in the past has funded 'The New Directions' programme for worker education on hazards (see A. Watterson (1982), 'American Trade Unions and Occupational Health and Safety', *The Industrial Tutor*, 3(7): 74–85. The Swedes also have a properly planned and reasonably resourced programme on the same subject (see K. Elgstrand, *Training and Education in Occupational Safety and Health in Sweden*, 1977).

6   Exceptional Boards on health and safety have in the past been the Construction ITB and the Plastics ITB.

7   GMBATU campaigns on noise, cancer, reproductive hazards; ASTMS campaigns on cancer and stress, VDUs and allergies; NGA campaigns on cancer, and LRD hazards booklets.

8   The HEC held a workshop in 1980 entitled 'Health Education in the Workplace' organised by Jane Randell and Dr James McEwan. This workshop gives the most comprehensive account of health education methods and developments in the workplace in Britain. The HEC's discussion document *Health Education in the Workplace* (1984) produced by Randell, Gail Wear and McEwan opens up debate on the way forward and suggests links between health education in the workplace and in the community. There is perhaps some innocence in its belief in a 'scientific' exploration of health education practices and the ease with which employers, employees and other bodies will recognise and develop a common approach: however, it is a useful first step. (See Moran, Chapter 7, for a less favourable comment on this publication.)

9   The Sheffield Occupational Health project has produced a leaflet explaining its aims and methods. Details can be obtained from the Darnall Road Medical Centre, 246 Darnall Road, Sheffield 9. Similar projects have also been developed in Italy (see Giorgio Assennato and Vicente Navarro, 'Workers' Par-

ticipation and Control in Italy: The Case of Occupational Medicine', in *Health and Work under Capitalism*, ed. Navarro, V., and Berman, D. (1983), Baywood Publishing Company, New York.

# REFERENCES

Armstrong, P. and Nichols, T. (1973), *Safety or Profit*, Falling Wall Press, Bristol.

Booth, R. T. (1983), 'Machinery Hazards' in Ridley, J. R., *Safety at Work*, Butterworths, London.

Brown, E. R. and Margo, G. E. (1978), 'Health Education: Can the Reformers Be Reformed?', *International Journal of Health Services*, 8(1): 3–26.

Craig, M. (1981), *The Office Workers Survival Handbook*, BSSRS, London.

Crawford, A. (1984), 'Training is Legally Required by Health and Safety at Work Act', *Health and Safety at Work*, August 1984: 59.

Djang, T. K. (1942), *Factory Inspection in Great Britain*, Allen & Unwin, London.

Draper, P., Griffiths, J., Dennis, J. and Popay, J. (1980), 'Three Types of Health Education', *British Medical Journal*, 16 August: 493–5.

Foster, A. (1983), Personal communications and 'Hearing Protection and the Role of Health Education' in *Occupational Health*, 35(4): 155–9.

Gill, F. (1985), 'Prevention: The Name of the Game', *Occupational Health*, 137(9): 400–2.

Greenwood, S. (1984), *The Effects of Toxic Substances and Physical Agents on the Reproductive System*, Sheffield TGWU pamphlet.

Hale, A. (1983), 'Is Safety Training Worthwhile?' in *Proceeding of the Annual Conference of the Aston Health and Safety Society*, Birmingham.

Health and Safety Commission (1984), Consultative Document, *Control of Substances Hazardous to Health*, HSE, London.

Health and Safety Executive, *Manufacturing Industry Reports, 1977–83*, HMSO, London.

Legge, T. (1934), *Industrial Maladies*, ed. S. A. Henry, Oxford University Press, London.

McEwan, J. (1982), 'Health Education at Work' in A. Ward Gardner *Current Approaches to Occupational Health. 2*, Wright PSG, Bristol.

McEwan, J. (1984), 'Health Education in the Workplace' in J. M. Harrington (ed.), *Recent Advances in Occupational Health, 2*, Churchill Livingstone, Edinburgh.

Peto, R., letter, *New Statesman*, 10 October 1982.

Schilling, R. S. F. and Hall, S. A. (1973), 'Prevention of Occupational Disease' in R. S. F. Schilling (ed.), *Occupational Health Practice*, Butterworths, London.

Silverstone, R. and Williams, A. (1982), *The Role and Educational Needs of Occupational Health Nurses*, Royal College of Nursing, London.

Stellman, J. M. and Daum, S. M. (1973), *Work is Dangerous to Your Health*, Vintage, New York.

Watterson, A. E. (1984), 'Occupational Medicine and Medical Ethics', *Journal of Society of Occupational Medicine*, 34(2): 41–5.

Willis, P. (1977), *Learning to Labour*, Saxon House, Farnborough.

# CHAPTER 6

# POLITICS AND HEALTH IN THE SCHOOL CURRICULUM

Alan Cribb

## INTRODUCTION

A great deal has been written about the way in which social concepts and practices can be impregnated with ideologies. Analyses of *education* are given from within one or other conflicting value perspective (MacIntyre, 1973). Similarly the concept of *health* has a complex, relatively open-ended, and contestable meaning (Beardmore and Vlijm, 1984). Leaving this contestability unexplored encourages a spurious consensus about the legitimacy and importance of health education in schools. As is often the case, people are prepared to agree that something is 'all for the good' providing we are sufficiently vague about what it amounts to in practice. There is nothing wrong with consensus, but if we are concerned with establishing one, we must look for a genuine consensus which transcends acknowledged differences in emphasis and values. These differences are real; there are a host of choices to be made both in educational and curricular philosophy, and in the politics of schooling.

I shall concentrate upon the nature of one such choice by: (1) examining the ways in which some recent conceptions of school health education entail, or amount to, the political education of young people, and would thus be subject to popular controversy if widely and explicitly espoused; (2) examining why these conceptions pose broader challenges to the traditional norms of schooling. This choice does not therefore relate only to curriculum content, it also raises more far-reaching practical political issues about the appropriate goals of health education. Which structures and contexts are to be treated as fixed, and which are to be challenged?

The recent development of health education in secondary schools can be seen against two backcloths. It is part of a wider health movement, which includes a critique of medicalisation, and it is also part of a set of changes towards a new self-consciousness on the part of educators about the role of schools in the personal and social education of their pupils. In both cases these influences have resulted in a closer alignment between health education and education for political participation. Before examining the specific role of health education, it is worth reflecting upon some of the other pressures and movements which have influenced personal and social education.

## SOCIAL EDUCATION AND POLITICAL LITERACY

Of course schools have always affected personal and social development; moreover, this has always been acknowledged as a fundamental objective of schooling whether it be achieved through sport, religious instruction, school organisation, teacher-pupil relationships or 'the hidden curriculum'. The raising of the school leaving age and the change to a comprehensive system disturbed and questioned some existing traditions of schooling, and left many schools seeking a suitable culture and ethos to accompany the institutional changes that were taking place. At the same time the background conditions have been shifting and uncertain. There has been a decline in religious belief and the associated value nexus, sometimes seen as an example of a decline in authority of all kinds. The anonymous nature of urban society has posed a threat to established communities and identities which is sharpened by the speed of technological change and the increase in social and geographical mobility. There has been a positive attack on discriminatory practices, attitudes and values, and a growing emphasis on women's issues and multi-culturalism. More recently all these challenges to traditional norms have coincided with a crisis of unemployment and alienation for many young people. It is hardly surprising that in these circumstances there has been extensive deliberation about the wider relevance of academic subjects and the values and skills which the education system transmits, in short about whether and how schooling provides an adequate preparation for life.

The last two decades have seen a plethora of curriculum development projects in the humanities, social studies and life skills, looking not only at course content and teaching methods, but also at procedures of evaluation and assessment such as pupil profiles and records of personal attainment. It is impossible to separate out the degree to which health educators have caused or benefited from this activity. They have certainly been influential and well informed about all the key shifts in the personal and social education curriculum including an increased emphasis upon student-involvement work, decision-making skills, and more negotiated and open-ended curricula. Another rapidly growing sphere is vocational preparation funded by government agencies such as the Manpower Services Commission, which is designed to provide training and work experience for young people. This has involved the formulation of a whole philosophy of training based upon the idea of basic, transferable skills—a philosophy which is already having an influence on curriculum development within schools.

A priority which has emerged in both the school and further education sectors is the need for political literacy. The Further Education Curriculum Review and Development Unit has listed as one of the twelve main aims of vocational preparation the need 'to bring about sufficient political and economic literacy to understand the social environment and participate in it' (FEU, 1982: 41). Pring, in his analysis of social education in the school curriculum, writes 'it is difficult to see how any programme of personal and social education can ignore either the political values or the political skills required for participating in those activities and choices which affect one's own welfare' (Pring, 1984: 100).

This is the crux of the educational justification for teaching politics. Education exists, amongst other things, to develop people's autonomy, to give individuals the capacity to make choices and to act on those choices so as not to be entirely subject to their environment or their 'unconditioned drives'. It must therefore tackle public decision-making processes and institutions so these are not regarded as alien, over-determining structures which are irrelevant to the lives of the majority of people.

A good deal of work has been done to decide upon an appropriate style and substance for political education in secondary schools (Brennan, 1981; Crick and Porter, 1978). The term 'political literacy' is used to distinguish this work from the heavy academic, factual and institutional bias of British constitution or comparative politics. It stands for 'a compound of knowledge, skills and attitudes, to be developed together, each one conditioning the other' (Crick and Porter, 1978: 13). This compound can and should have a large factual content. However, it would fail if it tried to be entirely descriptive, for there is a need to introduce issues, to help pupils understand conflicts and other people's views, and for them to be able to express and offer justifications for certain stances. Its proponents make it clear that this is an objective which can be pursued through other subject areas. It is of relevance across the personal and social curriculum, including health topics, because it can be furthered by focusing on any suitable institutions and issues and, perhaps most important of all, because it aims to teach awareness and respect for procedural values such as tolerance.

## HEALTH AND PARTICIPATION

In order to discover the distinctive contribution of health education to personal and social development writers typically refer to the concept of health. This might be seen as providing the underlying rationale of the subject, yet it is notorious for generating controversy and complexity. It would seem most peculiar, however, to proceed with the business of health education without reflecting at all on the concept of health. A number of authors have attempted to illuminate and clarify this concept by distinguishing between a number of different theories or models (Nordenfelt, 1983; Strong, 1983; Smith, 1981). Smith suggests that there are at least four underlying models of health into which our different unreflective uses of the concept can be organised:

1   Clinical model, with health seen as the absence of signs and symptoms of disease.

2   Role-performance model, with health viewed as maximum performance of occupational and family roles.

3   Adaptive model, where the health is the capacity to adjust to changing circumstances.

4   Eudaimonistic model, where the healthy person is viewed as the self-actualising, fulfilled and fulfilling personality.

In turn those models suggest a number of alternative conceptions of health education, ranging from a relatively circumscribed field concerned with the prevention of disease, the use of screening facilities and the presentation of symptoms, to a subject which encompasses basic skills, emotional development, and ultimately all human competences and values.

There has, up until recently (Seedhouse, 1985), been very little systematic analysis of the various conceptions of health and the relationships between them. This work is important for everyone involved with health education because we each need to form a relatively clear picture of the appropriate shape and parameters of our concerns if we are to be effective in practice. There are two most important insights to come out of this kind of analysis. Firstly, if by health we mean that range of capacities which enable various forms of human fulfilment, from physical functioning, through social and occupational coping, to intellectual, emotional or aesthetic development, then almost anything can count as a health intervention, and all forms of education could be seen as health education. However esoteric the ends of certain forms of education might be they can always be seen as the means to some further or other development. Secondly, it follows from this that we have to make choices, preferably self-consciously, about the content and scope of health education. Any view that the proper scope of health or health education is a neutral, technical question is an error, and any supposedly neutral model is unacceptable because it must rest upon some unrecognised commitments, or preferences.

Along with the controversy and complexity about the nature of health goes the problem of the most appropriate forms of intervention to promote health. Even if we are dealing with the most restricted definition of health, there is a need for intervention at a number of levels because the causation of disease is multifactorial. Wood and Bradley discuss the spectrum of determinants of health and illhealth 'from the insensible to the material' (Wood and Bradley, 1985: 31), including biological attributes, culture and social structure. Within this spectrum are matters of public policy such as those relating to food manufacture or occupational hazards. Central to all these concerns is the relationship between the social class structure and inequalities in health and illness (Townsend and Davidson, 1982). So if health education were to equip individuals only to achieve better physical health for themselves and others, its subject matter could quite reasonably range from the biological and other sciences to legal, economic and social policy. There has recently been a growing recognition that politics and health are inseparable, that questions of health care policy cannot be treated separately from conflicting theories of distributive justice (De Jong and Rutten, 1983), indeed that 'the fundamental determinants of health and health care are political' (Scott-Samuel, 1979: 123).

These insights about the nature and causation of health are part of the much-rehearsed critique of medicalisation. The main target of this critique is the dominance of a clinical reductionist model— which tends to reduce patients to a collection of physical systems, or to passive consumers permitted to give consent to professionals, or to isolated individuals abstracted from the social, economic and cultural systems which largely explain their lot in life. Granted that this critique itself can take a rather reductionist form and can itself be overstated, it has nonetheless gained sufficient currency in many quarters to have become something of an orthodoxy. What is less widely agreed upon is the extent to which more preventive, holistic, integrated and participatory forms of health care can and should be developed within and outside the existing systems. One clear consequence of the critique of medical dominance is that effective education is an essential component of any care which fully recognises and respects individual autonomy and circumstances. It is ironical that health education has itself been subject to limitations of medicalisation in the way it has tended to confine its role to education about individual health behaviour and disease avoidance (Vuori, 1980), when there is no obvious limit to the potential for education if health care is to be genuinely participatory. There is no good reason to confine participation to an involvement with one's own symptoms or treatment, or lifestyle. This ideal has been accepted and disseminated by the World Health Organisation in their new programme for 'health promotion'; its basic principles are set out as follows:

> Health Promotion is the process of enabling people to increase control over, and to improve, their health ... involves the population as a whole in the context of their everyday life, rather than focusing on people at risk for specific diseases ... is directed towards action on the determinants of causes of health ... combines diverse, but complementary, methods ... aims particularly at effective and concrete public participation. (WHO, 1984).

## THE CHANGING FOCUS OF SCHOOL HEALTH

These are some of the issues and circumstances which have influenced a gradual shift in the centre of gravity for the theory and practice of school health education. There has been a shift from a concentration on hygiene and other aspects of physical fitness towards a concentration on promoting a more healthy lifestyle as a whole and the recognition that this involves changes in attitudes, values and skills. The influential recommendations of the Schools Council and Health Education Council (1976) are that health education should not become the exclusive domain of one teaching specialism. Rather, a core course in health education should form only part of an overall school policy, co-ordinated by a senior teacher. The associated curriculum material 'takes as its theme the need for individuals to consider their own values and relationships before making decisions affecting health. The emphasis is on why people behave as they do, rather than on basic health information, though this is also provided' (Reid, 1982: 9). These ideas are now well established in health education theory and it is because of them that health education researchers and developers have been involved in a much larger undertaking than merely 'adding on' new content or topics to the established school curriculum. Because of their medical links school health educators have made exceptionally strenuous attempts to assess or evaluate the problems and benefits which stem from their work, and this in turn has entailed a rigorous interest in educational processes and objectives. It is relatively straightforward to measure specific changes in pupils' knowledge, but attempts to define, achieve and evaluate changes in attitudes, conceptual or social skills, locus of control, or self-esteem are fraught with difficulties.

Beyond all the methodological difficulties there is the fundamental shift that the prevailing model of health education has become manifestly concerned with *values*. Embodied in recent health education programmes are (1) views as to what kind of attitudes, self-image, dispositions, lifestyle, and skills are good for individuals; (2) judgments of priority as to which faculties or capacities are the most important, or more worthy of time and attention. These may be assumed, or stated as objectives, or unintended outcomes of practice. Health education is thus undeniably a value-laden subject. To teach about and for 'health' is apparently to threaten no-one; however, to admit to an involvement in value education is to invite popular controversy and professional obstacles. It is very tempting to rely upon the surface neutrality and the positive connotations of the concept of health, but it is vital to face up to the moral and social dimension if only to be self-conscious about the substance, coherence and clarity of the values which are being promoted. This self-honesty also raises the question of whether or not an exclusive interest in individual and interpersonal values and issues is an adequate response to people's experiences of health and illness in the face of the growing understanding of the social and political determinants involved.

One of the salutary effects of contemporary curriculum development is the wider appreciation that fixed subject divisions are not always compatible with educational objectives, and nowhere is this more applicable than in that part of schooling actually aimed at personal development. It is obviously absurd to try to provide separate units of moral education, multi-cultural education, community education, careers education and health education. These issues or subject areas, along with political education, are only abstractions which pick out aspects from a complex and interdependent whole. Education 'for looking after ourselves' must involve work which is drawn from, and relevant to, many of these concerns. Some authors are now discussing a model of health education in schools which explicitly includes political education. Tones writes of the potential role of schools 'in self-empowering and generating political and social awareness' (1983: 127) as part of a review of new directions in education and health promotion. Beattie describes 'education about environmental and political limits to health' as one approach to school health education:

> Its key feature is to educate for an understanding of the ecology and politics of health, to increase awareness of the forces within the social, economic and legal environment which constrain the choices any individual can make in matters of health and to improve 'political literacy' in these areas, through study of those features of public policy that determine health (eg. housing standards, welfare benefits, traffic control, advertising codes ... etc.) (Beattie, 1984: 14).

*To summarise:*

1   The scope of school health education is a matter for debate.

2   Health educators are already thoroughly committed to education in and about values.

108

3   It is educationally and professionally unacceptable not to be self-conscious about this, and worse still to rely on the careless image of health as 'a good thing'.

4   Some school health education overlaps with the goals of political literacy, and there is a choice whether or not to acknowledge and develop these links.

This is a choice which cannot be dodged. The internal rationale of modern health promotion, which centres so much around the idea of self-empowerment, leads inexorably to the issue of political literacy. To speak of self-empowerment invites scepticism about any 'autonomy' which is entirely passive with regard to the political process. Similarly, the related and growing emphasis upon community action and self-help as part of the wider health education movement directly introduces the need for organisation, advocacy and political action into the public domain of health care. Those whose responsibilities include schooling are thus practically forced to consider how these broader movements should be reflected in the full-time education of young people. However, the ultimate reason why the issue cannot be dodged is that if it is not faced honestly and openly, it will nevertheless be acted upon in practice. What is the case for health is also the case for politics: you cannot completely avoid teaching political lessons simply by neglecting to do so in a deliberate and systematic way. It is possible to 'educate' for political deference or apathy by excluding young people from the public arena. Similarily by default it is easy to give the impression that health is essentially the responsibility of the individual patient or health professional. Medicalisation cannot simply be explained by reference to the power of the medical profession. The maintenance of political influence of this kind requires a particular set of factors, and it is arguable that one such factor is the education system's failure to explain the community and political basis of health.

## THE CONSERVATIVE CURRICULUM

Yet the case for advancing a 'radical' model of school health education is not clear-cut. There is already a tension between many of the tenets of recent health education and a number of established and influential perspectives on the curriculum. Part of the necessary task of abandoning any superficial consensus about school health education is to acknowledge this tension. To plan for the future whilst ignoring alternative views and interests about education would be arrogant and narrow-minded. It would also be clumsy and ineffective—as if real changes might be brought about without trying to understand and engage with the more conventional forces and structures involved.

Foremost amongst these structures is the examination system which has immense power over school life:

> It is paradoxical that in a system where teachers are so proud of their freedom, they tolerate domination of the curriculum by examinations which are externally controlled. In such a situation the control of the examinations system is of crucial political importance. For example, decisions made about 16-plus and 18-plus examinations have very far-reaching effects on the curriculum and its organisation (issues such as setting, streaming and options structures) (Lawton, 1980: 106).

Examinations are believed by many to be the only guarantee of educational standards, and the only way of monitoring teacher success. They tend to define the amount of time, effort and prestige that is attached to subjects and topics within schools. This effect is independent of the wishes of particular teachers who may be anxious to stress broader objectives. Their efforts to transcend the particular demands of examination syllabuses are undermined by the socialising effects of parents, employers and higher education which 'teach' that non-exam work is not really important. The simple fact that timetabling is centred around examination courses can mean that only some pupils get ready access to non-exam work, and that they are likely to see it as second-rate. On the whole health educators have seen themselves as having responsibility for 'preparation for life' rather than for academic success, and they have been understandably reluctant to compromise with the proponents of examinations, yet this entails huge constraints upon the further expansion of school health education and the influence of its methods and objectives.

There are a number of other educational pressures against curricular reform; these do not form a simple pattern and they often diverge. One is the continuing stress that some educational theorists place on the primacy of basic expository teaching:

It is the failure of school to promote indispensible skills like literacy and numeracy; it is the failure of schools to disseminate general factual knowledge, which is the root of the problem. It is precisely the ignorance on the part of much of the population of basic 'facts' of law, politics, literature and science which is so disturbing (O'Keefe, 1981: 34).

Such writers would see the attempt to spread creative and interpretive skills, or to foster reflection upon attitudes and values, as laudable additional objectives which should not interfere with the transmission of core skills and responsible behaviour. There is always a worry that ambitious curriculum developers will try to get people to run before they can walk, and that in a desire to promote broad personal development they might fail in every specific.

Another important constraint upon educational change is the lobby for traditional academic subjects. Partly this can be understood as the expected behaviour of vested interests in teacher education and the teaching profession. However, it also consists of an important educational argument which is a direct challenge to radical health education. This argument can be stated as an argument for irrelevance in the curriculum:

The more irrelevant a subject, the more lasting is the benefit it confers. Irrelevant subjects bring understanding of the human condition, by forcing the student to stand back from

it. They also enhance the appetite for life, by providing
material for thought and conversation (Scruton, 1983).

By abstracting from the local and the concrete, and by subjecting
oneself to a 'discipline' and its refined theoretical perspective it is
possible to gain intellectual skills, and an understanding of issues,
which can be completely missed by a focus on the immediate or
the instrumental. This perspective is related to the argument about
the primacy of expository teaching; there is a widespread fear that
the essentials of a good education can easily become hopelessly
diluted by too much diversification.

One other type of argument which sometimes has a conservative influence on the schooling system is that which deals
with the relevance of education to the marketplace. This is a hazy
area: sometimes certain things are valued highly by the world of
employment simply as a result of the prestige they are already
given by the education system. However, there is a set of
accomplishments, namely literacy, numeracy, and technical
knowledge and skills, which are valued as key resources in the
economic system. Those who stress the role of the education
system as a service sector insist that education should at least in
part be geared to delivering suitably qualified young people to
the labour market, and they often have a very narrow concept of
vocationalism.

All of these diverse, but broadly 'conservative' pressures on
education, need to be seriously considered by those who wish to
advance school health education. How far is it educationally
sound, or politically expedient, for them to identify themselves
firmly with new teaching methods, subject areas, or controversial
objectives like political literacy?

It is necessary to acknowledge what substance there is in the
various forces against curriculum reform. Health educators must
be prepared to learn from others. When appropriate, they can be
conscientious about maintaining academic standards and reinforcing theoretical skills, as well as ensuring and highlighting the
vocational relevance of their work. This conforms with the model
of school health education as a co-ordinated activity which relies

upon existing traditions and specialisms. There are also some indications that the general tenor of schooling is moving in a way which will enable health education to assume an increasing role. New and influential examinations and courses are breaking with traditions. The General Certificate of Secondary Education, the Technical and Vocational Educational Initiative, and the Certificate in Pre-Vocational Education are placing weight upon such things as student-involvement work, group work, practical skills, and non-examination assessment. It appears that many of the lessons of recent educational and curriculum research are beginning to have a far-reaching effect on mainstream schooling. One example is the Department of Education and Science (DES, 1985) policy document which argues that where possible science education should be made relevant to pupils' everyday experience, and should aim to prepare them for adult life, and that teaching and assessment methods should recognise the importance of practical and problem-solving skills. This is an obvious opportunity for health educators to make some impact.

One could argue, then, that the goals and values of modern health education and mainstream schooling are moving into line, and that a successful compromise of teaching objectives and methods is slowly being achieved. But there are two major reasons to suppose that the tensions between health education and traditional schooling will increase. One reason is the general hysteria attached to the idea of politics in the classroom and the genuine fears of pupils being indoctrinated. This is a problem which can partially be overcome by a clarification of the aims of political literacy which are not to be mistaken for education in party politics or ideology. The other reason, which in fact has more substantial ramifications, is that education for participation can be seen as a real threat to existing school organisation and the power relations between teachers and taught. Thus, any compromise between health education and traditional schooling might be uneasy and unstable unless health educators give a wide berth to avowedly political work.

# CLASSROOM POLITICS—THE REAL CHOICE

Pring describes how education authorities are sensitive to schools taking the political element of personal and social education seriously, and gives examples of local bans imposed on subjects with political significance (1984: 100). In a recent report called *Education and Indoctrination,* Scruton, Ellis-Jones and O'Keeffe produce a sustained educational case for this kind of sensitivity, and call for 'a ban on politically contentious subjects' (Scruton *et al.*, 1985: 49). This report is a thorough critique of those who seek to reduce the education system to a political instrument, and of politicised 'subjects' in which a particular political stance is assumed and promulgated. They define indoctrination as the domination of subjects by foregone conclusions and loaded language which are based on a closed system of dogma, and they contend that political indoctrination is already widespread in British education. These arguments are important but they are not arguments against political literacy; they are aimed at ideological bias in the teaching of subjects such as history or economics. Teaching for political literacy is not only different from the transmission of ideologies, it is a positive safeguard against it. The resistance to the politicisation of school subjects amounts to a recognition that political and moral values are already embodied in the curriculum (Rutter, 1979), and that the conditions for political indoctrination exist whether or not there are lessons called 'political education'. To make the topic overt, and to teach politics as 'the creative conciliation of differing interests' (Crick and Porter, 1978: 4), and as practical ways in which disagreements and different interests are represented and regulated, helps to undermine the would-be indoctrinator. Similarly, the danger of political indoctrination creeping into other subjects is reduced by making their political content as plain and public as possible. Those who instinctively react against the teaching of politics in schools should be reminded that the other influences to which young people are subject, including that of the home, are by no means free from bias and distortion. If the political components of the curriculum are less disguised, this facilitates the introduction of controls, such as changes in teacher education, and collective responsibility for the content and teaching of certain courses, which in turn minimise the risk of these kinds of distortions being repeated in schools.

In order to curtail the emotive equation of political education with indoctrination it is also necessary to distinguish between politics and party politics in a clear and persuasive way:

> 'politics' is usually misunderstood to refer to the activities of politicians, parties, parliaments and governments, and all the dreary bickering and bargaining associated with them. That is not what is meant here. . . . Politics consists of all the activities of cooperation and conflict, within and between societies, whereby the human species goes about obtaining, using, producing and distributing resources in the course of the production and reproduction of its social and biological life (Leftwich, 1983: 2, 12).

There is a popular, but narrow, use of 'politics' to refer to the activities of a small group of individuals only. It is often even further restricted to that part of their activities in which they are trying to persuade or win support for a principle or programme. According to this sense even major aspects of public policy-making are described as 'not political' if they are not subject to ideological controversy. This limited use completely fails to recognise the way in which all groups have power relationships and means of resource allocation, and thus all individuals by their involvement in social and economic relationships are to some extent 'participating' in politics. The objective of political literacy is to make this participation more self-conscious, well informed and skilful.

The distinction between politics and party politics helps to illuminate the diversity of subject matter relevant to health education. Whilst there is scope for teaching about national structures and government policies, the objectives of political literacy are served at least as well by a focus on institutional, regional or community issues. Those wishing to provide some education for health and political literacy are by no means confined to considering the effects of general social inequalities or social policy on health and illness. They can choose from a host of topics such as: the impact of health and safety regulations on a local environment; the relationships between doctors, other health professionals and patients; the processes of resource allocation in a health district; sex roles and the responsibilities of parents; the organisation of meals and recreation within the school; the 'economics' of drug-pushing and so on. Of course the introduction of these, or any other health topics, into the school curriculum must rest upon thorough research which takes into account all relevant educational variables such as age, instructional methods, and co-ordination and coherence with other syllabuses. Similarly all such work would need to be evaluated for its effectiveness in conveying information, affecting perceptions, and enhancing self-empowerment.

The most telling argument (discussed above) against those who want to keep politics and schools apart is that, over and above questions of ideology in the curriculum, the very structures and socialising forces of schooling can 'teach' political lessons. This is not only the view of those who regard schools as an agency for legitimating the prevailing social and economic power relations (Miliband, 1969). A Schools Council project team looking at ways to improve social studies teaching suggests that

> Schools may tend to be authoritarian establishments where deference to authority is encouraged rather than an ability to see conflicts of interests and values, especially if that conflict is with school policy. Some schools may even convince pupils that real and important conflicts do not exist (1981: 72).

There should be no pretence that schools are independent from politics, otherwise it is possible that they will cultivate only alienation, deference, or quietism. In this way they constitute a barrier to self-empowerment, rather than an avenue for its enhancement. This raises the key question for health education and political education: if they are both directed at the self-empowerment of individuals, how far should they be concerned with bringing about structural changes to increase opportunities for participation in the education system?

Many of the shifts in teaching methods and materials have been in this direction, bringing about more student involvement and negotiation, and focusing more attention on issues which are relevant to those being taught. For example, the Humanities Curriculum Project (Ruddock, 1983) has challenged classroom roles by experimenting with teachers acting only as procedural, and not as substantive authorities. In the Humanities Curriculum Project the teacher is required to assume the role of a 'neutral chairman' and to facilitate the use of curriculum materials by pupils. Yet the idea of self-empowerment would seem to entail at least the potential for a change in the attitude and behaviour of teachers towards pupils *outside* the classroom, and in the organisation of school affairs. The real value of teaching about issues of immediate relevance is not that these may engage pupils' interest, but that they may engage pupils' action, and that there may be some opportunities for them to affect things and 'make a difference'. For this reason a number of education theorists (Entwistle, 1971; Ungoed-Thomas, 1972) have suggested that more pupil democracy is an important means of political education. There are serious obstacles to this goal given the statutory duties of teachers and education authorities, yet it highlights the crucial challenge for all health educators, particularly those interested in political literacy.

> The real difficulties of political education are likely to lie not in areas of bias and indoctrination but in its encouragement of action. There are still some who appear to want 'good citizenship' without the trouble of having citizens (Crick and Porter, 1978: 41).

The effectiveness of health education is dependent upon individuals taking on responsibilities at least for their own health, and where possible for that of the wider community. There must therefore be a readiness on the part of health educators, even within schools, to share responsibilities, and to respect and respond to the values and choices of those they teach. It could be argued that, in practice, this would require a profound change in the relationships between teachers and pupils, and would amount to a threat to existing authority and power relations.

Some health educators may feel it is unwise to associate themselves with objectives which suggest support for radical changes to the education system, and some may even feel that these questions lie beyond their concerns. However our choice of health education raises the whole question of how traditional or radical schooling should be. There is a case for confining school health education to the transmission of knowledge and competences which relate directly to the individual's lifestyle and physical welfare. This might restrict the opportunities for ideological bias, and stop basic health information about drugs or disease getting lost in a sea of perspectives and contexts. Providing those who teach it are conscious of social and political determinants, and can communicate something of the limitations of an individual lifestyle approach, health education is broad enough to become established in the mainstream of schools in a worthwhile form that does not foreground the political dimension. It can be viewed as a pragmatic question—which approach will best foster the development of health education in schools? However, we must be clear that there are wider choices being made. Should health educators reinforce the present schooling system as it tends to reproduce itself, or should they be trying to break this process of reproduction?

## REFERENCES

Beardmore, J. A. and Vlijm, L. (eds) (1984), *Health Education and School Biology*, European Communities Biologists Association, London.

Beattie, A. (1984), 'Health Education and the Science Teacher: Invitation to a Debate', *Education and Health*, 2 (1).

Brennan, T. (1981), *Political Education and Democracy*, Cambridge University Press, Cambridge.

Crick, B. and Porter, A. (eds) (1978), *Political Education and Political Literacy*, Cambridge University Press, Cambridge.

De Jong, G. A. and Rutten, F. F. H. (1983), 'Justice and Health for All', *Social Science and Medicine,* 17 (16): 1085–95.

DES (1985), *Science 5–16: A Statement of Policy*, London.

Entwistle, H. (1971), *Political Education in a Democracy*, Routledge & Kegan Paul, London.

FEU (1982), *Basic Skills.*

Lawton, D. (1980), *The Politics of the School Curriculum,* Routledge & Kegan Paul, London.

Leftwich, A. (1983), *Redefining Politics*, Methuen, London.

MacIntyre, A. (1973), 'On the Essential Contestability of Some Social Concepts', *Ethics*, 84.

Miliband, R. (1969), 'The Process of Legitimation—II', *The State in Capitalist Society*, Weidenfeld & Nicolson, London.

Nordenfelt, L. (1983), 'The Concepts of Health and Disease', a paper presented to the Society for Social Medicine, 27th Annual Meeting.

O'Keeffe, D. (1981), 'Labour in Vain: Truancy, Industry and the School Curriculum', in Flew, A. *et al.* (eds), *The Pied Pipers of Education*, The Social Affairs Unit, London, pp. 29–42.

Pring, R. (1984), *Personal and Social Education in the Curriculum*, Hodder & Stoughton, London.

Reid, D. (1982), 'Into the Mainstream', in Lee, J. (ed.), *A Guide to School Health Education*, The Health Education Council, London.

Ruddock, J. (1983), *The Humanities Curriculum Project: An Introduction*, Centre for Applied Research in Education, Norwich.

Rutter, M. (1979), *Fifteen Thousand Hours*, Open Books, London.

Schools Council (1976), *Health Education in Secondary Schools*, Evans/Methuen, London.

Schools Council (1981), *The New Approach to the Social Studies*, Schools Council Publications, London.

Scott-Samuel, A. (1979), 'The Politics of Health', *Community Medicine*, 1: 123–6.

Scruton, R. (1983), 'Why Politicians are All Against Real Education', in *The Times*, 4 January 1983.

Scruton, R., Ellis-Jones, A. and O'Keeffe, D. (1985), *Education and Indoctrination*, Education Research Centre, Harrow.

Seedhouse, D. (1985), 'The Need for a Philosophy of Health', *Explorations in Medicine*, 1 (2), and forthcoming papers in 2 (1) and (2).

Smith, J. (1981), 'The Idea of Health: A Philosophical Inquiry', *Advances in Nursing Science*, 3: 43–50.

Strong, P. M. (1983), 'Three Social Science Approaches to the Concept of Health', a paper presented to the Society for Social Medicine, 27th Annual Meeting.

Tones, K. (1983), 'Education and Health Promotion: New Direction', *Journal of the Institute of Health Education*, 21: 121–31.

Ungoed-Thomas, J. R. (1972), *Our School,* Longman, London.

Vuori, H. (1980), 'The Medical Model and the Objectives of Health Education', *International Journal of Health Education*, 23 (1).

WHO (1984), *Health Promotion—A Discussion Document on the Concept and Principles*, Supplement to Europe News, No. 3, WHO Regional Office for Europe, Copenhagen.

Wood, P. H. and Bradley, E. M. (1985), 'The Origins of Ill Health' in Smith, A. (ed.), *Recent Advances in Community Medicine 3*, Churchill Livingstone, London, pp. 11–37.

# CHAPTER 7

# RADICAL HEALTH PROMOTION: A ROLE FOR LOCAL AUTHORITIES?

## Ged Moran

Mainstream practice of medicine has come under sustained attack in recent years from a variety of radical perspectives. Although critics vary in emphasis, certain themes emerge repeatedly. Medical practice is seen as dominated by individual curative approaches to the exclusion of structural, preventive interventions, an obsession which too readily slides into blaming the victims for the unhealthy end-results of circumstances over which they have no control. Organised in rigid hierarchies, it is permeated by the cult of the expert, preferring passivity and compliance amongst its consumers rather than active partnership and the development of self-knowledge. Since it refuses to challenge the structures and social relationships which create illhealth, it is often reduced to offering patients the technological or pharmacological 'fix', or the guilt-trip—or both.

Observing the daily workings of the NHS, or listening to the national political debate with its tired litanies of who spent what and who did or didn't make cuts, it might seem that the variety of radical criticism has made little impact. But when the BBC can offer its Reith Lectures as a platform for one such critique (Kennedy, 1981) and when growing numbers of people turn at their own expense to a wide range of 'alternative practitioners', it is clear that concern about current medical practice extends well beyond small groups of idealists or cranks.

In theory, health education should be well placed to respond to these concerns, since its professional skills hinge on the dissemination of knowledge about health, and its emphasis has traditionally been placed on prevention rather than cure. In practice, however, conventional health education is neither theoretically nor institutionally equipped to respond appropriately. It has placed its major emphasis on achieving voluntary changes in individual behaviour through expert interventions which, while purportedly politically neutral, neglect the wider social and economic forces affecting health over which isolated individuals have little or no control. By uncritically echoing the values of much medical practice, health education can easily end up in precisely the same blind alleys, with the same risk of resorting to victim-blaming and professional distancing. Indeed, it could even be argued that much health education practice is positively counter-productive, since by overlaying medical 'knowledge' with the professional skills and values of education or marketing, it actually reinforces rather than bridges the gap between 'experts' and 'consumers'. Dr Kildare plus Saatchi and Saatchi is a formidable combination with which to subdue the feckless.

Institutionally, health education lacks a secure professional and political base. Despite its change of location from local government to the NHS in 1974, it has always been part of a specifically medical hierarchy led successively by the Medical Officer of Health and more recently the District Medical Officer. Whilst accepting the medical model may protect its flank against professional attack, it still leaves health education marginal in terms of prestige and resources. At the same time, its political base looks increasingly shaky. Lay members of health authorities have tended to operate on the vague assumption that health education is about 'prevention' and therefore 'a good thing' both morally and financially. It also offers them a convenient and cheap solution whenever a new moral panic (glue-sniffing, teenage sex, heroin abuse) requires the authority to be seen 'doing something'. However, since issues of this kind are particularly unsuited to narrowly medical approaches, health education staff face a quite impossible set of demands even in the long-term, let alone within the short time-scales usually demanded. This in turn makes health education peculiarly vulnerable to two strands of attack from the right: an ideological objection to interference by the 'nanny state', and post-Griffiths managerialism with its heavy emphasis on easily-demonstrable 'cost-effectiveness'. The result can only be growing scepticism at member level and growing demoralisation among staff.

One response to these conflicting demands has been to retreat into technique, pursuing the credibility which comes from 'scientific rigour' by devising ever more methodologically complex micro-studies with a heavy emphasis on evaluation. However interesting these studies may be, they cannot possibly resolve the problems faced by conventional health education. In part this arises because the studies themselves often have very limited wider applicability precisely because they are so methodologically cumbersome. More importantly, however, the technical complexity of such approaches obscures still further the inappropriate values on which much health education is based; in particular, issues such as the relationship between inequalities of power and the social causation of ill health are conspicuously absent.

A more recent phenomenon has been the sudden mushrooming of 'health promotion teams' and 'positive health teams' in place of conventional health education departments. At first sight this appears a much more promising answer to radical critics. Certainly definitions and statements of objectives of health promotion such as 'to improve or protect health through behavioural, biological, socio-economic and environmental changes' (Catford and Nutbeam, 1984), contain strong elements of structural analyses alongside the more familiar individualistic approaches. Even if the precise implications of these analyses are not always spelt out, it makes a welcome change to see health authorities adopt policy statements such as 'Health promotion is a combination of activities which include education, legislation, economic and fiscal measures, mass media, marketing, professional intervention and community development which bring about changes in health' (Greenwich DHA, 1984). Similarly, open acknowledgment of a political role 'to influence central government, regional and national bodies to obtain necessary social changes (including legislation where appropriate) for healthier living' (South-East Thames RHA, 1984) represents a new departure for most health authorities.

Timescales appear to be realistic; some specific policies may be more coherently thought through, there is a willingness to draw on a wider range of skills in devising and implementing programmes (including such dangerously radical-sounding elements as community development); and many of the individuals involved seem more energetic and forward-looking than their predecessors. At the very least, the emergence of health promotion has forced many RHAs and DHAs to talk about health education in much greater depth, has attracted increased resources from inside and outside the NHS, and has gained much favourable media coverage in a number of areas. These are all significant achievements, even if the distinction between health promotion and self-promotion gets rather blurred in some cases.

Nevertheless, serious doubts remain about the potential for health promotion to move health education practice in a genuinely radical direction. For if the major determinants of illhealth are rooted in wider social and economic relationships, radical practice has to be explicitly geared to changing those relationships. While health promotion policy statements could be interpreted as endorsing this focus, and individual practitioners may be very committed to it, they remain trapped within an institutional framework which operates on very different assumptions. Health authorities take a perverse pride in the primacy which they attach to technocratic and professional values, and in the determination with which they avoid involvement in anything which might remotely be labelled 'political'. In these circumstances, health promotion initiatives which seriously challenge power relationships within health care delivery are likely to be strangled at birth by the medical profession, whilst initiatives which challenge health-damaging power relationships elsewhere in society will fall foul of the self-imposed ban on 'political activity'. All too easily, the health promotion approach may be forced back to the lowest common denominator, concentrating its energies on the individualistic elements of the overall programme, and leaving the structural approaches as little more than pious aspirations. The likeliest end-product yet again is the mixture as before—albeit marketed with considerably more flair and possibly more resources than previously.

Such pessimism about the possibilities for radical change within the NHS may seem premature. But to sketch even in very general terms a framework for radical practice is to demonstrate the gulf which separates it from current approaches. For example, radical health practice would

- be clearly focused on the structural causes of illhealth *and* on the possibilities for change;

- be located in the power networks which can work for such change (including arenas such as trade unions, tenants associations and other pressure groups);

- be geared towards the sharing of knowledge about health, rather than allowing it to be monopolised by professional elites;

- reassert the importance of people's subjective knowledge about their own health;

- find ways of channelling that subjective knowledge into NHS planning to complement the technocratic approaches of statisticians and epidemiologists;

- attempt also to influence the activities of other health-relevant agencies such as local authorities and employers.

Such a framework contrasts sharply with the mainstream of health education practice at both national and local levels. For although recent initiatives such as the limited funding of the journal *Radical Health Promotion* suggest an uneasy awareness by the Health Education Council that conventional approaches have serious limitations, major campaigns remain strongly consensual in their basic assumptions and individualistic in orientation. For example, the discussion document *Health Education in the Work-*

*place* (HEC, 1983) lays heavy emphasis on the role of 'expert' health education professionals whose activities are 'explored scientifically' and endorsed by 'thorough evaluation'. Working-class people whose health experiences are so starkly catalogued in the Black Report are blandly redefined as 'groups with special needs [who] may be easier to reach effectively with health education messages in the workplace', and any suggestion that good health practice at work may conflict with the pursuit of profit seems to represent an unfortunate 'preconceived idea'. Totally absent from the document is the slightest acknowledgment that securing safer working conditions has been and continues to be a bitter struggle between employers and employed, and that the return of mass unemployment significantly shifts the balance of power towards the employer. Instead, the document stresses the need for 'the co-operation and involvement of all parties in the planning process', whilst employers are reassured that workplace health education is 'not necessarily expensive' and indeed offers 'increased productivity and, potentially, cost benefits'. In its reluctance to consider the power imbalances between employers and workers, its faith in 'experts' and its casting of employees as the passive consumers of health education messages, the document is an instructive example of conventional health education approaches.

Against this background one can only salute the efforts of those NHS workers in a variety of disciplines who struggle to develop genuinely radical approaches in the face of the entrenched orthodoxies. It is hardly surprising, however, that much of the pioneering work in areas such as community development and the women's health movement is being carried on outside the NHS. There are, however, enormous problems of obtaining funding for such work (especially secure long-term funding) and of access to NHS decision-taking. But it can also offer the benefits of independence from medical domination, and the opportunity both to redefine the scope of health education and to renegotiate the relationship between professionals and consumers. Ironically, if we are to support the isolated few within the NHS who are working for long-term change, the best place to focus our energies may often be outside its formal structures.

# LOCAL AUTHORITIES AND HEALTH PROMOTION: RE-INVENTING PUBLIC HEALTH

One area which merits particular examination is the potential role of local authorities in advancing radical health promotion initiatives. This is not to argue that local authorities are the only or even the most important arenas for such activity: there are serious problems inherent in any attempt to reshape their approach to health issues. Nevertheless, given that a handful of authorities have at least begun to consider health questions more seriously, some opportunities for experiment are opening up. What sort of demands should health activists be making of local authorities?

The single most important, most difficult and probably most unlikely step local authorities could take would be to rebuild their own relationships with their local communities. There is no point whatsoever in criticising health authorities for being remote, undemocratic, authoritarian, over-professionalised and dominated by white male middle-class values when so much local authority activity demonstrates exactly the same faults. Renegotiating the relationship between local state and local people—assuming it is possible at all—is likely to be a long and painful process, and even among those authorities who recognise the importance of this issue there is no unanimity on how to go about it. (For example, there have been widely different approaches to issues such as decentralisation, relations with the black community, sexual equality and the use of grant-making powers.) Nevertheless, even very limited progress in making existing structures and services more accessible and responsive will inevitably have spin-off benefits elsewhere, since it will both raise expectations of a right to influence decisions by major public authorities, and develop the skills of democratic participation. The current structure and attitudes of health authorities would be hard-pressed to survive such changes in attitude.

Secondly, local authorities should be systematically reviewing their own activities specifically for their health implications. Historically health considerations were a major factor in the expansion of local authority activity, enshrined in major pieces of legislation such as the 1872 Public Health Act. The Health Committee, responsible both for public health and community health services even after the introduction of the NHS, enjoyed considerable status within the local authority. Its Chief Officer, the Medical Officer of Health, was granted specially protected employment status as a guarantee of independence (a privilege now reserved for Chief Constables); and the publication by the MOH of an Annual Report was a statutory requirement. Whilst the quality of MOHs inevitably varied widely, the health function was an absolutely central part of the local authority's activities, and structures existed which allowed significant innovations such as the introduction of antenatal care to be pioneered by individual authorities. More recently, however, and particularly since the abolition of the MOH in the 1974 health and local government reorganisations, health has almost disappeared from the agenda of many local authorities. Environmental Health Departments, lacking status and resources but expected to cover a heterogeneous range of responsibilities from communicable diseases and soil pollution to housing conditions and aspects of occupational health, have rarely been able to fill the gap, even though their skills are often more relevant than specifically medical skills. Many local authorities thus find themselves without any institutional focus for the systematic discussion of health issues, and the public health tradition dating back over a century is rapidly being eroded. Revitalising this tradition, with its recognition of the material causes of illhealth and its emphasis on collective, preventive action rather than individualised curative interventions, should now be a major priority for local authorities.

Renewing this public health tradition is, however, likely to be a painful process for many authorities. For as the causes of illhealth are rooted in wider social and economic structures, local authorities have to face the possibility that they may often be part of the problem rather than part of the solution. For example, at the turn of the century when most housing was privately owned, it was easy enough for socialists to emphasise the connection between housing and health as an argument for major devel-

opments of council housing. Eighty years later, when some of the
worst housing and some of the worst landlords are Labour councils
themselves, there is a substantial vested interest in *not* highlighting
those self-same connections.

Even where authorities are willing in principle to accept major
criticisms of their past activities, the short-term consequences of
doing so may appear demoralising. It would hardly be surprising
if even the best-intentioned housing department, trapped between
the enforced sale of its best stock and the massive cuts in funding
for new stock or major repairs, lapsed into narrowly defensive
rationing of the residual stock, too overwhelmed by the sheer
extent of unmet housing need even to go on cataloguing and
publicising it. In earlier years some of the better Medical Officers
of Health played a key part in attracting political attention and
resources into housing precisely by emphasising its significance for
health. Since the majority of their successors in NHS community
medicine have effectively abdicated this responsibility, local authorities and voluntary groups have no option but to do it for
themselves if the condition of the housing stock is to re-gain its
former importance on the national political agenda.

A third role for local authorities is the funding of local groups
working on health-related issues. This funding might be in the
form of a community health worker for a particular project, or a
grant towards running costs, or support for a particular one-off
initiative such as a health festival. The groups themselves might
represent very different interests: a women's health group, a hospital campaign group, a black group, a workplace group, a tenants
action group. Inevitably, they will themselves come into conflict
with the council from time to time. Nevertheless, the local authority should be looking to support groups who are attempting to
develop new approaches to health provision and planning, and
who seek to draw upon and share the very considerable knowledge
of and interest in health which the existing structures are quite
incapable of mobilising.

Fourthly, local authorities can make available specialist skills
where these are appropriate. For example, a group campaigning
for a Well Woman's centre might want access to planning depart-

ment population analyses. A hospital campaign group might need a legal opinion on some procedural manoeuvre by the health authority, or advice from the public relations department on how to develop local media contacts. Virtually any group with a health interest may need a straightforward explanation of the more arcane elements of health service planning such as 'RAWP' or 'bed-norms' if they are to avoid being blinded by pseudo-science. In each case the local authority can play a useful facilitating role: not attempting to take over particular groups, but making it possible for them to campaign more effectively by the provision of specific skills or information.

## CHANGING THE NHS AGENDA

All these initiatives lie outside the NHS structure itself, but local authorities also have a pivotal role in changing the formal health agenda in a variety of ways. Precisely because elected councillors are relatively public figures engaged in an overtly political activity, they are far more likely than unelected and often anonymous DHA members to receive information or demands about health services, whether through constituents, party or voluntary groups, trade unions, or the local authority machinery itself. In a properly democratic NHS structure, such demands would flow automatically to the health authority. But if that democratisation is ever to be achieved, local authority members need to play a leading role in voicing the demands of people excluded or ill-served by the labyrinthine NHS planning process and the values which underpin much NHS practice. And in doing so they need to recognise that reconstructing a *political* agenda for health in place of the professionally dominated one is considerably more complex and time-consuming than simply engaging in an annual set-piece debate about cuts or private medicine.

It would be naive to underestimate the difficulties of repoliticising the public debate about health in any fundamental way: both the structures and the ethos of the NHS serve to buttress the professional monopoly of power. But local authorities are not without resources of their own with which to begin challenging that professional monopoly. For example, they could choose to devote some resources to obtaining independent information about health needs and provision, instead of relying on the crumbs offered by health authorities. They can draw on a far wider range of groups in formulating alternative policies on health—especially where they are willing to adopt relatively informal approaches to consultation. They also have guaranteed—if limited—access to formal NHS structures through representation on health authorities, Joint Consultative Committees and Community Health Councils, access which can be used to give support to those NHS workers trying to develop radical approaches.

Underlying these neglected organisational advantages the most important asset is that the legitimacy of local authority representatives rests on explicitly political foundations: they claim a right to speak entirely independent of the rights derived from professional expertise. Potentially at least they are fundamentally different from other health authority members who, appointed by patronage and lacking any independent basis of authority, find themselves marginalised by the combined assaults of the Secretary of State and the professionals. It is a depressing tribute to the existing medical hegemony that local authority representatives are so often indistinguishable from the rest, allowing themselves to be dominated by the professionals to a degree quite unthinkable within their own local authorities. Accepting the dominant definitions of health as 'non-political', they often attach low priority to health authority attendance, disdain such routine organisational devices as group meetings, rarely initiate agenda items of their own and are almost completely unaccountable for their actions to the people they supposedly represent. Simply to remedy these deficiencies would be a useful first step towards reclaiming health as a political issue, making it possible to raise systematically issues such as health and social class, unemployment, sexism, racism and the need to change the balance between individual and structural interventions.

Clearly there are major problems in attempting to develop the health role of local authorities in radical directions. Very many authorities whole-heartedly share the individualised, victim-blaming approach to illhealth; others do not see health as a local authority issue, and among the minority who are trying to redefine their stance on health a good number have been subjected to rate-capping or even abolition. In many areas therefore it would be a waste of time for health activists to devote much energy to local authorities (except in a purely adversarial sense). But where authorities are beginning to show a renewed interest in health, health promotion workers should be seeking to develop links. They may well find that the political independence of local authority members allows controversial issues to be raised from outside the NHS more easily or more critically than from within.

Even with a potentially sympathetic local authority, the diffi-culties of building such links are considerable, particularly where senior NHS staff are uninterested in or even hostile to such approaches. One essential starting-point for health promotion workers is to recognise that awareness at senior levels of the NHS of the health importance of local authority activities is depressingly narrow, frequently extending little further than complaints about the non-availability of local authority services to speed hospital discharges. By contrast, there can be few health visitors, especially in inner-city areas, who are unaware of the vital importance of housing or leisure facilities for the physical and mental health of mothers and children. If this awareness is to influence NHS policy, health promotion workers would need to play an educative role amongst their NHS colleagues, both by personal propagandising and by helping grass-roots workers to make their voices heard.

Formal structures also offer some opportunities for building local authority links. Health promotion sections of Strategic and Operational Plans should emphasise the importance of local auth-ority functions and identify potential areas for joint working. Health promotion staff should press for their authorities to use Joint Consultative Committees to question local authorities on a regular basis about major health issues such as housing policy, the quality of local authority catering, or the possibilities of health education in schools expanding into the mainstream curriculum instead of remaining merely a low-status optional extra. Such approaches should be supported by ensuring that health promotion groups at both officer and member level include strong local authority representation; conversely, health promotion staff should be aware of opportunities to contribute to planning forums elsewhere in the NHS and in the local authority.

These formal, often extremely bureaucratic channels need to be complemented by the day-to-day practice of joint working. A major reorientation of existing health education practice in the direction of community development approaches would undoubtedly bring much closer contact at a local level with social workers, community workers, voluntary groups, and local politicians and political activists. Such contacts will not always be harmonious, particularly where local authority services or the lack of them are a major cause of health problems, but radical health promotion activists simply cannot afford to be over-fearful of political involvement.

Less obviously controversial, but in the long term extremely politically significant, are issues already featuring increasingly prominently on health promotion agendas which would greatly benefit from joint approaches with local authorities. For example, some health authority food policies amount to little more than a mechanistic transplanting of the NACNE recommendations into the hospital diet (National Advisory Committee on Nutrition Education, 1983). This belated step is welcome, but it falls well short of understanding the potential for food policies identified by a number of local authorities (Sheffield Health Care Strategy Group, 1984; GLC Economic Policy Group, 1984; Greater Manchester Food Policy Unit, 1984). In particular, enabling the community at large to eat more healthily raises issues ranging from EEC subsidies and national taxation policies to planning, employment, transport and distribution systems, food-labelling and the division of labour within the home. Health promotion workers and nutritionists need to be contributing to these wider debates instead of limiting themselves to improving NHS institutional catering. Parallel considerations arise in areas such as drug or alcohol abuse, where effective strategies are unlikely to be developed without an awareness of the social pressures which result in increasing resort to 'drugs of solace' (Cameron and Jones, 1985).

## HEALTH PROMOTION WORKERS: IN OR OUT OF THE NHS?

To emphasise the health promotion potential of local authorities in terms both of political legitimacy and of service provision inevitably raises the issue of whether staff would be more effective within the local authority rather than the NHS. Certainly many local authorities are already engaged in work which might be labelled as health promotion whether at a micro-level, such as organising courses for food handlers, or in more ambitious attempts to prepare long-term strategies on food or to research health inequalities. Local authority staff such as social workers and community workers often intervene in ways which radical health promotion workers would recognise, for example, organising tenants' groups on neglected estates or bringing together isolated and depressed mothers to make demands for improved facilities. Furthermore, the local authority health role is potentially separable from the medically led, curative ethos which dominates the NHS. If local authorities do succeed in revitalising the public health tradition, they are unlikely to revert to the pre-1974 model with the unchallenged primacy it gave to the medical profession. Instead, authorities will be looking to more broadly based health promotion initiatives, drawing on a range of disciplines including planning, research, environmental health, community work and social work and possibly including representation from other statutory and voluntary agencies such as the NHS (Unit for the Study of Health Policy, 1979). Were such a development to occur, it would greatly expand the opportunity for health promotion workers to exert real influence from within the local authority itself.

More immediately however, the local authority base presents a range of problems, both organisational and political. Organisationally, local government in much of Britain is not a unitary structure; instead, different functions are located in different tiers of government. A desire to relocate existing health education staff into local government would require an essentially arbitrary decision as to whether a base at county level alongside activities such as social services, education, and strategic planning is preferable to working at district level alongside housing, environmental health and leisure. At the same time, severing the links with the NHS carries penalties as well as advantages. A substantial health promotion task remains to be done in and around the health care services themselves, both in expanding the knowledge patients have about their own bodies and in re-orienting the approach of many NHS professionals to the care they are providing. Such tasks, already daunting, would almost certainly become even more difficult in the short term from outside the NHS.

Politically, the local authority base is sometimes no more hospitable to radical initiatives than the supposedly 'non-political' NHS. For while the local authority ethos is an explicitly political one, the privilege of overt political activity does not automatically extend to staff themselves. As many social workers and community workers have found to their cost, in-house critics of local authority policies run severe risks of being marginalised or even disciplined if they persist too long in their opposition—particularly if they do so in public. Since local authorities are frequently at their most defensive in precisely those areas which are most likely to interest health promotion workers, particularly housing, activists might rapidly meet the same fate as previous generations of troublesome employees.

That neither the NHS nor local authorities offer an entirely satisfactory base for politically informed health promotion work is hardly surprising; the tensions inherent in working in and against the state have already been well documented (London–Edinburgh Weekend Return Group, 1980). Rather, a realistic awareness of the limitations of these structures should persuade health promotion activists that to press for any single organisational model is misconceived. A willingness to experiment with different structures according to different local needs and opportunities is far more likely to be productive in the immediate future. Thus where the more politically aware Community Health Councils are already involving themselves in health promotion activity, NHS workers might find with them a more congenial base than they now have in the district hierarchy. Clearly such possibilities would not appear overnight: in the short-term the informal development of links and of joint working may suffice. But in the longer term it may well be worth considering the CHC as a potential base if health promotion workers are to remain within the NHS—particularly if they are adopting community development approaches to their work. At the very least, to share the somewhat protected contractual status of CHC staff might strengthen their position where they are challenging the policies of the DHA within which they work. More generally, to argue actively for a range of different bases for health promotion work is to build on the existing reality, acknowledging the diversity of approaches already adopted in both the statutory and voluntary sectors as a source of strength and innovation.

To talk about changing the nature of local authority services, or using the local authority to improve access to NHS decisions may seem a very long way from traditional health education practice. Yet the existence of this gap merely underlines the extent to which health education has become constrained within a narrow and ultimately self-defeating definition of the proper scope of its activity. A radical approach, taking as its starting point a materialist explanation of the causes of illhealth, is bound to be concerned with the health impacts of local authority activities. Similarly, a commitment to expanding people's control over their own health and the agencies which provide health care (a central objective for any sort of health education) inevitably raises questions about how to make the best use of the existing, profoundly undemocratic structures. To do so would undoubtedly raise the predictable accusations of 'being political' from those content with the status quo. Not to do so is of course equally a political position—but in the current climate it too carries serious risks. For even the most scrupulously 'apolitical' health education practice will not be immune from demands to demonstrate that it can deliver the goods, if it is to defend even its existing meagre level of funding. If it is to meet this challenge effectively—let alone obtain the additional resources which a serious commitment to health promotion demands—health education will need to earn friends wherever it can find them. It could do a great deal worse than start looking towards local authorities.

## REFERENCES

Cameron, D. and Jones, I. (1985), 'An Epidemiological and Sociological Analysis of the Use of Alcohol, Tobacco and Other Drugs of Solace', *Community Medicine*, 7: 1, February.

Catford, J. and Nutbeam, D. (1984), 'Towards a Definition of Health Education and Health Promotion', *Health Education Journal*, 43: 2 and 3.

GLC Economic Policy Group (1984), *Food For a Great City: GLC Strategy Towards London's Food Sector*. Strategy Document No. 335, GLC, London.

Greater Manchester Food Policy Unit (1984), *A Food Policy in Greater Manchester*, Manchester Polytechnic.

Greenwich District Health Authority (1984), *Draft Annual Programme 1984*.

Health Education Council (1983), *Health Education in the Workplace: A Discussion Document*, Health Education Council, London.

Kennedy, I. (1981), *The Unmasking of Medicine*, Allen & Unwin, London.

London–Edinburgh Weekend Return Group (1980), *In and Against the State*, Pluto Press, London.

National Advisory Committee on Nutrition Education (1983), *A Discussion Paper on Proposals for Nutrition Guidelines for Health Education in Britain*, Health Education Council, London.

Radical Health Promotion Collective (1985), *Radical Health Promotion*, No. 1.

Sheffield Health Care Strategy Group (1984), *Food and Health: Sheffield Conference Report.*

South-East Thames Regional Health Authority (1984), *Outline Regional Strategy 1985–94.*

Unit for the Study of Health Policy (1979), *Rethinking Community Medicine,* Guy's Hospital Medical School, London.

# CHAPTER 8

# COMMUNITY HEALTH EDUCATION: A TIME FOR CAUTION?

## Alison Watt

Community health education, the attempt to take health messages out of the classroom or clinic and to ground them in people's own environments, interests and daily lives, is generally considered to be rather a good thing. It demonstrates a new vitality in health education as a discipline, encouraging a creative interchange between once distant health education units and their local communities.[1] It acknowledges that illhealth is not caused by a failure to comply with the moral imperatives of our social order, that the analysis is now considerably more sophisticated—and the solutions therefore considerably more complex. It represents, then, an understanding amongst a profession hitherto cast in a mould of individualism, of the value of engaging the collective interest, trust, and participation of the people who experience the poorest health, if the causes of such illhealth are to be in any way properly tackled. Given this encouraging progression, why am I suggesting that community health education be regarded with caution?

My first reservation is concerned with the way in which the *term* community is interpreted and applied. This, I shall argue, has substantial implications for the practice of community health education as a method. The second reservation is one that is more anticipatory than actual, yet if the pattern we are currently witnessing in community health education is to continue, this

139

reservation will soon become actual. It is concerned with the development of health promotion, and the bearing that this has, and may have, on the practice of community health education

What is to follow will be a consideration of the term community, with the suggestion that its very use can insidiously debilitate and prohibit a potentially progressive practice. This will be followed by an examination and comparison of the dynamic introduced when community health education becomes community *development* in health education. The significance of this will then be assessed in terms of the criticism health education has faced in its more traditional form, and the scrutiny the discipline is now under following the advent of health promotion.


## A CONSIDERATION OF THE TERM COMMUNITY


The focus here is the generalist use of the term community, and it is notably distinct from abstracted theoretical discourse. It is used in an everyday sense with increasing frequency, and within an array of contexts. We hear of the black community, the local community, community transport schemes, community life, community work and community development. Whilst there seems not to be any logical link between any of these concepts, there is, within the term, a recognition of something shared. A community, therefore, of whatever nature, evokes images of groups of people with recognised and recognisable boundaries, sharing something in common. The sharing might be of interests, of a demographic factor such as race, sex or age, or of a religion, subculture, or locality. The variations are infinite. Most importantly however, the image evoked is a *warm* one, and it feels positive, generating a sense of conviviality, harmony and mutual support. This, then, is the way in which the term community is most frequently used.

What happens when this understanding, this interpretation of community, is applied to health education? Interestingly, the *practitioners* experience a sense of warmth, a sense of conviviality and harmony in their new style of work. 'Reaching out to the community' has become the satisfied litany of every well-meaning health education officer (HEO). This satisfaction is compounded by the drip-effect of the general awareness of inequalities in health, prompting an understanding by HEOs of the need to depart from victim-blaming. Community health educators therefore feel excited as well as warm, because they perceive themselves to be doing something progressive.[2]

An important caveat must be made here. There are some health education officers who fall well clear of my sharp caricature. They have responded to the literature recommending the adoption of community *development* principles and methods as an important strategy for tackling structured health inequalities (for example: Freudenberg, 1978; Mitchell, 1982; Hubley, 1979; Fisher and Cochrane, 1982; Rosenthall, 1983; Greetham, 1982; Somerville, 1985) and they have implemented effective and appropriate programmes. (See, for example, Black, 1985; Drennan, 1985; Meade and Thorpe, 1985.) They are, however, in a small minority of the 500 HEOs in England and Wales—a profession generally in constant search of a method of practice that will counter sustained and ingrained criticisms of ineffectiveness. Ironically, as examples of the minority community health education activities spread along formal and informal HEO networks, these new methods are seized by the remaining majority, and then often reproduced without adequate understanding or preparation. In other words, they are implemented incorrectly, of use only to the implementers, who experience the symbolic and largely mythical sense of community (Bainton, Clifford, Frosh *et al.*, 1985) and a misguided sense of progressiveness.

To return to the use of the term community. Those health education officers who are working in the community and who *do* subsequently experience the community spirit must be engaged in communities where such a spirit exists. These communities will typically be middle-class, and suburban and rural. A community spirit will *not* immediately be found amongst people who are easily identifiable as suffering the worst health. These people generally live in poor housing, in areas where there is high unemployment, racial tension, inadequate recreation, education, shopping and social service facilities, and high levels of anger at such societal mistreatment. This anger is often expressed in crime and other anti-social behaviours (Harrison, 1983). Therefore, people who live in decaying council housing, experiencing high rates of vandalism, sexual and racial attacks, do not trip between each other's doors borrowing cups of sugar and minding each other's children. They do not live harmoniously, and they do not readily trust one another. Of course they can and do, but the processes required to establish such relationships are of a different order to the simple community spirit (Gough, 1979).

It can be seen then, that if HEOs wish to respond to the charge to direct resources where there is the greatest need, they are going to have to work in areas where it is well acknowledged that considerable skills are required if the work is to be sensitive, appropriate, and not counterproductive (Gulbenkian Foundation, 1968; Henderson and Thomas, 1980). Why is it important for HEOs to direct their resources to areas of the greatest health needs, and what would community health education look like if it were to properly do that?

## HEALTH EDUCATION: MEETING WHOSE NEEDS?

At the level of deciding on the allocation of *limited* resources it would seem self-evident that HEOs direct their resources to those with the greatest health needs. Indeed there is within the profession a recognisable rhetoric supporting this concept. The simplicity of this position is of course complicated by the lack of a common understanding as to what constitutes a *health* need, and in relation to whose assessment of need is the most valid. A major problem posed for health education officers by the evidence supporting the significance of social factors in the production of health and illness is that the boundaries of health—and by implication of health education—are pushed to the widest shores of conception. Where to begin, let alone where to end?

Compounding this dilemma is the process by which health *needs* are typically defined. Within the NHS, it is generally assumed that health needs are best assessed by health professionals, the parameters of such assessments being defined and regulated by medical practitioners. This normative approach to needs indicates not only that doctors have tremendous influence in assessing and prioritising health needs (Friedson, 1972) but also that unless they *ratify* an expressed health need, it ceases to exist (Cooper, 1975). If, for example, a man presents complaining of persistent headaches, unless the doctor concerned agrees with his symptomatology and can find some evidence for it, the condition, in terms of attracting treatment, ceases to exist. In relation to community health education, if it is to be effective, it must begin by recognising that people's *own* assessment of their health needs is the most valid starting point for any programme of action.

Further problems faced by HEOs when prioritising their work are the claims made by other health professionals, and in particular by doctors, on the time and resources of health education officers. Despite management changes introduced by the Griffiths Report (Haywood, 1985), most HEOs remain nominally if not actually accountable to their District Medical Officer. HEOs are therefore frequently called upon to respond either to the latest issue to catch the medical interest—such as AIDS or drug misuse—or to issues which persist despite clinical intervention, and to which health education is subsequently instructed to turn—such as a district's high infant mortality rate. Even the drawing up of plans by health education units is expected to reflect the district's priorities, and furthermore to lend support to them. The scope for HEOs to define their own professional agenda is limited.

These are therefore the two major constraints on surpassing the rhetoric of directing health education resources towards the greatest health needs. There is, however, a structural imperative within all of this, increasing the likelihood that HEOs will want to push for community health education, whatever their political understandings of health and illness.

The delivery of NHS health care, in *whatever* form, has been

143

dominated recently by the negotiations around the allocation of limited resources to a perception of infinite demands (Culyer, 1976; Doyal and Pennell, 1979). Health education, as we have seen, is no exception to this ritual, and indeed faces disproportionate scrutiny and budget-paring in comparison with its more established *treatment*-based competitors (Jones, 1985). Health Education Officers are consequently expected to pick up substantial responsibility for the prevention of disease and promotion of health on remarkably limited finances. Given this constraint, it is no surprise that health education is struggling to prove its effectiveness. The picture is further complicated by the misdirection of some of the already limited health education resources (Gray and Blythe, 1979).

What we are observing, therefore, is a health education service within the NHS that is firstly severely underfunded, and secondly, charged with the responsibility of solving many of the currently intractable health problems faced by the curative sector. It is precisely because HEOs have consistently been unable to demonstrate effectiveness as a result both of this underfunding and of a poorly developed theoretical base (see for example Draper *et al.*, 1980; Brown and Margo, 1978), that the discipline has accepted with notable willingness the demands made by the medical profession to solve, by prevention, its more thorny curative problems. In other words, to meet the *medical* profession's needs. This is now particularly the case as community medicine gains a stronger position in the ranks of the medical hierarchy. There is always the hope within health education that a medically supported programme will successfully address the problem, will meet the various health needs, and will therefore underpin a discipline caught in an impossibly vicious circle.

So despite cutbacks, health education continues to limp along because of the irrefutable logic in preventing rather than treating, yet it is never funded adequately to implement this massive undertaking because it has not, to date, proved effective. It has not, therefore, to date, met health needs in areas where the incidence is particularly high, it has not met its own needs to establish itself as a successful profession, and it has not met the medical profession's needs. Consequently, health education is constantly searching for its forte, for a success that will end this tautology. It is for this reason that the trend to look to the community is emerging. Yet until the theoretical base of community health education is strengthened, until practice reflects an adequate theory, the quest for salvation in the community will remain fruitless.

To summarise so far, the problem is that the feelings and images of warmth and support evoked by the term community in its generalist use, are not ones that will be found when working in those areas where there is the greatest social disadvantage, and where there are the greatest health needs. So to point resources at 'communities'—whenever medical permission for such an approach has been secured—because that is the current thing to do, and because it makes the practitioner feel as warm and progressive as the term community itself, is not directing resources towards those in the greatest need. This will continue to be the case for as long as we have communities set in the social squalor of structured inequalities.

It is at this point that community *development* in health education enters the discourse. In order to be effective, in order to apply a practice that is both informed by an understanding of inequalities in health, and that attempts to tackle them, community health education must draw upon the principles of community development.

## COMMUNITY DEVELOPMENT IN HEALTH EDUCATION

Community development can be traced to colonial development in the 'Third World'. The practice of an overseas worker mobilising highly disadvantaged communities into collective action—via public health, acute health, and agricultural strategies—was transferred back into Britain in the late 1960s when poverty was 'rediscovered' (Rosenthall, 1983). In particular, inner-city decline and decay attracted concern, prompting a dual but polarised response. On the one hand the welfare rights movement in its various manifestations was established, and on the other, local authorities became larger, more hierarchical, and with a greater investment in corporate management. This climate of distanced local authority provision, the failure of urban planning, and increasing industrial alienation, generated substantial amounts of neighbourhood activity (Higgins, Deakin, Edwards et al., 1983). The colonial concept of mobilising for collective action was seized, 'participation' became a crucial aim, and principles of British democracy were scrutinised. Hence, community development refers to a process that seeks to:

> extend the democratic potential of our political system to all those who are presently little involved in decisions taken on their behalf. The complex nature of modern government has resulted in more and more decisions resting solely in the hands of elected representatives and public officials. As a consequence, the less organised and articulate sections of the population— and this could be of any class—have had less attention paid to their needs, especially matters affecting their environment. Certainly in some cases it is no accident that motorways are routed through less affluent neighbourhoods or that council tenants become the guinea pigs for architects' experiments in housing development (Harris et al., 1978: 5).

Community development therefore uses as its baseline an analysis of social inequity. All activities attempt, implicitly or explicitly, to challenge the 'Matthew Effect'—to close the gap between the haves and the have-nots (Lorber, 1984). There is therefore a concern to address inequalities, not only because of an ideological commitment to an equal society, but, more prosaically, because of the unacceptable consequences of inequality for those who are squashed at the bottom. Community development workers therefore listen to people's experiences and needs, and attempt to assist these people to gain access to the arenas in which decisions are made that actually produce and reproduce the quality of their lives.

It can be seen then, that application of the term community is far more specific in community development than in its more generalist use. 'Community' refers to those people who have to make disproportionately high demands on the social welfare services, and who are therefore in the position of having decisions about fundamentally important aspects of their lives being made *for* them. They cannot, for example, choose where to live, as their housing options are subject to council availability. They cannot choose if or where to work. Their options will be determined by the labour market. They cannot choose a 'good' school for their children—because they cannot choose where they live, and they will have limited means for transport. The examples could continue, and would increasingly be seen to inter-relate. It is this point that is important, for we are observing the effects of structured inequalities from which it is so difficult to escape. It is inappropriate to resort to the ideology of bootstrap pulling, yet this is so often the case, and carries with it a conservative political expediency.

In the health arena, community development workers are concerned with inequalities in health—differentials in health status between the classes. The inverse relationship between class and health demonstrates itself not only in morbidity and mortality rates—that is the lower the class the higher the sickness and death rates—but also in access to health care (Tudor Hart, 1971). Access as a concept includes the social inappropriateness of the health service for certain categories of people, as well as geographical issues of access. For example, mothers of small children are higher users of the health services precisely because of their small children, yet travelling on public transport with a pushchair and two toddlers, at least one of them poorly, is a marathon exercise. Once at the doctor's, there are rarely toys for the children, let alone crèche facilities. If the woman is working-class, the patronising which she can expect to receive as a woman will be increased (Roberts, 1985). If she is black, she can expect to receive another layer of covert or overt hostility (McNaught, 1985). Furthermore, whether male or female, working-class patients are referred by GPs to specialists only half as much as middle-class patients with the same disorder (Blaxter, 1976), despite having twice as high an incidence for some diseases (Mitchell, 1984). Social access to health care can therefore be seen to be in part determined by health professionals—who typically sit comfortably in a class system that deprioritises lower social classes. Such deprioritisations have a substantial bearing on health differentials. It is precisely these sorts of issues with which community development health workers attempt to get to grips. What does their work look like in practice?

Most community development workers are employed by a neighbourhood centre or settlement, or occasionally as specialist community workers by the local authority. Geographically, they work to a neighbourhood, although the nature of their work may sometimes be better described as issue-based. They will typically be accountable to a management group of the centre, on which will sit residents of the neighbourhood as well as more traditional managers. In summary their job descriptions will indicate that their major task is to help people in their neighbourhood to identify their health needs, and to assist them in seeking to have them met. It is not the task of these workers to impose their own values, nor to take a leading or authoritative role. Their work is centred in the understanding that residents in disadvantaged areas will only gain control by taking control—not by following a leader who decides on their behalf. Because of the wide variety of people's health interests and needs, the work that is undertaken is extremely diverse.

Take as an example a worker based on an estate where there is a high proportion of elderly residents. A number of them might express feelings of loneliness, and that they no longer know what to expect from their bodies as they change with age. The worker would then propose the forming of a pensioners' health club, and would test the idea with the other elderly residents and the other neighbourhood workers. If it is met with approval, a venue such as the tenants' hall would be found, and the first meeting advertised throughout the estate. Between the worker and the group, a programme of health activities and learning would be drawn up, the pensioners taking on as much of the decision-making and organisation as was practicable. There are many groups such as this, although all have different emphases. One group in Brent, for example, in addition to running pensioners' health courses, was successful in persuading the District Health Authority to improve its chiropody service (Kerrison, 1985).

A centrality of community development health projects is the recognition of the value of the group process. The sharing of experiences and knowledge, and the discovery by an individual that she or he is not the only person suffering in such a way, is therapeutic in itself. This sharing also helps to lessen the guilt people experience when ill—a guilt generated by the way in which an individual is typically held responsible for becoming ill (Crawford, 1977). The community development health worker will be sensitive to all of this, and will ensure that there is time for people to talk, and will encourage them to trust and validate their own knowledge and experiences. The worker will also encourage them to voice their criticisms of the health services. This forms part of the process of enabling people to have a greater say in their treatment when they do have to use the health services.

Another task of many community development health workers is to promote, within the neighbourhood, an awareness of health issues in such a way that people can see for themselves the value of participating in the local delivery of health services. Hence some neighbourhoods might identify the prospective building of a health centre as a facility in which they would like to be involved (Stockwell Health Project, 1981). Another might decide that, as the local hospital does not provide adequate food for Asians, action should be taken to have this remedied (Cornwell and Gordon, 1984).

The possibilities for involvement are endless. As noted, some workers work only with a particular group in a neighbourhood, for example with young mothers—whereas some work in the neighbourhood generally. The issue of common concern, however, is that people living in disadvantaged areas particularly experience their lives and therefore their health as something over which they have little control. It is the challenging of this state of affairs that community development health workers are pursuing. For of course their motivation is not one of empty agitation. It is the realisation that much of today's medical care is both ineffective and inappropriate for people who suffer the disadvantages of our societally produced inequalities.

## COMMUNITY DEVELOPMENT IN HEALTH EDUCATION

I have intentionally allowed this description of community development health work to draw attention to those aspects that are regarded by many health professionals, especially doctors, as unacceptable. A tendency when writing for an audience that may include the medical reader is to strain out the sensitive bits. As the attempt here is to analyse why it is that health education officers have failed so far—in the main—to implement a community health education informed by community development, I have had by necessity to include the less palatable components. For whilst much of the failure comes from the earlier described combination of a poorly developed theoretical base, and an inclination towards the community simply because it represents something warm and progressive, lack of autonomy is also an important restriction. It does not require too careful a consideration to realise that community development in health constitutes a disruption to the order and equilibrium of medical dominance. Whilst HEOs are by no means unanimously inclined to contribute to any disequilibrium, those that *do* perceive medical hegemony as not necessarily in the interests of health find it extremely difficult to proceed with any counter-measures. (See Wendy Farrant and Jill Russell, Chapter 9.)

It would be useful to know precisely how health authorities operate to discourage participation by health education units in community development health education. For whilst I have said that if done properly it constitutes a challenge to medical dominance, it need not be an unhelpful challenge. On the contrary, those medical practitioners who do support and participate in people's health as well as illness, and in people's increasing knowledge and interest in their health, find it a stimulating and rewarding experience. (See for example: Somerville, 1985; Fisher and Cochrane, 1982; Scott-Samuel, 1982.)

Furthermore, in practice, community development in health education looks far less seditious than many believe it to be. It is logically difficult to defend a position that excludes the recipients and purchasers of a service from decisions about its delivery. All that community development health projects attempt to do is to enable people to understand that principle, and to then apply it to their own health needs. I am saying 'all' because grass-roots work is by definition small scale and localised. It might help to illuminate this point by comparing two relaxation classes. The first will be a venture instigated by a health education officer who wants to 'do' health education in the community. The second will be by an HEO employing a community development approach.

The relaxation class 'done' in the community would appear in seed form as a response to the medical literature—and subsequent popularisation of that literature—concerning stress as a pathological agent. The District Medical Officer or the District Health Education Officer would then decide that a suitable form of action would be relaxation classes for the local community. A meeting would be held with appropriate professional representation, the proposal examined in the light of long-term aims and objectives, and the budget scrutinised. After ratification, a venue would be sought—perhaps a church hall or a school room, or an anteroom off the library. A physiotherapist, occupational therapist, or health education officer would be approached to conduct the classes, and a ten-week programme would be drawn up. Posters would be produced advertising the class, and displayed in local health centres, libraries, and the post office. Health visitors would be alerted to the class and instructed to tell their patients. The class would run, and, if there was sufficient attendance—albeit mainly middle class—it would be considered a success. If attendance was poor, suspicions about such an approach would have been confirmed and would be filed away for future use when considering another proposal for a 'community' venture.

The relaxation class in the community development model would be presented as an idea from a local group to a worker with access to resources. The idea might have emerged spontaneously and independently, or in response to a community worker asking a group what it wanted to do next. It might also have been the *idea* that became the pivot for the formation of the group—for example a number of women in a Mothers and Toddlers club talking about feeling tense and deciding to set up a relaxation class. On approaching the local health education unit, the process of ratification would be similar to that above. The implementation of the classes would be quite different, however. The neighbourhood would be alerted via networks or workers and volunteers, and a suitable, accessible venue would be agreed upon such as a tenants' hall or a community centre. Decisions such as this would be made jointly. One crucial element of the venue is that it would have crèche facilities. Discussion about who would lead the classes would include the possibility of the participants taking it in turns to do so. Implicit in this process would be a rejection of anything didactic or patronising. The classes would be planned to be open-ended until the need for them dissolved. Arrangements for any subsequent funding would be discussed, and individuals would agree to explore the various options. Publicity would be extensive and would include door-knocking and leafleting on the estates near to the venue.

At this level then, it can be seen that whilst the two approaches are quite different, the community development approach is in fact sensible, and far more likely to succeed. It seems, on the face of it, curious that it raises as many medical objections as it does. Given that it is sensible, why are so many health education officers implementing it incorrectly? It is necessary to scrutinise the ways in which health education has traditionally been practised in order to understand why so few HEOs have the skills necessary for the proper implementation of community health education. As we have seen, much of health education practice is informed by medical imperatives and ideologies. I shall therefore move on to summarise the most salient features of what is now becoming a rather familiar chronicle of criticisms of conventional health education. This will elucidate the heritage that HEOs need to slough off before they can begin to attempt community development in health education.

The basis for this criticism lies in three years of work as an attempting to establish a community development project—a converted double-decker bus which we took to the more disadvantaged estates in Lambeth to offer and develop health knowledge with women with small children. As part of the work we encouraged users of our project to voice their experiences both of the health services generally and of health education in particular. We did this in order to try to meet the women's needs as best as we could. We pieced together this critique over the years, and it suffers from loss of vitality, condensed as it now is into a formal framework. The information was collected through a series of recorded talks, notes made by the women, and accumulated observations of health education practice generally.

## THE LIMITATIONS OF CONVENTIONAL HEALTH EDUCATION

The first, and perhaps most pervasive limitation of health education is that it *individualises* health. It holds the individual responsible for his or her health with an analysis that takes no account of those social factors beyond an individual's control. This in itself is unhelpful, as the root of the problem remains. Of equal importance is the side effect of blaming the individual for failing to resolve a structural problem that actually requires a coherent and collective response. This syndrome, commonly termed victim-blaming, can be seen to *cause* illhealth because it provokes guilt. The problem is compounded by the class distribution of health. In addition to the inversely high morbidity and mortality rates in the lower social classes (Townsend and Davidson, 1982) middle- and upper-class attitudes serve to hold, in particular, the working-class sick as responsible for their illhealth. Hence:

> Many professionals have always been inclined to blame the 'feckless' for their misfortunes. Whether it is inadequate child rearing practices, failure to attend family planning or ante-

natal clinics, spending the week's wages on alcohol, or giving the children too many sweets. Now as the daily lifestyle message is disseminated through the medical and popular press as well as in official publications, health professionals have every encouragement to intensify their inclination to 'victim-blaming' (Mitchell, 1982: 172).

The guilt that is produced by being held responsible for something beyond an individual's control can be emotionally debilitating. Pensioners, for example, who are told to clear bronchitis by turning up the heating, and who already cannot meet the bills, feel they are failing. Similarly, Asian women are held responsible for their children's rickets, and hence feel guilty. Interestingly, when large numbers of indigenous English children had rickets, the governmental response was a Vitamin D supplement to margarine, yet no such measures are being taken with chapati flour. (See Pearson, Chapter 3, for further discussion.) Any examination of standard health education materials will provide further examples of individualism. Glossy posters of glossy families do not help us to tackle our health problems.

The second limitation to conventional health education can be summarised as one of *elitism*. Health educators tend to operate from the assumption that people's health knowledge is extremely limited. This is to some extent a health educator's self-justification, but it is also a denial of different cultural approaches to health, and of lay intelligence. This attitude creates a relationship with dynamics of active expert and passive consumer. Like guilt, passivity is an unhelpful and uncreative condition.

Thirdly, conventional health education operates *separate* from the people it is attempting to serve. This can be seen to be an impositional form of practice, as little if any attempt is made to assess what people want to know or need to know. Instead, packages of information are drummed up, often quite irrelevant to people's experiences. Ironically the subsequent rejection of such inappropriate information by the 'targeted audience' serves to compound the professionals' suspicions that people are not interested in helping themselves.

The fourth limitation concerns *values*. The dominant values within our society are white, male, and middle class. Most health education materials rigorously reproduce these values, and therefore fail to speak to the majority of people for whom they are designed. Shining and happy middle-class homes, with attractive, white young parents, represent an unobtainable stereotype to those who have few, if any of these variables. The result is that these materials are perceived to be for someone else. Someone like the woman in the poster.

The *political* determinants of health constitute the fifth limitation. This has already been touched upon in the discussion about individualising health, but there is a further element. Health educators typically refuse participation in any activity that they perceive to be political, because health is health and politics is separate from that, and is for politicians. (See Farrant and Russell, Chapter 9.) What such an approach fails to recognise is the political power embodied within any activity concerned with the allocation of limited resources. There is no absolute truth concerning society's priorities that inform such decisions. They are made subject to any number of agendas, and by people who typically have little in common with the lower socio-economic groupings, or with socially oppressed minorities. Furthermore, the health educator's decision not to become involved in, for example, tackling the council about inadequate safe play provision because that would be political is, of itself, a political statement. Hence, the failure to challenge the status quo implicitly supports and reproduces the status quo—an undeniably political position.

Finally, and almost as a summary of the above points, health educators tend to regard health as an objective *thing*, that one does or does not have. Quantification of this thing is prolific. The balancing of the diet, the quest for the normal weight, blood pressure, skin texture, sexual practice, and so forth, dominate the majority of health educators' messages. Health however is not a thing. To quote Anne Murcott:

It could be thought that debate about defining health would lead progressively to an ultimate and universal designation.

155

Given sufficient discussion, refinement and reworking a true definition of health should at last be revealed. But it turns out not to be so. This is an unattainable goal, and attempts to achieve it will remain frustrated. For it becomes evident that 'health' is never confined to the realms of biology. Wherever definition is ventured, health is seen to be a state valued not in nature but in society (Murcott, 1979: 34).

It must be stressed that the intention here is to identify the deeply entrenched problems faced by HEOs, many of which arise from their lack of autonomy and professional status, rather than superficially to blame and lament. Nonetheless, the problems remain. The critique of conventional health education is difficult to ignore. The general picture is one of misapplication of already limited resources, and methods that fail to address the roots of today's health problems. Whilst it is known that a small number of HEOs across the country are attempting to depart from conventional health education, precisely how many, and how they became able to do so has yet to be established—although a programme of research is underway.[3] Community development in health education is by no means the only solution to some of these problems. It is certainly the solution to any community health education approach, and yet hopes of achieving this solution may now possibly be further out of reach. Ironically, it is the advent of health promotion that prompts this concern.

## HEALTH PROMOTION AND COMMUNITY HEALTH EDUCATION

The term 'ironically' is used because underpinning the concept of health promotion is a recognition of the role the community has to play—indeed must play—if *health* as a concept is to be pursued, rather than the avoidance of sickness. Hence:

Health promotion involves the population as a whole in the context of their everyday life rather than focussing on specific diseases. It enables people to *take control over* and responsibility

for, their health as an important component of everyday life –
both as spontaneous and *organised action* for health (WHO 1984:
3. Emphasis added).

And:

In order to make primary health care universally accessible in
the community as quickly as possible, maximum community
and individual self-reliance for health development are essential
... such participation is best mobilised through appropriate
education (Alma Ata, 1978, quoted in Jones, 1985: 23).

Indeed, the World Health Organisation sees health promotion as
historically linked to community development:

The growth of health promotion has been built on public
rather than medical-professional interest. It is linked to a
growing interest among the general public in positive health,
in personal growth, and in community development (WHO,
1982: 41).

Why does this most encouraging recognition of, and commitment
to, the community cause concern? At first glance, the prominence
of the role of the community in health promotion would seem
to be progressive, and to strengthen the chances of community
development becoming a method worthy of investment in terms
of resources and training. My reservations are threefold, and, as
stated earlier, are prospective rather than actual.

Firstly, in the way of most semi-professions or occupations
jostling for position, there is a tendency to seize new ideas, try
them on for size, and to then discard them in the quest for change
from without rather than from within. In these instances, the
body of knowledge remains unaltered, except to perpetuate a
wisdom that concept x does not hold the solution, and that it
should therefore be abandoned. Like other earlier developments,
health promotion is now regarded by many health education
officers as the solution to a declining discipline. In theory there is
no reason why this should not be the case, as it does necessitate

internal change as well as the more straightforward absorption of a new regime. Of course, however, if implemented hastily and incorrectly, it is destined to fail—even as a method, let alone as a salvation. In terms of community health education, the focus on the 'community' in health promotion is serving to accelerate the already substantial interest in the community, thus increasing the chances of hasty and inappropriate implementation.

Secondly, whilst I hold no fundamental quarrel with health promotion as a concept, the concern earlier expressed in relation to health educators failing to take on board the practical implications of acknowledging, and tackling, the social production of health and illness, has an equally substantial bearing on health promotion. Certain aspects of health promotion come worryingly close to the individualism, elitism, separatism, patronism, and political conservatism uncovered in conventional health education. So we can now witness various strategies of what might be called 'health by numbers' where the common goal is to identify as many victims of unhealthy 'lifestyles' as possible, and to encourage subsequent behaviour changes.

In the same way as the technique of painting by numbers breaks the total into numbered sections, removing the capacity for sensitive and creative expression, aspects of health promotion mirror that process of multiple individualism. The marketing devices and improved technologies employed by some health promotion programmes to create a sense of personalisation for large numbers of people, like the superficially glossy accomplishment of painting by numbers, actually results only in decontextualising. So people lose their identity, and lose their particular social characteristics that determine their health needs. Needless to say, these health needs are then unlikely to be met. Furthermore, such strategies mark a significant shift from equally recent attempts to conceptualise health holistically.

There is no reason why this sort of individualistic approach should attract any less criticism than its predecessor. However, the appeal of health promotion to conventional health educators, and to the bulk of the medical profession, can be seen to be twofold. If implemented without care, it departs little from the philosophy of conventional health education, and is hence comfortable in its familiarity. Similarly, if implemented without any attempt to identify causality in health and illness, it is non-threatening and can be regarded as apolitical. The higher level of health promotion, focusing on various legislative changes, can be tolerated as overtly political because of its distance from the everyday politics that HEOs more typically encounter and often attempt to avoid.

Thirdly, the Manpower Services Commission has recently begun to encourage the NHS, and in particular HEOs, to act as agencies for its expanded Community Programme (CP). At a recent conference,[4] discussion ranged over the value of CP health promotion projects for both health education as a discipline and for today's unemployed youth. It was noted that this is the biggest pot of extra-NHS monies for health education to date, and that it will be difficult to resist. Whilst presenters of two CP projects already in existence demonstrated a rigour in their application (South Sefton Dental Health Scheme, and Mersey Region Travelling Health Fair Scheme), and one receives, annually, over £1 million from the Community Programme, there is no evidence to suggest that other units will have the necessary skills to implement projects with sensitivity. The discipline is not yet sufficiently solid in getting to grips with the social production of health and illness to be able to usefully employ any number of young people for periods of only one year per person, each expected to do some health-related activity for the benefit of the community. The management problems alone are formidable. With an even greater sense of foreboding we face the prospect of inexperienced people performing tasks known to require substantial skills in order to be properly implemented. The potential dangers in all of this for health education generally, let alone for the method of community development in health education, strike me as considerable— another angle on health by numbers.

## TO CONCLUDE

In summary, health promotion, like community health education, can be regarded as a good thing. Both, however, must be implemented with extreme care and caution. The focus on the community as generated by health promotion now increases the vulnerability of community health education to incorrect application. In order to avoid the possibility of reproducing twice over the shortcomings of conventional health education, we may need to begin by scrutinising our own attitudes and behaviours. This will take us one step closer to the roots of the problem than is allowed by the more familiar search for behavioural change in people for whom it is either not possible, or where the change merely addresses the symptoms and not the causes.

It is easy for some to take a rather cynical or bored '1970s' air about community development, perhaps because their bread is buttered by newer fashions. The reality, however, is that the community development in health *external* to the NHS is gaining in vitality. Over ten thousand local health initiatives are known to exist in England and Wales,[5] a remarkable indication of both people's interest in health, and also, in many instances, of unmet need. This community health movement presents a most persuasive development because it constitutes a potential challenge to medical dominance. For this reason, community development, as one element of the community health movement, and as an effective method for adoption by health education, requires support from *within* the NHS. The NHS will then be better placed to address the fundamental problem of meeting people's health needs.

If this chapter has read negatively, negativity has not been the intention. Rather, it has been written from a conviction in the value of the community health education as an important and effective health education method, and from a concern that we find and learn from its full potential.

## NOTES

1   The focus throughout this chapter is on health education as practised by Health Education Officers—employees of the

National Health Service, and located within Health Education Units.

2　The evidence for this was collected whilst working as an HEO on a community development project, and visiting, nationally, groups of HEOs for workshops on community health education.

3　A. Watt, 'The Nature and Extent of Participation by Health Education Units in Community Health Education', in progress.

4　Health Education Council one-day Conference at the King's Fund Centre, 19 July 1985: 'Using Manpower Services Commission Resources for Health Promotion and Health Education'.

5　Community Health Initiatives Resource Unit, 26, Bedford Square, London, WC1.

## REFERENCES

Bainton, R., Clifford, P., Frosh, S. *et al.* (1985), *The Politics of Mental Health*, Macmillan, London.

Black, D. (1985), 'Community Development and Health Issues', *Radical Health Promotion*, 1, Spring 1985.

Blaxter, M. (1976), 'Social Class and Health Inequalities' in Carter, C. O. and Peel, J. (eds), *Equalities and Inequalities in Health*, Academic Press, London.

Brown, E. R. and Margo, G. E. (1978), 'Health Education: Can the Reformers be Reformed?', *International Journal of Health Services*, 8(1).

Cochrane, M. and Fisher, B. (1983), 'Peckham Health Project: Raising Health Consciousness', *Community Development Journal*, 18(2).

Cooper, M. H. (1975), *Rationing Health Care*, Croom Helm, London.

Cornwell, J. and Gordon, P. (eds) (1984), *An Experiment in Advocacy*, The Hackney Multi Ethnic Women's Health Project, King's Fund, London.

Crawford, R. (1977), 'You are Dangerous to Your Health: The Ideology and Politics of Victim Blaming', *International Journal of Health Services*, 7(4).

Culyer, A. J. (1976), *Need and the National Health Service*, Martin Robertson, London.

Doyal, L. and Pennell, I. (1979), *The Political Economy of Health*, Pluto, London.

Draper, P., Griffiths, J., Dennis, J. and Popay, J. (1980), 'Three Types of Health Education', *British Medical Journal*, 16 August 1980.

Drennan, V. (1985), *Working in a Different Way*, Paddington and North Kensington Health Education Unit, London.

Fisher, B. H. and Cochrane, M. (1982), 'Peckham Health Project, Raising Health Consciousness', *British Medical Journal*, 284: 1843–1845, 19 June.

Freudenberg, N. (1978), 'Shaping the Future of Health Education: From Behaviour Change to Social Change', *Health Education Monographs*, 6(4).

Friedson, E. (1972), *Profession of Medicine, A Study of the Sociology of Applied Knowledge*, Dodd Mead, New York.

Gough, I. (1979), *Political Economy of the Welfare State*, Macmillan, London.

Gray, M. and Blythe, M. (1979), 'The Failures of Health Education', in Atkinson, P., Dingwall, R. and Murcott, A. (eds), *Prospects for the National Health Service*, Croom Helm, London: 89-101.

Greetham, J. (1982), 'Community Development through a Community Health Project' in *Association of Community Workers: Talking Point*, No. 42. Gulbenkian Foundation (1968), *Community Work and Social Change*, Longman, London.

Gulbenkian Foundation (1968), *Community Work and Social Change*, the report of a study group on training, Longman, London.

Harris, P., Blackmore, M., Blackmore, E. *et al.* (1978), *Evaluation of Community Work*, London Council of Social Service.

Harrison, P. (1983), *Inside the Inner City: Life Under the Cutting Edge*, Penguin, Harmondsworth.

Haywood, S. C. (1985), 'An Essay in the Government of Health; Griffiths or Status Quo?' *Social Policy and Administration*, 19(1).

Henderson, P. and Thomas, D. (1980), *Skills in Neighbourhood Work*, Allen & Unwin, London.

Higgins, J., Deakin, N., Edwards, J. *et al.* (1983), *Government and Urban Poverty*, Basil Blackwell, Oxford.

Hubley, J. (1979), *A Community Development Approach to Health Education in a Multiply-Deprived Community in Scotland*, Paper presented at the Tenth International Conference on Health Education.

Jones, L. (1985), *An Overview of the Health Promotion Function*, Bradford and Airedale Health Education Unit.

Kerrison, S. (1985), 'Are Your Feet Killing You?' in *Age Well Ideas Pack*, Health Education Council.

Lorber, J. (1984), *Women Physicians, Careers, Status and Power*, Tavistock, London.

McNaught, A. (1985), 'Black and Ethnic Minority Women and the National Health Service', *Radical Community Medicine*, Spring 1985.

Meade, K. and Thorpe, P. (1985), 'Running a Pensioners' Health Course', in *Age Well Ideas Pack*, Health Education Council.

Mitchell, J. (1982), 'Looking After Ourselves: An Individual Responsibility?', *Royal Society of Health*, 4.

Mitchell, J. (1984), *What Is To Be Done About Illness and Health?* Penguin, Harmondsworth.

Murcott, A. (1979), 'Health as Ideology', in Atkinson, P., Dingwall, R. and Murcott, A. (eds), *Prospects for the National Health Service*, Croom Helm, London.

Roberts, H. (1985), *Patient Patients: Women and their Doctors*, Pandora, London.

Rosenthall, H. (1983), 'Neighbourhood Health Projects—Some New Approaches to Health and Community Work in Parts of the United Kingdom', *Community Development Journal*, 18(2).

Scott-Samuel, A. (1982), 'Community Development Outreach and Health Association Community Workers', *Talking Point*, 33, March.

Somerville, G. (1985), *Community Development in Health: Addressing the Confusions*, King's Fund, London.

Stockwell Health Project (1981), *Mawby Brough—A Health Centre for the Community?*

Townsend, P. and Davidson, N. (eds) (1982), *Inequalities in Health: The Black Report*, Penguin, Harmondsworth.

Tudor Hart, H. (1971), 'The Inverse Care Law', *Lancet*, 1: 405-12.

World Health Organisation (1978), *Primary Health Care*, Report of the International Conference on Primary Health Care, Alma Ata, 6–12 September 1978, Geneva.

World Health Organisation (1982), Summary Report: *Working Group on the Concepts and Principles of Health Promotion*, Copenhagen.

World Health Organisation (1984), *Health Promotion: A Discussion Document on the Concepts and Principles*, Copenhagen.

# CHAPTER 9

# COMMUNITY INITIATIVES IN HEALTH EDUCATION PUBLICATIONS: A ROLE FOR HEALTH EDUCATION OFFICERS?

Wendy Farrant and Jill Russell

We certainly need more information about health—but of a different kind. We need to understand how this society is dangerous to [our] health. And each of us needs to decide what we can realistically do under these difficult conditions to increase our confidence and to work for improvements in our health (Kenner, 1985).

## INTRODUCTION

The individual behaviour-oriented, prescriptive model of conventional health education, that is the subject of criticism in other papers in this collection, is clearly reflected in both the content of the conventional range of health education publications, and in the social relations of their production and use. Analyses of the content of such publications reveal an ideology that locates the causes of illhealth within the individual, that emphasises the supremacy of medical knowledge, and, at the same time, that reinforces the predominant, white, middle-class and male values of our society (see, for example, Kenner, 1985). In addition, research into the production and use of health education publications reveals a system that is generally dominated by pro-

165

fessional assumptions and decision-making, with a notable lack of consumer input (Farrant and Russell, 1985). The end result is a mismatch between health education publications and the health concerns, experiences and self-defined needs of the lay public.

In this chapter we use health education publications as a case study for an exploration of the possibilities for, and constraints upon, progressive innovation in health education policy and practice. Specifically, we are interested in the potential role of publications within a community development approach to health education (see Chapter 9) and in the current and potential role of local health education units in supporting community initiatives in the production of health education publications. Throughout the chapter we draw upon findings from a recent research study, which involved a postal questionnaire survey of all health education officers in post in 1982, and an in-depth interview survey of twenty heads of local health education units. The research was carried out as part of a wider study of the production, distribution and use of Health Education Council (HEC) publications (Farrant and Russell, 1985).

## THE SCOPE FOR INNOVATION

It was clear from our research interviews with the small minority of health education officers who are committed to a community development approach to health education, that community health projects at present have little, if any, use for the conventional range of health education publications that are stocked by health education units:

> There is a total mismatch between our politics, priorities and policies and HEC publications, in so far as the HEC is entrenched in *only* providing information concerned with individual responsibility and ignores the political environment—the socio-economic reasons for the major areas of disease causation. Useful publications would consist of a complete set of information, comprehensible to the group

concerned, which covers the full range of causes of disease/ill-health—including areas beyond body maintenance—which feature the social causation of ill-health. In addition, stress would be laid on the definitions/needs of community groups. The analysis would accept that 'health' and 'health education' are political concepts—which require political remedies, concerned with social change.

The major use for HEC publications that was identified by community development health workers was in the context of consciousness-raising discussions about the ideology of the health education message:

> We use very few HEC—if any, in fact—leaflets and posters except if we're doing sessions on, broadly, aspects of victim blaming, sexual stereotyping, the politics of health information.

> Posters which embody moralistic messages about individual responsibility and blame *can* be useful as trigger for discussion.... The main value of HEC posters and leaflets is that they offer an excellent sample of the world as seen by a government-funded and DHSS-engineered quango: ie stressing individualism, bad habits, inadequacy, and victim-blaming.

So, what would a health education publication that evolved out of, and usefully supported, a community development approach to health education look like? And how would it differ from the traditional range of health education materials stocked by health education units? As an illustration, we have reproduced in Figure 1 two posters on the same subject (drug prescribing). The first poster—'Take a pill Mrs Brown'—was produced by the See Red Women's Workshop—a collective of women designers who work with groups of women in the community to produce informative, consciousness-raising posters on issues that have been defined as important by women themselves. We choose this example because the See Red Women's Workshop health posters were frequently mentioned to us as useful by community devel-

*Figure 1* Comparison of health education posters on drug prescribing, produced by the See Red Women's Workshop and by the Health Education Council.

opment health workers who were interviewed in our research study. The other poster was produced by the HEC. The HEC poster has now been discontinued, but it nevertheless provides a useful example in terms of highlighting the essential features of the conventional model of health education and the differences between this model and a more community-oriented approach.

The HEC poster was produced centrally by the publications section of the Council. Consultation about the content of HEC material is, on the whole, restricted to the medical profession and specifically to doctors within the medical section of the HEC and high-status representatives of professional bodies outside the Council. Increasingly, discussion also takes place with the DHSS, who informally, if not formally, 'approve' the content for publication. There is often little or no consultation or feedback from professionals in 'the field' and even less from the groups at whom the messages are being directed—the lay public. This consultation process effectively results in HEC publications reflecting and disseminating an official and establishment ideology of health and medical thinking, and failing to take seriously lay knowledge (Farrant and Russell, 1985, 1986).

The HEC poster on drug prescribing was produced in support of a joint campaign by the HEC, the DHSS and the British Medical Association. The aims of the campaign were described in the HEC (1979: 14) *Annual Report* as follows:

> The primary objective of [DHSS and BMA] was to cut the costs of medicines prescribed by general practitioners and to reduce pressures on doctors to over-prescribe. The Council's [HEC's] complementary objective was to promote acceptance by patients that not all consultations with their general practitioners should end with a prescription; and hence to embark on the formidable process of weaning the public off their dependence on others for the discharge of a responsibility which, at least in principle, the great majority can and should carry for themselves.

The HEC poster clearly illustrates the 'victim-blaming' ideology of conventional health education messages. It is the patient who has to change his/her expectations and be prepared to leave the doctor without a prescription—despite the availability of research evidence to show that, far from patients demanding prescriptions, there is a high level of patient dissatisfaction with the over-readiness of doctors to prescribe pills (see, for example, Dunnell and Cartwright, 1972). In addition, the poster serves to reinforce the professional expertise and judgment of the doctor and the status quo of the doctor–patient relationship—'you can be sure that if you really need one [a pill], you'll get one.'

The alternative poster was produced by and for women. At the See Red Women's Workshop, initial ideas for posters evolve directly out of women's daily experiences and are then developed through discussions with health and/or women's groups working on the particular subject. In this way, the production process itself is consciousness-raising—the presentation of an issue for a poster or pamphlet requires that feelings and needs be translated into a broader, community-defined, political issue.

In contrast to the victim-blaming ideology of the HEC poster, the alternative poster produced by and for women locates the prescribing and taking of medicines within their social and economic context. The focus of attention is shifted from the patient on to both the doctor and the drug manufacturers. At the same time, the alternative poster challenges the passive role of the patient ('ask your doctor exactly what you are being prescribed'), confronts the social control function that the medical profession exercise ('don't let them keep us bottled up'), and implies the need for collective and not individualistic solutions to tackle the issue of drug-prescribing and taking.

A central question for our research was what are the possibilities for, and constraints upon, the type of approach that is reflected in the alternative poster discussed above being incorporated into state-funded health education?

# LOCAL PRODUCTION OF HEALTH EDUCATION PUBLICATIONS—AN ALTERNATIVE APPROACH?

In our research interviews with heads of health education units, we explored their views in relation to the production of local health education publications, the publications which the health education unit had been involved in producing, and the process of local production of publications.

All of the heads of the health education units in the interview sample saw a role for locally produced health education publications and most (17 out of 20) were directly or indirectly involved in local production. However, involvement in local production of publications did not necessarily imply an alternative, more community-oriented approach. The reason most frequently given by heads of health education units for becoming involved in local production was to satisfy a demand for materials from local professionals that could not be met by existing national publications:

> We mainly produce something where there's a demand and a gap [in national publications] that needs filling.... It's something I didn't originally want us to spend time on, but we were pressurised into it.

> I've spent a small fortune on them (publications produced by the health education unit) filling in gaps ... but it has brought us goodwill with other health professionals.

We asked the heads of the 17 survey health education units that were involved in local production about the process of initiation and production of publications. The most common response to the question 'Who does the original idea for a leaflet or poster usually come from?' was health professionals. Only 4 respondents mentioned the lay community as a source of ideas for publications. Furthermore, once the health education unit had decided to produce a publication, the process of production at local level tended to be a microcosm of the top-down, professionally dominated

172

process of production of HEC publications. Copywriting of publications produced by health education units was most usually the responsibility of a health education officer, working in collaboration with local medical and other professional experts and sometimes writing from a medical brief. Publications were generally designed in-house by the health education unit technical and graphics staff, or sometimes commissioned to outside designers, with designers usually working under the general supervision of a health education officer. The role of health education unit staff, in writing and designing publications, was described by respondents mainly in terms of ensuring that the publication was appropriate and accessible to the 'target audience', but the views of the target audience were rarely canvassed:

> It's difficult because of the difference between what they [other health professionals] *think* the public will understand and what *we* think people will understand. Consultants produce [drafts of publications] at the level of scientific journals. We want to bring it down to the level of the Daily Mail.

There was generally little, if any, attempt to involve consumers directly in the production process. In response to the question 'Who is likely to be consulted about the contents and design of a leaflet/poster?' all those interviewed mentioned medical and/or other professional experts, but only 3 made any reference to representatives of the target audience. Some respondents cited isolated examples of a publication being pre-tested on the target audience, but this was not usual practice. It was also unusual for any evaluation of the publication to be carried out after it had been produced. As one respondent put it: 'The demand for [the publication] is our evaluation. If there are no takers for it then we let it die.' The comment just quoted begs the question of whether demand for publications by professional health educators bears any relation to consumer-defined need.

The professional domination of the processes of initiation and production of local publications tended to be reflected in the content of publications. From the health education units that we visited for the interview survey, we collected a total of 118 leaflets and posters that those units had been involved in producing. A content analysis of these leaflets and posters revealed that, in terms of subject matter, ideology, and style of communication, the locally produced publications did not, in the main, differ in any fundamental way from publications produced by the HEC. The subject matter of over 80 per cent of the leaflets and posters fell within the broad medically defined topic areas of the HEC publications catalogue, the most popular topics being, in order of frequency, nutrition, pregnancy and childbirth, baby care, fitness and health, smoking, dental health and drug abuse. The orientation of the locally produced publications was predominantly individualistic, with a notable absence of any reference to the social causes of illhealth. Also the imagery of the majority of the locally produced publications was often retrograde in comparison with more recent publications by the HEC, in terms of the dominance of white, male, middle-class values. For example, of the 57 leaflets which included illustrations of people, only 6 showed a non-white person; babies and doctors were almost always referred to as 'he' and the images of some of the publications were blatantly sexist.

There were, however, some notable exceptions to the general pattern of local production of publications described above. In the course of our interview survey and our other contacts with health education officers, we encountered some encouraging examples of local publications being produced on the basis of developmental research with the target audience. Some health education officers have been involved in the production of local publications that have been innovative in challenging dominant social values and power structures and in addressing health issues that are defined as important by people themselves. For example, some health education units had collaborated in the production of local publications on housing, dampness and health, on sickle cell disease and on abortion and other aspects of women's health. Perhaps even more encouraging, some health education units are beginning to challenge traditional social relations of publications' production, by extending their resources and facilities to support local community initiatives in the production of health education publications.

## ATTITUDE OF HEALTH EDUCATION OFFICERS TOWARDS SUPPORT OF COMMUNITY INITIATIVES

We asked heads of health education units what they saw as the advantages and disadvantages of local community groups producing their own health education leaflets and posters, and whether the health education unit had a policy and/or experience of supporting community initiatives in the production of health education publications.

Two-thirds of respondents saw some potential advantages to community groups producing their own publications, the main perceived advantage being the relevance of the materials so produced to the health concerns and lives of the local population:

They're in a better position than us to find out what the real needs are.

The more you get down to grass roots the more responsive it is to local needs.

They're directed to our people and relate very much to the way in which they see things.

They know what information they want, they're aware of the life style and vocabulary.

Some respondents also stressed the educational value of the experience of being involved in the process of producing publications, and others referred to the cost effectiveness of using the health education unit resources in this way:

It's involving local people in decision-making. The learning process is very important. They learn as much from producing material as from what is produced.

... giving money to voluntary groups is effective because

175

you're making or enabling use of free labour as it were. If you give £50 to a group, it makes an enormous amount of difference to what can get done, but it makes precious little difference in our unit.

The majority of respondents said either that their health education unit had had experience of supporting community initiatives in the production of health education publications or that their unit would be open to providing such support. However, these respondents differed in terms of the extent to which they saw the health education unit's role as *supporting*, as distinct from *controlling*, community initiatives.

Some health education units were prepared to extend their support without strings, mainly in the form of loan of printing and photocopying facilities, help with design, or sometimes through financial assistance or (to quote one respondent) by acting as 'a progressive/supportive facilitator'. Whilst these health education units might make their professional expertise available to the community group, they accepted that their advice might not be wanted:

> We never say 'no'. We may try to get them to amend it to be a positive health education thing, but if they don't take our advice we still don't say 'no'.

> They don't like us interfering. We try to advise them but they usually don't want to know because it cramps their style.

Other health education units interpreted 'support' in terms of the health education unit intervening more actively in or, in some cases, taking over the production process. Some health education units made their extension of support conditional upon the community group's health message fitting in with professionally defined concepts of health education, or upon the groups being seen to be amenable to professional guidance:

> I'm all for helping them if they say what they want and let us get on with it.

It depends on whether or not it's health education ... [one group] wanted us to produce a leaflet that was purely political, about NHS resources: it didn't promote health.

It was clear that for some respondents, the very concept of community groups producing their own materials was seen as a threat to the professional control and autonomy of the health education unit:

Most of the [community groups] don't know much about it [producing publications] and they don't always consult [with professionals]—they don't see a *need* to consult.... It's like saying 'what are the advantages of me lecturing on chiropody?' People should know their limitations.

It's difficult to control the content [of publications produced by community groups]. They're resentful of professional involvement. [One group] wanted to *use* my support and no way. We have a lot of autonomy in health education and it's very easy to abuse it.

More fundamentally, support of community initiatives was perceived by some respondents as posing a potential threat to the health education unit's relationship with the health authority, which was seen as being dependent upon the health education unit maintaining a position of political neutrality:

You've got to be careful. They [community groups] can be radical.

A lot of community groups are political.... We have to be cautious.... My bosses expect me to have a middle-of-the-road philosophy.... Once you start showing your colours politically in this job it can go wrong for you.

In order to explore further health education officers' feelings about the political implications of supporting community health initiatives, we asked respondents what their response would be (assuming there was no problem of resources) in the hypothetical case of a request for support from:

(a)   'a group that was producing a leaflet that implied conflict with the local health authority—for example a leaflet opposing a local hospital closure, or criticising local antenatal services', and

(b)   'a group that was producing a leaflet about the political and economic determinants of ill health—for example a leaflet on the way in which the tobacco industry encourages smoking, or a leaflet explaining what government, as opposed to individuals, could do to improve the nation's health—for example, reducing the risks of coronary heart disease through controls over the food industry, etc.'

The most common response to part (a) of the above question was an unqualified 'no':

I wouldn't touch it.

That's politics, not health education. I'm employed by the health authority. I wouldn't see it as my role.

If it was something that I personally agreed with I'd bend over backwards to try and find some way of helping them find the right people who could do it. But I would not, as a manager of the service, do it within this office and have the service implicated.

You have to have some loyalty to your employer. I don't want to be used as a political animal. I know there is a move [in health education] towards thinking we should be used to promote change, but I won't act in a subversive way . . . I know there are shortcomings in the services, but I don't join a group arguing for change like that.

The only respondent who replied with an unqualified 'yes' to part (a) of the question was the head of a health education unit that had already been involved in a confrontation with the health authority about local services. The remaining respondents were less certain about what their reaction to the request for support would be:

I don't know where you should draw the line. Ante-natal clinics are something we're concerned about, so I would want to give some help, yet I'm funded by the NHS. Drawing the line's a problem in health education.

Responses to part (b) of the above question were more mixed with approximately equal numbers of respondents saying (with varying degrees of qualification) that they would or would not agree to a request to support the production of a leaflet on the political and economic causes of illhealth and the role of government in improving health. The variety of responses to this question are a clear illustration of the issue of 'drawing the line' in health education, referred to by the respondent quoted above:

I'd keep out of it. I won't be used.

It's not a health education message ... we can only give the health education aspect.

I can see the worth of that information. You're talking about national food policy [but] I'm not sure it's our responsibility. You're in danger of putting over personal opinions—political opinions.

That's fine. That's politics with a *small* 'p'.

We should be able to help, because many health issues are not under individual control and it's important to increase awareness, but we're not supposed to be a political body so it could cause problems. We should be pressurising the government ourselves in those respects, and if there's not time to do it we could help others to.

I wouldn't see that as political necessarily. It's so definitely a national health education topic that I would quite definitely see that we could produce that without disturbing the political applecart.

You could validate an involvement in issues like that. You have to be political animals a little, even within the NHS.

Most health education officers were conscious of the potential conflicts of an NHS-funded health education unit using its resources to support community initiatives in the production of health education materials. They differed, however, in the extent to which they saw such conflicts as an avoidable or inevitable feature of the role of a health education officer.

Some attempted to make a clear separation between their work and politics, and were critical of health education officers who were beginning to adopt a more overtly political stance:

> I won't be involved politically. I keep out of the political side. I don't allow it to come into the Department—you're really in trouble if you do.

> Personally, I think some health education units are getting far too politically involved.

For others, politics was seen as integral to the concept of a health education service committed to improving health and health care institutions and to reducing social inequalities in health. For these health education officers, the question was not one of whether to get involved with community health initiatives, but rather of how to tread what they all acknowledged to be the political tightrope of being an NHS service employee involved in supporting the production of publications which might be critical of local health services or challenge official definitions of health issues and health priorities. The strategies employed by these health education officers included: using medical and social research evidence and local statistics to argue the case in terms which are acceptable to the health authority; pointing to the statutory requirements of health education units to support all agencies carrying out health education, including voluntary agencies; eliciting the support of sympathetic and respected health professionals; and, ultimately, accepting that it is sometimes less problematic for the health authority if the health education unit's support of community health initiatives is covert.

## CONCLUSION

In this chapter we have looked at the potential role of publications within a more community oriented approach to health education. We have illustrated how, in terms of the process of production, the content and the ideological function of the information, such publications would, and indeed do, look very different from the conventional range of state-funded health education publications stocked by local health education units. Health education officers are, in theory, in a position to bring together state resources and local groups of people expressing needs for health information and so enable the production of more community oriented publications. In practice, however, it would seem that the potential of health education officers for supporting such progressive innovation is often constrained by concerns over 'professionalism' and assumptions about the need for 'political neutrality' in health education. The fallacy in this argument of political neutrality, of course, is the assumption that conventional health education is *not* political:

> The indisputable though subtle effect of concentrating educational efforts on individual prevention or prevention by early detection, and the relative neglect of the potential of education for social intervention, conveys the message that illness and disease are preventable or curable only by individual methods. By conveying a message of this sort, health educators divert attention from the opportunity for social prevention and from the relationship between forms of social organisation and the prevalence of illness (Tuckett, 1979).

A small but growing number of health education officers is now challenging traditional health education practice and showing us that 'professionalism' does not automatically imply control, and that health information cannot be divided into the 'political' and the 'politically neutral'. We have illustrated some of the contradictions and dilemmas that inevitably confront a health education unit that chooses to use its resources to support community initiatives in the production of progressive and challenging health education publications. But we hope also to have underlined the significance and importance of such innovation in helping to redress the distribution of information (and thereby, ultimately, power and control) between professionals and lay groups in society.

## ACKNOWLEDGMENTS

The research on which this chapter is based was funded by the Health Education Council, and conducted at the University of London Institute of Education under the directorship of Alan Beattie. The views expressed here are those of the authors. We are indebted to the health education officers who kindly agreed to be interviewed for the study.

## REFERENCES

Dunnell, K. and Cartwright, A. (1972), *Medicine Takers, Prescribers and Hoarders*, Routledge & Kegan Paul, London.

Farrant, W and Russell, J. (1985), *Health Education Council Publications: A Case Study in the Production, Distribution and Use of Health Information*, Health Education Publications Project, University of London Institute of Education, London.

Farrant, W. and Russell, J. (1986), *Beating Heart Disease: A Case Study in the Production of Health Education Council Publications*, Bedford Way Paper, University of London Institute of Education, London.

Health Education Council (1979), *Annual Report*, 1978/9, HEC, London.

Kenner, C. (1985), *No Time for Women*, Pandora Press, London.

Tuckett, D. (1979), 'Choices for Health Education: a Sociological View', in Sutherland, I. (ed.), *Health Education: Perspectives and Choices*, Allen & Unwin, London.

# CHAPTER 10

# HEALTH EDUCATION AND GENERAL PRACTITIONERS: A CRITICAL APPRAISAL

## Michael Calnan, Mary Boulton and Anthony Williams

### INTRODUCTION

It has recently become popular to emphasise the importance of general practitioners as health educators, both in the prevention of disease and in the promotion of healthy living (RCGP, 1981). This concern, with much of the impetus coming from within the profession itself, is less of a new departure than a revitalisation of an interest that can be traced to the beginnings of the National Health Service. As early as 1950, a British Medical Association report portrayed GPs as specialising in continuous and preventative care, and in health education (BMA, 1950). A subsequent report of the General Practice Steering Committee argued that these specialisms should be seen as 'unique' and 'positive' features of a future general practice (BMJ, 1952). Interest in this area gained further momentum in the 1960s with the translation of the notion of continuity of care into a practical concern for early diagnosis (McWhinney, 1964) and with the re-definition of roles and boundaries within general practice that accompanied this (Jeffreys and Sachs, 1983; Armstrong, 1985). Thus, by the 1970s a number of authors were pointing to the attributes of general practice which made it the 'natural setting' for health education (Calnan and Johnson, 1983) and were calling for an increased role in health education for general practitioners (Stott and Davis, 1979).

In this chapter, we examine in more detail the assumptions

that general practitioners should be more extensively involved in health education and that they can be effective in this role. The first part of our analysis considers the current rhetoric of prevention in general practice, in particular that embodied in the various reports and documents published by the Royal College of General Practitioners. The second part, drawing upon the authors' own empirical research, looks at current *attitudes* to health education among GPs and patients and then investigates its actual *practice* in the context of medical consultations.

## THE ROLE OF GPs IN HEALTH EDUCATION: CURRENT VIEWS OF THE RCGP

Current interest in the role of GPs in health education derives largely from a series of Reports produced by the Royal College of General Practitioners between 1981 and 1983. In response to the publications on prevention from the Department of Health and Social Security in the mid-1970s, the RCGP set up its own Working Party to consider the issue in the context of general practice. Five Reports were eventually produced which looked at the role of GPs in prevention in general (RCGP, 1981a) and in four specific substantive areas (RCGP 1981b, c, d and 1982). Whilst not constituting 'policy' documents in the strictest sense, these Reports were an attempt by the College to provide a clear statement of what it felt the field of interest should be in general practice.

In setting out the types of 'worthwhile preventive activities' for GPs, the authors of the main Report (RCGP, 1981a) delineated three main arenas in which they could be active. The first involves patients who present themselves in the consultation. That is, with each patient who consults, the GP can extend the traditional content of the consultation to provide a preventive component. In addition to the prevention of complications of the presenting problem, the types of activities recommended include opportunistic screening for presymptomatic diagnosis of other problems and health education about lifestyle issues, particularly smoking.

The second arena is the practice population as a whole. Because each GP is responsible for a defined population of registered patients who may be divided into 'risk' groups according to age/sex characteristics (for example, girls of 10, men over 35) or medical criteria (for example, hypertensives, diabetics), he or she is in a position to monitor the health of such groups and to provide appropriate preventive interventions. This approach is seen as a radical innovation for general practice because it involves GPs in thinking in terms of *groups* at risk, taking the initiative in contacting them and co-operating more closely with other members of the primary health care team in providing the service. Once again, however, the focus is on personal preventive advice given to individual patients in the context of the one-to-one consultation.

The third arena, which is only briefly and tentatively described, is the local community. The GP's responsibilities here involve working with professionals in other institutions in the community. A GP may, for example, co-operate with school teachers in teaching about 'relationships', 'sexual love and childbirth', 'healthy living', 'preventing disease' and 'using the health services'. Aside from this example, however, little is said in the introductory Report about the role of GPs in the community and it is seldom referred to in the subsequent Reports.

Criticisms of this initiative from the RCGP have been made on a number of levels. Some have interpreted it as another example of the creeping medicalisation which is inherent in western industrial society. It is argued that the medical profession—or one segment of it—is furthering its empire by attempting to claim jurisdiction over people's lifestyles, or those aspects of lifestyle which are claimed to influence disease. Others have suggested that the Royal College of General Practitioners' crusade in the area of prevention is a further attempt to maintain or enhance their professional identity independent of hospital medicine. For example, as Honigsbaum (1985: 826) states:

They [the RCGP] fear most any move that will carry general practitioners closer to hospital medicine, so much so that it might be fair to describe their proposals as the 'keep general practitioners busy in the community' school. For them, almost any activity will do as long as it leaves general practitioners free from entanglement with consultants.

Honigsbaum also doubts the potential success of the present RCGP drive, since it focuses on education and exhortation to involve GPs, without any attempt to change the system of remuneration to reward their involvement in preventive activities.

Others have criticised the RCGP's initiative because of the inherent individualism in its approach to disease prevention and health promotion (Davies, 1984). While the main Report presents GPs as becoming involved in progressively wider arenas of activity, the view of their roles in each arena is in fact narrow and limited. The emphasis is almost exclusively on GPs dealing with individual patients in the one-to-one consultation. The kinds of issues which are discussed are therefore those which are best suited to personal advice in this setting: aspects of lifestyle and personal health choices. Broader issues of 'social conditions and standards of living' (RCGP, 1981a: 9) are recognised as having a fundamental influence on health and illness but seem to be largely ignored as inappropriate or unrealistic topics in the context of general practice. Instead, in the aetiology of preventable disease the focus is on individual patients and their families whose *behaviour* is seen as the main factor that the GP can influence. The role of GPs, therefore, is restricted to that of educating patients and their families about personal health habits, and motivating them to change these when appropriate.

Implicit in this individualistic approach, which is inherent in health policy more generally in the UK, are two assumptions about the production of health and how it might be controlled (Graham, 1979). Firstly, the medical model of disease causation and disease management dominates as the emphasis is placed on individual causes which in this case are individual or family lifestyles. Secondly, the individuals are assumed to be able to control their own lifestyle and to be able significantly to improve their health in this way. Doubt has been cast on the validity of these two assumptions, which together constitute a form of 'victim-blaming' since the effect is to shift the responsibility for disease causation, cure and care away from broader socio-economic factors on to the individual who suffers illhealth (Labonte and Penfold, 1981).

More specifically, not only does evidence suggest that socio-economic factors influence patterns of lifestyle but it also suggests that there are other socio-economic influences on health outcomes which might be independent of lifestyles (Doyal, 1979; Townsend and Davidson, 1982). For example, social class differences in health status might be explained, at least in part, by the less favourable living and working conditions of manual workers which expose them to greater physical hazards. Moreover, the stress generated by financial problems, housing problems and problems associated with employment may contribute directly to higher rates of illness.

Additionally, recent empirical research (Graham, 1984) has shown that there are strong barriers to the adoption of preferred health choices, particularly in conditions of socio-economic disadvantage. Many people are simply not in a position to alter their lifestyles or health decisions in response to GPs' advice and encouragement. Moreover, the relevance of 'good health' as defined in conventional health education terms might be of limited significance in some social circumstances where, for example, cigarette or alcohol consumption is based on rational rather than idiosyncratic premises. For women in particular, smoking and/or heavy drinking may be a rational way of coping with the pressures of living in conditions of social and economic adversity (Jacobsen, 1981).

On yet another level, further criticisms have been made of the RCGP initiative for ignoring trends and patterns within general practice which may themselves undermine even the limited value of its individualistic approach. The first concerns the present organisation of general practice. If health education with the individual patient is to be effective, then relationships between doctors and patients need to be personal ones and their continuity needs to be maintained. At first sight these elements appear to be particularly strong in general practice. However, the development of group practices and the greater use of deputising services has led to an increasing impersonality and distance between general practitioner and patient. GPs are no longer the 'personal doctors' which it is often claimed they once were and patients may be less inclined to 'comply' readily with their advice. This loss of personal involvement on the part of GPs may be less of a problem if other members of the primary health care team were to become involved in personalised care but there is little evidence that this is happening.

A second set of criticisms concerns the variations in patterns of demand for general practice services and the variations in the quality of care given to certain groups. For example, for a complex set of reasons, women use general practitioners more than men, but the relative health 'risks' suggest that there needs to be a refocus on men (Townsend and Davidson, 1982). Similarly, there are cultural and sometimes racist barriers to help-seeking amongst ethnic minorities living in this country, as Maggie Pearson demonstrates in Chapter 3. To overcome this, health education needs to be both sensitive to different cultural beliefs and alert to institutionalised racism in the delivery of health care. The range of ethnic backgrounds among general practitioners is as yet very narrow and their knowledge of, and sensitivity to, cultural variations is not well developed. Finally, there is evidence of a higher consumption of hazardous substances in social classes IV and V compared with other social classes; yet there is also evidence that working-class groups receive less medical information in general practice consultations than their middle-class counterparts (Pendleton and Bochner, 1980). Clearly, it is important to make health education more accessible and relevant to the widely differing, and often neglected, needs of *all* groups within a multifarious society.

## ALTERNATIVE ROLES FOR THE GP

In their preoccupation with the role of GPs in the consultation, the authors of the College Reports give little attention to alternative ways in which they could be involved with their patients. Only in the Report on the prevention of psychiatric disorders is mention made of a wider role for GPs. Here the subcommittee suggest that GPs are in a unique position to understand community needs and therefore 'well placed to encourage community development' (p. 13), for example, through patient participation groups. The criticisms of the individualistic approach reviewed above point to the importance of considering more carefully such alternative, collectivist approaches which can better take account of the broader issues involved in health and illness.

There are at least two strategies for health education within the notion of 'collectivism' which could have implications for the role of the general practitioner (Beattie, 1983). Both approaches identify a role for health education in encouraging social change although they differ in the degree to which the approach is directive. The more directive of the two strategies would involve general practitioners and the primary health care team in a public agenda-setting exercise. The aim would be for health professionals to increase the awareness of their patients and others in the local community about the forces within the social, economic and legal environment which limit the choices that individuals have in matters of health. General practitioners, therefore, might be involved in attempting to educate the public about the need to press for change through legislation or through other public policies. Such change, it is argued, would contribute towards the creation of a healthier environment *per se*, which would in turn enable people to adopt a 'healthy' lifestyle if they so chose. The drawbacks of this approach, however, are those inherent in all 'top-down' strategies of community action. That is, the models of illness causation and of appropriate intervention which dominate are likely to be those of the health professionals rather than those of the community which they are meant to serve. The pressures which are brought to bear are therefore likely to reflect the interests of health professionals and to perpetuate the effective disenfranchisement of the lay members of the community.

The second collectivist approach is less directive in that emphasis is placed on ideas and issues generated by local groups and local people rather than on needs expressed by professionals. The role of the primary health care team in collaboration with other health professionals, such as Health Education Officers, would be to provide resources (skills, facilities, support, etc.) to local people to enable them to develop their own structures for effective action in meeting health needs. This approach, however, is also not without weaknesses. The recent proliferation of 'self-help groups', as one of the three categories within the community health movement (Watt, 1984), may appear as a positive response to local needs but these are seldom concerned with social change and many accept prevailing individualistic notions and medical models of health. Furthermore, there is a tendency towards over-reliance on '*volunteering*', that is, the use of unpaid voluntary helpers, to tackle problems that should be the responsibility of the statutory services (Beattie, 1983; Watt, 1985).

While there are certain drawbacks in both these 'collectivist' approaches, they offer GPs additional—or alternative—roles and clearly warrant further attention. Before commenting further on the relative value of the various approaches, however, it is useful to look at the views and practices of the participants in general practice and to consider what doctors and patients feel are acceptable and useful approaches.

## PARTICIPANTS' PERSPECTIVES: THE VIEWS OF GPs AND PATIENTS

It is characteristic of formal debates, such as those in the RCGP documents, that they rarely address the perspectives of the actors involved. Since they specify a broad and at times controversial role for general practitioners, an assessment of where individual doctors stand in relation to these issues is of some relevance. Of equal importance are the views of patients concerning the acceptability of GPs as a source of advice about health matters.

## (a) The doctors' perspective

Previous surveys (e.g. Jamrozik and Fowler, 1982) have shown that GPs are 'interested' in health education, but tell us little about how they conceptualise health education and how they view their role in relation to others or the difficulties and constraints they perceive in putting it into practice. These issues were explored in a recent study of attitudes to health education among 34 advisers and course organisers in two regions in south-east England (Williams and Boulton, 1985; Boulton and Williams, 1985). This group of doctors is responsible for postgraduate and continuing education in general practice in the two regions, including the planning and running of specialist courses and the organisation of vocational training schemes. They therefore occupy a position of influence in relation to present and future trends in general practice and for this reason were considered more likely to have thought about the issues involved in health education and prevention. For the same reason, however, they cannot be considered 'typical' of the GPs in the two regions.

The doctors were asked to comment on how they saw themselves and others functioning in the three arenas of activity identified in the RCGP documents. All saw prevention and health education as an important activity for the practice. However, those that had personal reservations about its acceptability and practicality were more inclined to see it as the role of others within or attached to the practice (for example, health visitors and practice nurses). Those with fewer reservations viewed their involvement in shared and complementary terms, with the doctors providing health education in consultations and acting as co-ordinators of a wider practice involvement. However, very few had any clear idea of the kind of role they could play in the community and knowledge of the roles and practices of other agencies and groups was very limited. Prevention and health education were, in essence, seen as a new domain of 'medical' expertise and were

191

therefore largely viewed as practice-based activities.

The way the doctors defined health education showed considerable variation and their responses characterised four different approaches to health education. The first group, about a quarter of the sample, viewed health education as a new technical service to build into practice routines, for example, organising an effective screening programme and records checklist. They emphasised their role in promoting behaviour changes in individual patients, especially in relation to lifestyle and the use of the GP service. Unlike several of their peers, this group of doctors had few qualms about the acceptability of this kind of activity to patients and saw the constraints largely in terms of structural and situational factors, such as practice management and the availability of appropriately motivated and trained staff.

These doctors stood in marked contrast to a second group (again about a quarter of the sample) who perceived health education in terms of the need to be 'responsive' to the patient's presenting problems. The emphasis in their approach was on 'explanation' which promotes understanding and helps the patient to cope and to make sensible choices. They showed considerable reservations about the more opportunistic forms of health education and prevention, in which the doctor's agenda assumes precedence over that of the patient. Accordingly, they were more likely to see health education on lifestyle issues as intrusive and moralising, as too narrowly physical and as beset by contradictions and uncertainties stemming from the epidemiological evidence on which it is based. Interestingly, it is this group who most often pointed to the important role of social (as opposed to individual) factors in the aetiology of disease and the constraints these impose on behaviour.

A third group of doctors (about a fifth of the sample) argued for an 'integrationist' approach. This would combine most aspects of a 'technical service' approach—which addresses longer-term behavioural outcomes—with one which meets the immediate needs of the patients in terms of explanation and understanding. Their rationale for this rested in particular on a notion of 'effective teamwork' and the application of new approaches to communication (Pendleton *et al.*, 1984; Tuckett *et al.*, 1985). It is members of this group who had been most influenced by the RCGP initiatives and who had most actively sought to develop policies for their own practices. Not surprisingly, they viewed the constraints on practising health education as emanating largely from doctors: in particular, from their erroneous perception of patients' expectations of doctors and of their lay views as barriers to understanding.

The final group (about a third of the sample) saw prevention and their role as health educators in more restricted terms. Health education was a part of their daily work but they defined it mainly in terms of problem-related interventions on smoking, weight and occasionally alcohol. Some participated in limited screening exercises, but few were willing to become involved in a more general promotion of health where this was apparently unrelated to the patient's presenting problem. In several instances this reflected a lack of knowledge of any of the recent RCGP initiatives on prevention. The purpose of explanation was seen largely in terms of achieving compliance. For these doctors, the disruptive effect of health education on the doctor–patient relationship and the 'resistance' of patients in terms of their lack of interest in and ability to understand medical issues, were seen as largely immutable barriers to effective health education by the GP.

## (b)  The patients' perspective

The idea that patients do not want or are upset by health education in the consultation was certainly not reflected in the results of a study done by Calnan (1985) into women's perspectives on health education and health promotion. This exploratory study involved interviews with 30 women from social classes I and II and 30 women from social classes IV and V. Respondents were asked, in a series of questions about taking responsibility for health promotion, whether they would like their family doctor to be involved. Two factors emerged strongly from this study.

Firstly, the majority of the 60 women (78 per cent) thought that their general practitioners *should* play a part in health promotion and the most frequently mentioned activity was giving advice; the second most frequently mentioned activity was carrying out health checks. Of those women who did see a role for general practitioners in health promotion, just over a third (36 per cent) said that their doctor should, but did not, carry it out. The reasons given by patients for this lack of involvement were the doctor's attitude, lack of the doctor's time or the fact that they only consult when they are sick. Another 8 per cent said that another person in the primary health care team should carry out this role.

Secondly, the vast majority of respondents (90 per cent) felt that, along with their general practitioner, the government *also* had a role to play in health promotion. The most popular measures were provision of cheaper recreation facilities, improving the range of services available and the quality of services in the NHS, providing health education and providing wider publicity about the range of facilities available.

## (c)    The practice of health education in the consultation

While the descriptions of their attitudes and approaches convey the way doctors and patients view health education, more direct observation of consultations is needed to provide a picture of what health education actually takes place. A comprehensive study of this subject was carried out by the Health Education Studies Unit and involved tape-recording 1470 consultations in a sample of surgeries carried out by 16 doctors in south-east England (Tuckett *et al.*, 1985). Two main approaches were used to assess the health education content of a sample of these consultations.

Firstly, taking a broad definition of health education, each consultation was considered for the extent to which the doctor tried to help the patient understand the issues relating to the presenting problems. Four main topics were distinguished: diagnostic significance, treatment, prevention and social or psychological implications of the problem. Assessments were made to establish whether, during the consultation process, the doctors indicated their views on each of these topics, and when they did, whether they explained their views more fully and whether they took account of the patients' views in their explanations.

The results of this analysis showed that general practitioners' efforts to increase their patients' knowledge of health issues by providing information and explanations in their consultations were limited and unsystematic. While they stated their diagnosis and treatment advice in almost all the consultations, the GPs mentioned preventive measures in only one quarter of them and virtually never discussed social or psychological implications. A more elaborate explanation of *any* of the topics was given in only a third of the consultations and in only a third of these did the doctor try to respond to the patient's own ideas.

The second approach involved looking more specifically at the main 'lifestyle' issues which GPs identify most readily with health education: smoking, diet and alcohol consumption. Each consultation was assessed firstly in terms of the opportunities it provided for such health education and then in terms of the discussion that occurred and the advice that was given. The investigation distinguished between opportunities for *problem-related health education*, where the nature of the patient's problem itself raised one of these topics, and *non-problem-related health education*, where the doctor could take the initiative and raise such topics with the patient, independently of the main presenting problems.

The results of this analysis (Boulton and Williams, 1983) showed that a large proportion of consultations provided opportunities for problem-related education, particularly in relation to smoking. However, the vast majority of these opportunities were not used and at the most only a fifth of all the problem-related opportunities were used. Opportunities for non-problem-related health education were virtually never exploited.

The main conclusion to be drawn from this study is that the apparent interest in health education among leading figures in general practice does not seem to be reflected in the routine practice of health education among GPs in general. This conclusion is supported by other research, which also suggests that health education is not a priority for most doctors in most consultations. This would appear to be true for both 'lifestyle' topics (Fleming and Lawrence, 1981; Jamrozik and Fowler, 1982) and for more broadly defined educational issues (Boreham and Gibson, 1978; Pendleton and Bochner, 1980).

## THE STRUCTURE OF THE DOCTOR–PATIENT RELATIONSHIP

One possible explanation for the notable absence of educational exchange in consultations can be found in the structure of the doctor–patient relationship prevalent in British general practice at present.

The RCGP Reports, in emphasising the GP's role with individual patients in the consultation, also stress that the *kind* of doctor–patient relationship needed for effective health education is a more 'equal' one in which doctors help patients to help themselves. For example, the authors of the Report on psychiatric disorders recommend a counselling approach to all consultations, stating that 'Its basic purpose is to assist the individual to make his [sic] own decisions from the choices available to him' (RCGP, 1981c: 12).

The form of doctor–patient relationship which these Reports are describing appears to be a 'mutual-participation' type (Szasz and Hollender, 1956). In this type of relationship doctors provide resources such as advice, encouragement and support, which help patients to make their own decisions about how to control their health or change their health-related behaviour if they so choose. It is an equal partner relationship, although the basis of the two participants' power is different. The power of general practitioners comes from their more extensive knowledge of health and its control. The power of patients derives from the fact that they ultimately decide whether or not to follow the GP's advice.

This mutual-participation type of relationship, however, is not common in present-day general practice, at least according to empirical studies of doctors and patients (Stimson and Webb, 1975; Byrne and Long, 1976; Tuckett *et al.*, 1985). The most prevalent form of relationship is one characterised by a dominant and active doctor and a passive and dependent patient. This form of relationship naturally leads to a dominance of the perspective of the doctor over the patient. This unequal relationship is produced by the difference in the level of knowledge and expertise between doctor and patient and is perpetuated by the lack of information given by the doctor to the patient. Certainly, one of the most common reasons that patients give for dissatisfaction with doctors is the lack of information given to them about their complaints (Korsch *et al.*, 1968; Cartwright and Anderson, 1981).

Some attribute this problem to the poor communication skills of doctors which can be remedied by teaching these skills during medical training (Doyle and Ware, 1977). Others suggest that it is not sufficient to argue that doctors should be taught communication skills alone. The problem of information control in the doctor–patient relationship is tied up with issues of professional status, power and authority. A doctor's authority, it is argued, is diminished by the routine divulging of 'expert' knowledge, and information control acts as a means of prolonging uncertainty in the patient, thus maintaining professional status (Waitzkin and Stoeckle, 1972).

A further problem associated with professional status derives from the uncertainties inherent in scientific medical knowledge itself, which are perhaps most marked in the area of disease prevention. By changing the doctor–patient relationship into an equal relationship, doctors may be subjected to criticism as patients become more aware of the uncertainties in scientific medical knowledge. This may lead to increasingly critical patients, who may wish to change their general practitioners more frequently, and to increasingly reluctant doctors, who may not want to become involved in health education because of the considerable uncertainties in knowledge and the potential threat to their professional status that this entails (Black and Strong, 1982).

Clearly, the image of the doctor as health educator freely giving out information is not one which appears to have a realistic basis in empirical studies of doctor–patient relationships. However, the relationship may be tied up with the content of the consultation and it may change as a result of the shift from curative medicine to preventive medicine. Much will depend on how willing or how able both doctor and patient are to shake off their 'illness orientation'. More serious problems may arise if the present structure of doctor–patient relationships is more strongly influenced by professional identity than by the content of the consultation, since a mutual-participation type of relationship may not be conducive to the maintenance of a clearly bounded professional identity.

## DISCUSSION

The College initiatives on prevention view health education in general practice almost entirely in terms of 'advice giving' in consultations. This view is supported by empirical research, which demonstrates that GPs themselves see health education primarily as a practice-based initiative. There is a similar correspondence between the individualistic model of health conveyed in the literature on prevention in general practice and the way many GPs equate health education with advice on lifestyle. Recent innovations in consultation approaches (Pendleton *et al.*, 1984) may run the risk of reifying the consultation and conveying the view that patients' problems can be resolved by good communication alone. Clearly, there is a need to complement present initiatives and trends with approaches that are more collectivist and community based, but there are potential pitfalls and problems in simply exhorting GPs to get involved in community education programmes.

To begin with, while GPs may be acceptable sources of advice to laypersons in the context of consultations and the surgery, the extent to which this holds true if they translate their activities into the community remains unproven. Self-help groups, community action groups or community health projects may be more acceptable and effective in this context. Furthermore, community involvement would require a major paradigm shift for general practitioners: one-to-one consultation and contact with patients and their families is the *modus operandi* and main daily experience of GPs. In addition, many of the shortcomings and biases identified in the 'prevention in general practice' debate are common to medicine as a whole: the present system of selecting and training doctors, and their prevailing medical subculture, can both prevent significant changes from taking place.

Stronger arguments can be produced, however, for involving GPs in the production of co-ordinated local health policies, at a planning and developmental level. As the empirical research shows, GPs have few links with and limited knowledge of health education and preventive activity beyond the practice. One way of encouraging this approach would be to attach a *'facilitator'* to general practices. The facilitator could help GPs and other members of the primary health care team to develop links with the community, particularly with health education units as well as voluntary groups.

A more pressing and immediate concern for general practice is the discrepancy revealed by empirical research between the rhetoric of the present policy proposals and the reality of health education in the consultation. While the evidence suggests that both doctors and patients favour health education in the consultation, the amount of health education actually taking place appears to be smaller than it could be. Both doctors and patients identified barriers that limit the doctors' involvement in health education. Some of these may be overcome by changes in the organisation of general practice, but others may be more difficult given that they may involve fundamental changes in the nature of the doctor–patient relationship. For example, some doctors felt that the major barrier to health education in the consultation was the attitude of the patient, whereas some patients felt the problem lay with the attitude of the doctor. This discrepancy may provide another illustration of the likelihood of misunderstanding in the doctor–patient relationship because of the different perspective of the two parties. However, it has recently been argued (Tuckett *et al.*, 1985) that an understanding of the lay perspective is crucial for general practitioners, not just in relation to health education, but more generally in their dealings with patients. Unless this kind of change occurs, it is unlikely that they will be able to follow the policy of 'helping patients to help themselves', let alone helping people to gain greater *control* over their own health.

## BIBLIOGRAPHY

### Royal College of General Practitioners Reports

RCGP (1981a), *Health and Prevention in Primary Care, Report from General Practice 18*, London, RCGP.

RCGP (1981b), *Prevention of Arterial Disease in General Practice, Report from General Practice 19*, London, RCGP.

RCGP (1981c), *Prevention of Psychiatric Disorders in General Practice, Report from General Practice 20*, London, RCGP.

RCGP (1981d), *Family Planning—an Exercise in Preventive Medicine, Report from General Practice 21*, London, RCGP.

RCGP (1982), *Healthier Children—Thinking Prevention, Report from General Practice 22*, London, RCGP.

RCGP (1983), *Promoting Prevention, Occasional Paper 22*, London, RCGP.

### Other references

Armstrong, D. (1985), 'Space and Time in British General Practice', *Social Science & Medicine*, 20(7): 659–66.

Beattie, A. (1983), *Directions for the Development of Health Education in Relation to the Prevention of Coronary Heart Disease*, Coronary Heart Workshop at University of Kent, Canterbury.

Black, N. and Strong, P. (1982), 'Prevention: Who Needs It?' *British Medical Journal*, 285: 1543–44.

Boreham, P. and Gibson, D. (1978), 'The Informative Process in Private Medical Consultations: A Preliminary Investigation', *Social Science & Medicine*, 12: 409–16.

Boulton, M. and Williams, A. (1983), 'Health Education in the General Practice Consultation: Doctor's Advice on Diet, Alcohol and Smoking', *Health Education Journal*, 42(2): 57-63.

Boulton, M. and Williams, A. (1985), *Health Education and General Practice: General Practitioners' Perceptions of Difficulties and Constraints*, Paper given at Study Day on Health Education in General Practice, King's Fund Centre, London, 5 June.

British Medical Association (1950), *General Practice and the Training of the General Practitioner*, BMA, London.

British Medical Journal (1952), 'Report of the General Practice Steering Committee: A College of General Practitioners', *British Medical Journal*, 2: 1321.

Byrne, D. and Long, B. (1976), *Doctors Talking to Patients*, HMSO, London.

Calnan, M. (1985), *Lay Perspectives on Health, Illness and the Health Services*, Tavistock, London.

Calnan, M. and Johnson, B. (1983), 'Influencing Health Behaviour: How Significant is the General Practitioner?' *Health Education Journal*, 42(2): 34–45.

Cartwright, A. and Anderson, R. (1981), *General Practice Revisited: A Second Study of Patients and Their Doctors*, Tavistock, London.

Davies, C. (1984), 'General Practitioners and the Pull of Prevention', *Sociology of Health and Illness*, 6(3): 267–84.

Doyal, L. (1979), *The Political Economy of Health*, Pluto Press, London.

Doyle, B. and Ware, J. (1977), 'Physician Conduct and Other Factors that Affect Consumer Satisfaction with Medical Care', *Journal of Medical Education*, 52: 743–801.

Fleming, D. and Lawrence, M. (1981), 'An Evaluation of Recorded Information about Preventive Measures in 38 Practices', *Journal of the Royal College of General Practitioners*, 31: 615–20.

Graham, H. (1979), ' "Prevention and Health: Every Mothers's Business". A Comment on Child Health Policies in the 1970s', in Harris (ed.), *The Sociology of the Family: New Directions for Britain, Sociological Review Monograph 28*, University of Keele, Keele.

Graham, H. (1984), *Women, Health and the Family*, Wheatsheaf Books, Sussex.

Honigsbaum, F. (1985), 'Reconstruction of General Practice: The Failure of Reform', *British Medical Journal*, 290: 823–6.

Jacobsen, B. (1981), *The Ladykillers: Why Smoking is a Feminist Issue*, Pluto Press, London.

Jamrozik, K. and Fowler, G. (1982), 'Anti-Smoking Education in Oxfordshire General Practices', *Journal of the Royal College of General Practitioners*, 32: 179–83.

Jeffreys, M. and Sachs, H. (1983), *Rethinking General Practice: Dilemmas in Primary Medical Care*, Tavistock, London.

Korsch, B., Gozzi, E. and Francis, V. (1968), 'Gaps in Doctor–Patient Communication: Doctor–Patient Interaction and Patient Satisfaction', *Paediatrics*, 42: 855–71.

Labonte, R. and Penfold, S. (1981), 'Canadian Perspectives in Health Promotion: A Critique', *Health Education*, April 1981: 4–8.

McWhinney, I. (1964), *The Early Signs of Illness*, Pitman, London.

Pendleton, D. and Bochner, S. (1980), 'The Communication of Medical Information in General Practice Consultations as a Function of Patients' Social Class', *Social Science & Medicine*, 14a: 664–73.

Pendleton, D., Schofield, T., Tate, P. and Havelock, P. (1984), *The Consultation: An Approach to Learning and Teaching*, Oxford University Press.

Stimson, G. and Webb, B. (1975), *Going to See the Doctor*, Routledge & Kegan Paul, London.

Stott, N. and Davis, R. (1979), 'The Exceptional Potential in Each

Primary Care Consultation', *Journal of the Royal College of General Practitioners*, 29: 201–5.

Szasz, T. and Hollender, M. (1956), 'A Contribution to the Philosophy of Medicine: The Basic Models of the Doctor–Patient Relationship', *Archives of Internal Medicine*, 97: 585–92.

Townsend, P. and Davidson, N. (1982), *Inequalities in Health: The Black Report*, Penguin, Harmondsworth.

Tuckett, D., Boulton, M., Olson, C. and Williams, A. (1985), *Meetings between Experts: An Approach to Sharing Ideas in Medical Consultations*, Tavistock, London.

Waitzkin, H. and Stoeckle, J. (1972), 'The Communication of Information about Illness', *Advances in Psychosomatic Medicine*, 8: 180–215.

Watt, A. (1984), *Community Health Initiatives: Clarifying the Complexities*, Paper given at Conference on Community Health Initiatives, King's Fund Centre, London, 14 June.

Watt, A. (1985), 'Community Health Initiatives: Their Relationship to General Practice', *Journal of the Royal College of General Practitioners*.

Williams, A. and Boulton, M. (1985), *Concepts of Health Education in General Practice: The Views of Advisers and Course Organisers*, Paper given at Study Day on Health Education in General Practice, King's Fund Centre, London, 5 June.

# CHAPTER 11

# PREPREGNANCY CARE: WHOSE NEEDS COUNT?

## Sue Rodmell

The *Nursing Times* noted in 1983 that:

> prepregnancy care is something of a cottage industry . . . Much
> of the work is being done by interested individuals and it ranges
> from basic research to something as small, but significant, as a
> G.P. remembering to ask women whether they are trying to
> conceive when he [sic] prescribes any medication (*Nursing
> Times*, 15 September 1983: 239).

During the last two or three years, in discussions between health
professionals about ways of encouraging women to experience a
healthy pregnancy, the terms of prepregnancy care and preconceptual care have featured increasingly. Particularly for those
working 'in the community'—health visitors, community midwives and some general practitioners—interest has begun to focus
on the *anticipation* of pregnancy and on ways of practising health
education in this area.

In this chapter I want to take a closer look at the emergence of
prepregnancy care as a focus of interest, for community nurses
within the health service in particular, and to use this to highlight
some of the failings of conventional health education. I shall
suggest that the information presented through prepregnancy care

courses is not in itself unhelpful, but that the mode of delivery and presentation requires reassessment. The relevant questions are: What were the reasons for this new interest in health care before pregnancy? Where did it come from? What form did it take in practice? And what can be learnt from it?

## PRECONCEPTUAL COUNSELLING

To begin with it is important to make clear that my concern is not with a clinical service called preconceptual counselling. I am taking this to mean a service provided by medical practitioners in a clinical setting. Typical candidates for preconceptual counselling are women who have already experienced a problematic pregnancy, or who have a family history of genetic disorder or disability—women who are already identified as potentially or actually at risk themselves, or whose regular partner manifests fertility problems. These are patients in the conventional sense. They are treated by a specialist and can only receive this form of treatment by referral from their GP, a hospital doctor, or occasionally through self-referral (Chamberlain, 1980). Whilst clinicians offering preconceptual counselling may well incorporate the basic messages of prepregnancy care into their treatment programmes, this information is received within the context of a clinical procedure, and is therefore validated by the medical model. The treatment process is tailored to the specific needs of individuals or couples, and may involve genetic counselling, analysis of blood, urine, semen and ova (Hawkins, 1982). Infertility is a common reason for referral and recent developments in reproductive technology suggest that preconceptual counselling may become more widespread. The level of specialisation and success in treatment methods is leading to increased demand. To an extent this demand is being met through private-sector health care (for example, by *Foresight*) but this service is only available to those who can afford to pay a fee.

# PREPREGNANCY CARE

By contrast, prepregnancy care is a more generalised and broad-based intervention into the community and is practised by community nurses, particularly health visitors. Recipients are, therefore, not patients, but clients; they are seen not in a hospital clinic, but in the community, and they are unlikely to have a previous history of reproductive problems. They are, to all intents and purposes, healthy and well.

So what exactly constitutes a programme of prepregnancy care? Before we can answer this in any detail we must look at the recent history of antenatal care. For to a large extent the emergence of prepregnancy care is a predictable response to two distinct but related factors: firstly, what was seen by government bodies to be the relative failure of the antenatal services to prevent certain forms of foetal handicap; secondly, the persistent difference between the perinatal mortality rate in the United Kingdom and that of other developed countries, and of social class differentials in perinatal mortality rates within the United Kingdom itself.

## Foetal handicap

Influential research findings began to emerge in the late 1970s indicating that one of the possible causes of neural tube defects (e.g. spina bifida) and other congenital malformities may be a deficiency in vitamins and minerals in the diet of women at the time of conception (Smithells et al., 1977; Smithells et al., 1981; Wynn and Wynn, 1981; Renwick, 1982; Lawrence et al., 1983). Neural tube defects are understood to occur within twenty-eight days of conception, before a woman is aware that she is pregnant. The Wynns argued that many women, and not necessarily those with low socio-economic status, have an inadequate diet. In the early weeks of pregnancy this diet places the foetus at risk and may lead to one of the disabilities mentioned. Nutritional deficiencies have been linked to a range of outcomes, including subfertility, low birthweight and spontaneous abortion (Campbell and Gillmer, 1983). Studies have indeed revealed a strikingly high incidence of vitamin deficiency amongst certain social groups. For example, in a recent London study of 76 mothers of low socio-economic status, 95 per cent had deficiencies in vitamin B and vitamin D (Doyle *et al.*, 1982). These and other findings prompted the Medical Research Council to mount a 'random clinical trial of folic defects'—a controversial procedure involving the selection of women at risk through the previous birth of a spina bifida baby, and the division of these women into two groups, one of which is given the supplement whilst the control is not (Lawrence *et al.*, 1981).

The significance of nutrition was thus increasingly recognised in the incidence of preventable foetal handicap, and became a focus for both the statutory and voluntary sectors in their efforts to improve perinatal mortality rates. The concern of the voluntary sector was voiced by the Spastics Society, and subsequently by the Maternity Alliance with the National Council for Voluntary Organisations (Health and Handicap Group). The Spastics Society presented evidence to the *Social Services Committee on Perinatal and Neonatal Mortality* (headed by Renée Short, M.P.) to the effect that an annual figure of 'at least five thousand children are surviving with important handicaps' (DHSS, 1980: 663). There were subsequent reservations over the response to this figure which centre on the conflation by the Committee of perinatal *morbidity* with perinatal *mortality* (Chalmers, 1980; Russell, 1982). In effect the issue of the quality of life and the quantity of care was confused. This lack of clarity resulted in a series of recommendations which focused on the nature of the delivery of services to pregnant women, and also to the point at which pregnant women availed themselves of that service, rather than on ways of enabling women to achieve a nutritionally sound diet. In focusing on the quantity of care given and received by pregnant women, policy makers paid due heed to the importance of the perinatal mortality rate as a comparative measure of socio-economic progress; attention was at the same time diverted away from demands being made for a more equitable redistribution of resources towards women and children in lower socio-economic groups.

One of the criteria for measuring the socio-economic progress

## Table 1    Perinatal mortality per 1,000 live births

|  | 1960 | 1975 | % Decrease 1960–1975 | Annual % decrease 1971–5 |
|---|---|---|---|---|
| England and Wales | 33.5 | 17.9★ | 46.5† | 4.1 |
| Scotland | 38.1 | 18.5★ | 51.3† | 5.1 |
| Sweden | 26.2 | 11.1 | 57.7 | 7.3 |
| Norway | 24.0 | 14.2 | 40.8 | 5.1 |
| Denmark | 26.5 | 12.7★ | 52.1† | 5.5 |
| Finland | 25.3 | 13.9 | 45.0‡ | 5.9 |
| Netherlands | 25.6 | 14.0 | 45.3 | 4.3 |
| France | 31.8 | 19.5★★ | 38.7‡ | 4.8 |
| West Germany | 36.3 | 19.4 | 46.5 | 4.8 |

★1976, ★★1974, †1960–76, ‡1960–74

*Source*: Townsend and Davidson, 1982.

of a country is to assess its perinatal mortality rate (PMR) in relation to that of others. The PMR measures the number of stillbirths and deaths in the first week of life for every 1,000 live births. At the end of the 1970s the figures indicated that the PMR was not falling as fast in the United Kingdom as it was in other comparable countries. Interestingly, in the infant mortality rate (IMR) league table the United Kingdom was not doing very well either—slipping from 8th place in 1960 to 15th place in 1978 (Townsend and Davidson, 1982: 15). In measuring mortality rates in the first year of life, the IMR registers socio-economic standards rather than levels of hospital care and is, therefore, a more realistic measure of wider social forces.

Social class differences in perinatal and infant mortality rates were also marked, and were acknowledged by the Court Committee in 1977, when it was noted that the PMR had fallen by 45 per cent amongst the highest social classes between 1950 and 1973, but only by 34 per cent amongst the unskilled manual class (Townsend and Davidson, 1982: 70). Table 2  shows that more recently differences between social classes have not improved.

Redressing the structured inequalities which allow the IMR to remain relatively high requires more sweeping changes than rais-

Table 2    Perinatal deaths and low birthweights by
social class, England and Wales, 1981 and 1984
(legitimate births only)

| Social class | Total births | | Perinatal deaths per 1,000 live and stillbirths | | Birthweight under 2,500 gms per 100 live births | |
|---|---|---|---|---|---|---|
| | 1981 | 1984 | 1981 | 1984 | 1981 | 1984 |
| I | 41,252 | 39,640 | 8.5 | 7.1 | 5.5 | 5.5 |
| II | 122,932 | 115,180 | 9.7 | 7.9 | 4.8 | 5.5 |
| III | 260,259 | 243,090 | 11.2 | 9.0 | 5.9 | 6.25 |
| IV | 80,445 | 76,380 | 13.2 | 11.6 | 7.4 | 8.0 |
| V | 31,834 | 29,910 | 15.5 | 14.1 | 8.4 | 8.1 |
| All | 638,696 | 504,190 | 11.8 | 10.1 | 6.1 | 6.5 |

*Sources*: Birthweight statistics 1981, 1982, 1984. OPCS Monitor reference DH3 83/3 DH3 85/5 (OPCS 1983, 1985); Crown copyright 1983; 1985.

Infant and perinatal mortality 1981, 1984. OPCS Monitor reference DH3 84/2 DH3 86/1 (OPCS 1984, 1986); Crown copyright 1984; 1986.

ing technological activity in hospital labour wards. Thus, the recommendations of the Short Committee fell neatly into line with efforts to improve the PMR, whilst at the same time putting the onus on women to make sure they made use of the service provided. Subsequent health education activities were directly related to this effort, and aimed to encourage women to attend for antenatal care through a 'Baby' campaign—leaflets, posters, and a pregnancy care card—all of which adopted a patronising and trivialising tone (Kenner, 1984: 84).

There was one *legislative* change which was expected to assist women to attend for antenatal care whilst in paid work. Through the 1980 Employment Act, women were allowed to take paid time off work to attend the antenatal clinic. There were a number of loopholes in the Act which meant that women in small workplaces or in part-time work may be excluded, but the significance of this change should not be lost. Whilst there was no redistribution of resources to make the financial burden of pregnancy and childcare easier to bear, efforts were made to facilitate attendance at antenatal clinics (Daniels, 1981; Daniels, 1982; Rodmell and Smart, 1982).

The call for improvements in the delivery and outcome of health care provision for pregnant women acted as the rationale for proposals to bring forward the point of intervention by health professionals. No matter how soon women booked in for their antenatal care, this was not soon enough to prevent some problems during pregnancy. The realisation that women, and their partners, should be in their prime at the moment of conception presented something of a challenge to health educators—a challenge that is virtually impossible to meet, even with the best of intentions. Nonetheless, it was, and is, being attempted. In 1982 the Health Visitors' Association and the Royal College of Midwives issued a Joint Statement on Antenatal Preparation in which they put forward a 'vision of ideal arrangements'. Under these arrangements, health visitors were strongly recommended to 'give or inspire appropriate sessions on preparation for parenthood ... in schools and with all relevant groups within the community' (HVA/RCM, 1982). Despite, or indeed because of, this somewhat grandiose statement, prepregnancy care has remained more or less the cottage industry spotted by the *Nursing Times*. Efforts to implement programmes and courses have been sporadic and *ad hoc* because health educators have tried to mount such programmes without any clear idea of what they were and who they were for. The recommendations made by the HVA and RCM highlight many of the practical problems and ideological imperatives which underlie the call for prepregnancy care. It is to these that I now turn.

I shall argue that there is a set of inherent weaknesses in the professional demand for prepregnancy care which reproduce many of the failings of conventional health education described throughout this volume.

# THE IDEOLOGICAL BASE OF PREPREGNANCY CARE

## A typical programme

A prepregnancy care programme organised by NHS professionals may run for about 6 weeks, occupying a morning or an evening per week. It is aimed at prospective first-time parents, and may be advertised through the Family Planning clinic, Well Woman clinic or GP surgery. In many ways it typifies the 'top-down' approach to health education in the community, described by Alison Watt (Chapter 8). The need is normatively defined, with the imperative coming from the professional body through the nurse manager, and onwards to the fieldworker. It is genuinely considered to be 'a good thing', as is so much conventional health education, and practitioners initiate courses with fairly high hopes of a positive response from women in the locality.

A typical 6-week course will include advice and recommendations on:

(a) Contraceptive use—to come off the pill and change to a barrier method at least three months, and preferably five months, before trying to conceive, so that 'normal periods' will be resumed.

(b) Nutrition—changing to a 'healthy' diet, putting emphasis on wholesome, fresh and unadulterated foods, with the necessary nutrients and vitamins.

(c) Baby spacing—allowing sufficient time between pregnancies, at least one year between each.

(d) Tobacco and alcohol—stopping smoking and restricting alcohol intake to one or two glasses per week.

(e) Body maintenance—taking exercise regularly, perhaps cycling or swimming, and making sure of getting plenty of rest.

(f) Drugs—only taking medicines prescribed by a doctor, and trying ways of coping with stress other than taking tranquillisers.

All of this information is useful in certain contexts, and some of it is reasonable enough to be acted upon by a minority. As a package, however, designed to influence knowledge, attitudes and behaviour ('KAB' in health education parlance), it falls far short of a realistic programme of behavioural modification, even if one accepts that this is a reasonable goal for a health educator in the first place. Each component of a prepregnancy care programme exhibits some of the ideological imperatives of conventional health education, and as such it offers a cautionary example for those wishing to develop new methods of working.

## On behalf of others

Prepregnancy care reproduces the traditional health education message—'look after yourself'—but in this case it is not for women themselves, but for their future offspring. As has been argued in a number of recent works, women continue to act as the lynchpins of family health and welfare (Kenner, 1984; Graham, 1984; Roberts, 1985). They are constantly encouraged to keep themselves healthy in order to care for their various dependants—men, children, ageing parents. Helen Roberts points out that:

> If those who design health education leaflets are correct it is an awareness of her family commitments which is the most pressing reason why a woman should take care of her own health (Roberts, 1985: 88).

In this case, women are being advised to make sure they are fit before they have another dependent being. In encouraging a woman to look after herself before becoming pregnant, the health services and the medical profession persist in seeing her through her reproductive capacity, defining her in terms of her capacity for healthy childbearing; service provision caters to that perception with a commitment which far outweighs a commitment to the health of women in its widest sense. Women's experiences of illnesses which are not part of their reproductive capacity remain largely undocumented, as Linnie Price has shown recently in her examination of women and coronary heart disease. The factors associated with coronary heart disease—smoking, diet, exercise and hypertension—are typically identified with men's lifestyles, particularly of men in sedentary occupations. Health education efforts, however, are frequently directed at women who are asked to 'change their men to' a low-fat spread, for example. Attention is rarely paid to women's experience of coronary heart disease, despite its increasing incidence (Price, 1985). Overall, women's health resources remain disproportionately allocated to women during pregnancy and immediately after birth, and as Charmian Kenner points out, whilst Well Woman clinics focus on testing for cervical cancer and breast cancer rather than solely on pregnancy and childbirth, they fail to take account of more common health issues such as varicose veins, arthritis or migraine (Kenner, 1984: 41).

## To have and not to have

Pregnancy care programmes also manifest the tendency to present a package of advice on which only a minority can act, thus basically reinforcing the division between those who can and those who cannot, between those who have and those who have not. The danger of this elitism has been recognised by the Health Visitors' Association. In an editorial for the *Health Visitor Journal* in March 1984, June Thompson noted the middle-class involvement in prepregnancy care, and asks:

> Will it, however, remain a middle class phenomenon with the result that, in a few years time, there will still be a gap between the social classes regarding infant mortality and congenital malformation rates, only it will be attendance or otherwise at prepregnancy care clinics that will now be cited as a cause? (Thompson, 1984: 65).

There are many signs now that health educators working in the community are aware of the disparities between social groups. But there is still a tendency for elitism and patronisation to occur. There is an assumption built into prepregnancy care programmes (as indeed into most conventional health education projects), that women are ignorant about the essentials of parenting and that information should be obtained from trained health educators rather than from 'lay' sources, such as friends and relatives. A Health Education Council poster of the mid-1970s illustrates this approach by succinctly asking 'How can another woman make you pregnant?' The answer: 'Just by talking to you'. The remedy: 'friendly and accurate advice' from health professionals. The principle of traditional health education is that the *giving* of information in the form of strictures to do this and that is in itself sufficient. Once the information is made available then it is up to the receiver to make an informed choice about what to do. Built into this stricture, moreover, is a dismissal of structured inequalities in terms of the decision-making process itself. Whilst there is a recognition of class, race and age differentials in material terms, health educators rarely acknowledge that making a decision is in itself a struggle.

Take the example of diet, which features centrally in pre-pregnancy care. To expect a single woman without consistent support to make an informed choice about her diet even during her pregnancy, never mind for a year or so beforehand, is quite unrealistic. Moreover, there is much debate about the cost of a 'healthy diet'. One nutritionist argues that 'a good healthy diet need cost no more than an "average" diet' and goes on to compare two supermarket shopping baskets, one containing healthy choices and the other filled with prepackaged food. Both baskets cost the same but the healthy choices involve both a mental plan of the week's meals and considerable home preparation and cooking (Pickard, 1984: 51). In another recent work, Heather Bampfylde suggests to readers that although 'many women worry that eating well will be expensive, seasonal foods are always reasonably priced so there is no reason not to enjoy a healthy diet even on a tight budget' (Bampfylde, 1984: 32).

Countering this view is the study undertaken for the Maternity Alliance, by Lyn Durward. She showed recently that it is almost impossible for women on supplementary benefit to follow the recommendations for the daily amounts of food energy and nutrients identified by the DHSS in 1979 as essential for basic health maintenance (DHSS, 1979). Rather than estimate the cost of an 'ideal healthy diet', the Maternity Alliance study 'attempts to estimate the cost of diets currently recommended by hospital antenatal clinics and to relate this to income levels' (Durward, 1984: 4). The exercise was carried out in eight cities and the average cost of the diet was £13.87 per week, at 1984 prices. The researcher concludes that:

> For a couple on supplementary benefit expecting their first child, the woman's food would use up 28% of their income (excluding household costs) even if she were claiming free welfare milk ... a single householder will be left with only £13.10 to meet all her costs, apart from food and rent, if she is eating this diet (ibid: 14).

The recommendation to plan meals in advance, avoid food with additives and select fresh, seasonable vegetables displays an unawareness of the realities of women's lives. As Nickie Charles and Marion Kerr show in Chapter 4, it is not generally within the control of women to decide on family menus. It is the men in the family whose wishes are most often met, and most men display an intransigence over changes in regular meal provision. Moreover, for women living in hostel or bed and breakfast accommodation, the task of making 'an informed food choice' must appear a remote ideal. Some health educators have tried adopting an encouraging 'think positive' approach when faced with the undeniable lack of choice for many of their clients. For their clients, however, knowledge alone is insufficient if the means to act on it are denied. Indeed this process is detrimental to health because it paves the way for women to feel guilty and for professionals to engage in victim-blaming.

## Laying the blame

Much has been written about victim-blaming in the sociology of health and illness. An important point to make is that victim-blaming is both 'expert-defined' and 'self-defined'. Those who are made to feel inadequate may blame themselves for their failure, but victim-blaming can also take place *within* the 'failed' group.

In other words, victim-blaming acts in a doubly insidious way. It encourages those who are part of the 'failed' social group to blame themselves and each other whilst allowing those who are in control (of their own lives and those of others) to attribute blame to those whom they perceive to be 'failing'. This is not as overt and blatant as it sounds: victim-blaming is often couched in liberal, well-meaning rhetoric, but it invariably takes a white middle-class value system as the point of departure.

In prepregnancy care programmes there is much scope for victim-blaming. It is not only the difficulty in eating healthily that makes women feel inadequate. Many women, and particularly the young and vulnerable, have been praised for having the foresight to use the contraceptive pill. Now they are being told that if they want to increase their chances of producing a healthy baby they should switch to a barrier method—a *safer* contraceptive—because it is thought that the pill increases the chance of foetal abnormality, delayed fertility, poor pregnancy outcome and disturbed vitamin and mineral status in first pregnancies (Guillebaud, 1983). There are two points here. Firstly, the pill is prescribed for most women on the basis that it *is* safe and non-problematic. Only when pregnancy becomes a probability do health professionals switch to a position in which it is considered unsafe and undesirable. Secondly, this recommendation is made by health educators who fail to acknowledge fully the realities of established sexual practice in which the pill forms a routine part. To encourage women to use the pill and then to point out its problems and suggest a less pleasing alternative (the sheath or cap) is a guilt-inducing practice. To the receiver of this information, which is being given in a quite straightforward manner by an expert in such matters, the fact that they cannot take apparently simple advice makes for feelings of resentment, inadequacy and self-blame.

Similarly, one of the strongest recommendations made during pregnancy is to stop smoking. There is increasing evidence that it may inhibit foetal growth and result in a small baby. Women are put under tremendous pressure to stop smoking at this time, again, not for themselves but on behalf of another. Yet there is also evidence that an impending increase to the family adds to the stresses and strains which already exist (Graham, 1984). Women have described how smoking acts as a brake on other less socially acceptable forms of behaviour, such as hitting the children. As Jacobsen notes in her analysis of women and smoking:

> Smoking acts as a safety valve, an alternative to letting off steam. Women smoke not to accompany expressions of frustration and anxiety, *but instead of expressing those feelings* (Jacobsen, 1981: 32, her emphasis).

The pressure not to smoke may also be coupled with a recommendation not to take tranquillisers or other artificial stress reducers, but to find other ways of coping such as using relaxation techniques, or engaging in gentle sporting activities (Pickard, 1984). Again, these coping strategies are often quite inappropriate for women with one or more under-fives, living in an inner city area without play facilities and on a small income.

In one way or another, all the recommendations listed earlier are difficult to act on under conditions of powerlessness, poverty and disadvantage. Bearing in mind that it is the concern of policy makers and service providers to improve the rate of congenital disability and class differentials in mortality rates amongst the new born, it is ill advised and insensitive to suggest to precisely those most vulnerable a course of action they cannot follow.

I have argued that traditional health education imposes knowledge in a way which separates the 'expert' from the 'receiver' and also separates those who can from those who cannot. Typically, health educators construct a package of information and advice which they perceive, from their position as health professionals, to be necessary to improve people's health. As one health educator put if after organising a prepregnancy care course:

> I have devised a short course of talks for schoolgirls on this subject. It has proved so acceptable that I am sure that similar courses for teenagers, *at all levels of intelligence*, will do nothing but good (Johnson, 1984: 4, my emphasis).

The presentation of this package is made in the genuine belief

217

that the educator has something to offer the client. This belief gives rise to extraordinary situations in which health professionals will doggedly pursue an attempt to 'reach the community' when it should be quite clear that their efforts are being wasted. From various conversations with health visitors during teaching sessions and at meetings across the country, it appears that two situations can occur. In the first, a decision is taken to promote prepregnancy care by holding courses at local health centres. After several months, the health visitors report back to their sector that these courses are meeting with a very poor response. It is felt that lack of publicity may be the cause, and they recommend that the health education unit be approached to 'do a poster for each clinic'. The point to be made here is that once an initiative has been set in motion it proves extremely difficult for health professionals to admit that they got it wrong. Instead, there is a persistence in attempts to 'reach' the people who professionals are convinced need their advice. Hence a renewed effort through extra publicity. This approach is not confined to health educators. It is common across the health and social services, whenever an issue arises in which professionals believe that they can 'help the community', and huge amounts of energy are invested with philanthropic zeal, often for very little reward (for a more detailed analysis of the limitations of this type of approach see Alison Watt, Chapter 8).

In the second, the health educator has to confront the problem of attracting the 'right' target group. Efforts to publicise pre-pregnancy care courses through the leaflet and poster method seem doomed to fail. The most common approach is to select those practices which are considered least appropriate for a 'fit' parent and draw attention to them—smoking, drinking and over-eating—images of undesirability are conjured up and presented to the local populace in the hope that some of them will be suitably chastised into attending a course. 'Do you want a healthy baby?' 'Are you fit to be a parent?' Such questioning serves as a reminder to the more seasoned political activist that attitudes die hard.

This value-laden approach still prevails and is reproduced unthinkingly with what are claimed to be the best of intentions, in no way insensitive or offensive. The notion of fitness, becoming a proper parent, is very evident in prepregnancy care. 'Getting fit for pregnancy' has become the catch-all phrase which deserves some scrutiny. What is really meant by 'fitness' in this context? To be fit means to be healthy. But it also means to be appropriate for, to qualify for, to become competent for the task at hand. In order to become fit for pregnancy, prospective parents must qualify, they must show that they can indeed shoulder the responsibility. To become 'fit', certain individuals will be advised to drop their bad habits and replace them with good ones and it is the role of the health educator to instruct them in this.

## IMPLICATIONS FOR HEALTH EDUCATION

Conventional health education seeks to improve the adequacy of individuals in their negotiations with themselves and others. This adequacy is primarily defined through the dominant social order, and health education is concerned to make the 'inadequate' into acceptable social citizens. This is not imposed in a repressive or coercive way, but rather by using methods which are arguably more insidious by being well-meaning. It is through this ostensibly benign benevolence that health professionals act to reinforce conservative ideologies. That these ideologies are antithetical to health, that they exacerbate structural inequalities and perpetuate dependency on 'expert' definitions and imperatives, only serves to indicate their insidiousness.

By using prepregnancy care as an example, I have attempted to highlight the reproduction of many of the traditional failings apparent in conventional health education. As a feasible course of action, it is possible that prepregnancy care programmes will run out of steam. They are inherently problematic in their own terms, since those responsible for implementing them cannot identify a target group (all heterosexually active men and women?); nor can they get over the difference between prepregnancy care and antenatal care. Both labels are confusing for women, and even the British Medical Association could only offer 3 pages of information on the 'pre' part of the reproductive process, compared with 24 pages on actually being pregnant, in their new publication *Getting Fit for a Baby* (BMA, 1984).

What is instructive about this account of a health education programme is the alacrity with which it has been taken up and delivered to the community. There are two reasons why pre-pregnancy care offers a particular insight for more radical practitioners. Firstly, on the surface, it all seems a good idea. The argument goes—if health professionals know that certain situations have a part to play in causing certain outcomes, then surely it is their duty to transmit that infomation. Let us be clear about this. Much of the information contained in prepregnancy care *is* useful and should be shared. But it is not appropriate to single out certain sections of the population (even if this were to be possible) and impart this information to them because there has been a professional assessment that they 'need' it. Rather a redistribution of resources is required so that those in the greatest need have their needs met in a realistic fashion. Such a redistribution of resources is not easily realised, without a major shift in the level of intervention. That women and men are living in unhealthy environments is acknowledged by policy makers and health professionals, but simply to invest more funding into hospital and community care systems, in this case during pregnancy and childbirth, will not tackle the causes of unhealthy environments. Nor can it ultimately improve the outcome of pregnancies which become problematic. There seems little point in raising clinical input and medical intervention when many women come from, and go back to, lives of unrelenting poverty.

The identification of a prepregnant population which may 'need' health education leads to the second point at issue. For health professionals to voice a need for prepregnancy care is to implicitly acknowledge the basically *unhealthy* state of many women. It is precisely in an unhealthy society that there is a need for a special effort to 'get fit' for pregnancy. In a post-industrial society with highly advanced medical technology it is an indictment of the inequitable distribution of resources that doctors should find it necessary to warn women to be prepared for the *risks* which may be ahead:

These tragedies cannot always be prevented whatever care and precautions the mother-to-be and the medical staff take, but many are the result of things the mother has done without realising the dangers.... we now know that many would not happen at all if all intending mothers-to-be could be persuaded to get themselves fit before starting their baby (BMA, 1984: 3).

## REFERENCES

Bampfylde, H. (1984), *Countdown to a Healthy Baby*, Collins, London.

British Medical Association (1984), *Getting Fit for a Baby*, BMA, London.

Campbell, D. M. and Gillmer, M. D. G. (eds) (1983), *Nutrition in Pregnancy*, Royal College of Obstetricians and Gynaecologists, London.

Chalmers, I. (1980), 'Intensive or Extensive Care in Perinatal Health Services', *Community Medicine*, 2: 279–281.

Chamberlain, G. (1980), 'The Prepregnancy Care Clinic', *British Medical Journal*, 5 July: 29–30.

Daniels, W. (1981), *Maternity Rights: The Experience of Women*, Policy Studies Institute, London.

Daniels, W. (1982), *Maternity Rights: The Experience of Employers*, Policy Studies Institute, London.

DHSS (1979), *Recommended Daily Amounts of Food Energy and Nutrients for Groups of People in the United Kingdom*, Report on Health and Social Subjects, 15, HMSO, London.

DHSS (1980), *Second Report from the Social Services Committee: Perinatal/Neonatal Mortality*, HC 663–1 (1979–1980), HMSO, London.

Doyle, W., Crawford, M. A., Laurance, B. M. and Drury, P. (1982), 'Dietary Survey during Pregnancy in a Low Socio-economic Group', *Human Nutrition: Applied Nutrition*, 36A: 95–106.

Durward, L. (1984), *Poverty in Pregnancy: The Cost of an Adequate Diet for Expectant Mothers*, Maternity Alliance, London.

Graham, H. (1984), *Women, Health and the Family*, Wheatsheaf Books, London.

Guillebaud, J. (1983), *The Pill*, Oxford University Press, 2nd Edition, London.

Hawkins, D. F. (ed.) (1982), 'Prepregnancy Counselling in Obstetrics', *Clinics in Obstetrics and Gynaecology*, 9: 12–25.

Health Visitors Association/Royal College of Midwives, *Joint Statement on Antenatal Preparation*, 22 June 1982.

Jacobsen, B. (1981), *The Ladykillers: Why Smoking is a Feminist Issue*, Pluto Press, London.

Johnson, E. (1984), 'Preconceptual Care: A Course for Schoolgirls', *Midwife, Health Visitor and Community Nurse*, April 1984.

Kenner, C. (1984), *No Time for Women*, Pandora, London.

Lawrence, K. M. *et al.* (1981) 'Double-blind Randomised Controlled Trial of Folate Treatment before Conception to Prevent Recurrence of Neural Tube Defects', *British Medical Journal*, 282: 1509–11.

Lawrence, K. M., Campbell, H. and James, N. E. (1983), 'The Role of Improvement in the Maternal Diet and Preconception Folic Acid Supplementation in the Prevention of Neural Tube Defects', in Dobbing, J. (ed.), *Prevention of Spina Bifida and other Neural Tube Defects*, Academic Press, London.

Pickard, B. (1984), *Eating Well for a Healthy Pregnancy*, Sheldon Press, London.

Price, L. (1985), *The Social Construction of a Disease Category: Coronary Heart Disease and the Invisible Woman*, Paper to the London Medical Sociology Group, 16 October.

Renwick, J. H. (1982), 'Food and Malformation', *The Practitioner*, 226: 1479–1953.

Roberts, H. (1985), *The Patient Patients*, Pandora, London.

Rodmell, S. and Smart, L. (1982), *Pregnant at Work*, Open University, Milton Keynes.

Russell, J. (1982), 'Perinatal Mortality: The Current Debate', *Sociology of Health and Illness*, 4: 302–19.

Smithells, R. W. *et al.* (1977), 'Maternal Nutrition in Early Pregnancy', *British Journal of Nutrition*, 38: 497–506.

Smithells, R. W. *et al.* (1981), 'Possible Prevention of Neural Tube Defects by Preconception Vitamin Supplementation', *Archives of Diseases of Childhood*, 56: 911–18.

Thompson, J. (1984), 'Prepregnancy Care—Essential for All?' *Health Visitor*, 57: 64.

Townsend, P. and Davidson, N. (1982), *Inequalities in Health: The Black Report*, Penguin, Harmondsworth.

Wynn, M. and Wynn, A. (1981), *The Prevention of Handicap of Early Pregnancy Origin*, Foundation for Education and Research in Childbearing, London.

# BIBLIOGRAPHY

Acheson, D. (1985), Interviewed on *World at One*, Radio 4, 27 August 1985.

Advisory Council on the Misuse of Drugs (1984), *Prevention*, London.

Ahmed, A. and Pearson, M. (1985). *Directory of Maternity Initiatives for Black and Ethnic Minority Women*, Maternity Alliance, London.

Armstrong, D. (1985), 'Space and time in British General Practice', *Social Science and Medicine*, 20(7): 659–66.

Armstrong, P. and Nichols, T. (1973), *Safety or Profit*, Falling Wall Press, Bristol.

Atkinson, P., Dingwall, R. and Murcott, A. (eds), *Prospects for the National Health Service*, Croom Helm, London: 89–101.

Bampfylde, H. (1984), *Countdown to a Healthy Baby*, Collins, London.

Banton, M. and Harwood, J. (1975), *The Race Concept*, David & Charles, Newton Abbot.

Banton, R., Clifford, P. and Frosh, S. *et al.* (1985), *The Politics of Mental Health*, Macmillan, London.

BBC (1982), Seminar on the *Evaluation of Play It Safe!*, London.

Beardmore, J. A. and Vlijm, L. (eds) (1984), *Health Education and School Biology*, European Communities Biologists Association, London.

Beattie, A. (1983), *Directions for the Development of Health Education in Relation to the Prevention of Coronary Heart Disease*, Coronary Heart Workshop at University of Kent, Canterbury.

Beattie, A. (1984), 'Health Education and the Science Teacher: Invitation to a Debate', *Education and Health*, 2(1).

Ben-Tovim, G. and Gabriel, J. (1982), 'The Sociology of Race—Time to Change Course?' in Ohri, A. *et al.*, *Community Work and Racism*, Routledge & Kegan Paul, London.

Black, N. and Strong, P. (1982), 'Prevention: Who Needs It?' *British Medical Journal* 285: 1543–4.

Black, D. (1985), 'Community Development and Health Issues', *Radical Health Promotion*, 1, Spring 1985.

224

Black, J. (1985), 'Child Health in Ethnic Minorities: the Difficulties of Living in Britain', *British Medical Journal*, 290: 579–654.

Blaxter, M. (1976), 'Social Class and Health Inequalities' in Carter, C. O. and Peel, J. (eds), *Equalities and Inequalities in Health*, Academic Press, London.

Booth, R. T. (1983), 'Machinery Hazards' in Ridley, J. R., *Safety at Work*, Butterworths, London.

Boreham, P. and Gibson, D. (1978), 'The Informative Process in Private Medical Consultations: A Preliminary Investigation', *Social Science and Medicine*, 12: 409–16.

Boulton, M. and Williams, A. (1983), 'Health education in the general practice consultation: doctor's advice on diet, alcohol and smoking', *Health Education Journal*, 42(2): 57–63.

Boulton, M. and Williams, A. (1985), *Health Education and General Practice: General Practitioners' Perceptions of Difficulties and Constraints*, Paper given at Study Day on Health Education in General Practice, King's Fund Centre, London, 5 June 1985.

Brennan, T. (1981), *Political Education and Democracy*, Cambridge University Press, Cambridge.

British Medical Association (1950), *General Practice and the Training of the General Practitioner*, BMA, London.

British Medical Association (1984), *Getting Fit for a Baby*, BMA, London.

British Medical Journal (1952), 'Report of the General Practice Steering Committee: A College of General Practitioners', *British Medical Journal*, 2: 1321.

Brown, C. (1984), *Black and White Britain*, Heinemann, London.

Brown, E. R. and Margo, G. E. (1978), 'Health Education: Can the Reformers Be Reformed?', *International Journal of Health Services*, 8(1): 3–26.

Byrne, D. and Long, B. (1976), *Doctors Talking to Patients*, HMSO, London.

Calnan, M. and Johnson, B. (1983), 'Influencing Health Behaviour: How Significant is the General Practitioner?' *Health Education Journal*, 42(2): 34–45.

Calnan, M. (1985), *Lay Perspectives on Health, Illness and the Health Services*, Tavistock, London.

Calouste Gulbenkian Foundation (1978), *Community Work and Social Change*, the report of a study group on training, Longman, London.

Cameron, D. and Jones, I. (1985), 'An Epidemiological and Sociological Analysis of the Use of Alcohol, Tobacco and Other Drugs of Solace', *Community Medicine*, 7: 1, February.

Campbell, D. M. and Gillmer, M. D. G. (eds) (1983), *Nutrition in Pregnancy*, Royal College of Obstetricians and Gynaecologists, London.

Carter, C. O. and Peel, J. (eds), *Equalities and Inequalities in Health*, Academic Press, London.

Cartwright, A. and Anderson, R. (1981), *General Practice Revisited: A Second Study of Patients and Their Doctors*, Tavistock, London.

225

Catford, D. (1983), 'Developing A Strategy For Health Promotion', unpublished seminar paper.

Catford, J. and Nutbeam, D. (1984) 'Towards a Definition of Health Education and Health Promotion', *Health Education Journal*, 43: 2 and 3.

Centre for Contemporary Cultural Studies (1982), *The Empire Strikes Back*, Hutchinson, London.

Chalmers, I. (1980), 'Intensive or Extensive Care in Perinatal Health Services', *Community Medicine*, 2: 279–81.

Chamberlain, G. (1980), 'The Prepregnancy Care Clinic', *British Medical Journal* 5 July 1980: 29–30.

Charles, N. and Kerr, M. (1984), *Attitudes towards Feeding and Nutrition of Young Children*, Report to the Health Education Council, London.

Cochrane, M. and Fisher, B. (1983), 'Peckham Health Project: Raising Health Consciousness', *Community Development Journal*, 18(2).

Cooper, M. H. (1975), *Rationing Health Care*, Croom Helm, London.

Cornwell, J. and Gordon, P. (eds) (1984), *An Experiment in Advocacy*, The Hackney Multi Ethnic Women's Health Project, King's Fund, London.

Cowley, J. and Catford, J. (1983), 'Developing A Strategy for Health Promotion', *Health Education Journal*, 43.

Craig, M. (1981), *The Office Workers' Survival Handbook*, BSSRS, London.

Crawford, R. (1977), 'You are Dangerous to Your Health: The Ideology and Politics of Victim Blaming', *International Journal of Health Services*, 7(4).

Crawford, A. (1984), 'Training is Legally Required by Health and Safety at Work Act', *Health and Safety at Work*, August 1984: 59.

Crick, B. and Porter, A. (eds) (1978), *Political Education and Political Literacy*, Cambridge University Press, Cambridge.

Culyer, A. J. (1976), *Need and the National Health Service*, Martin Robertson, London.

Daniels, W. (1981), *Maternity Rights: The Experience of Women*, Policy Studies Institute, London.

Daniels, W. (1982), *Maternity Rights: The Experience of Employers*, Policy Studies Institute, London.

Davies, C. (1984), 'General Practitioners and the Pull of Prevention', *Sociology of Health and Illness*, 6(3): 267–84.

Dennis, J. *et al.* (1982), 'Health Promotion in the Reorganised National Health Service', *The Health Services*, 26 November 1982.

De Jong, G. A. and Rutten, F. F. H. (1983), 'Justice and Health for All', *Social Science and Medicine*, 17(16): 1085–95.

DES (1985), *Science 5–16: A Statement of Policy*, London.

DHSS (1976), *Prevention and Health: Everybody's Business*, HMSO, London.

DHSS (1979), Recommended Daily Amounts of Food Energy and Nutrients for Groups of People in the United Kingdom, *Report on Health and Social Subjects*, 15, HMSO, London.

DHSS (1980), *Rickets and Osteomalacia*, Report of a Working Party on

Fortification of Food with Vitamin D, Committee on Medical Aspects of Food Policy, HMSO, London.

DHSS (1980), *Second Report from the Social Services Committee: Perinatal Neonatal Mortality HC 663–1 (1979–1980)*, HMSO, London.

DHSS (1981), *Civilian Doctor Statistics*, HMSO, London.

DHSS (1981), *Prevention and Health: Avoiding Heart Attacks*, HMSO, London.

DHSS (1984), *Diet and Cardiovascular Disease*, Report of the Committee on Medical Aspects of Food Policy (COMA), HMSO, London.

Djang, T. K. (1942), *Factory Inspection in Great Britain*, Allen & Unwin, London.

Dobash, R. and Dobash R. (1980), *Violence Against Wives*, Open Books, London.

Dobbing, J. (ed), *Prevention of Spina Bifida and other Neural Tube Defects*, Academic Press, London.

Donovan J. (1984), 'Ethnicity and Health: A Review', *Social Science and Medicine*, 19(7): 663–70.

Doyal, L. and Pennell, I. (1979), *The Political Economy of Health*, Pluto Press, London.

Doyal, L. *et al.* (1980), *Migrant Workers in the National Health Service*, A Report to the SSRC, Departments of Sociology, Polytechnic of North London.

Doyle, B. and Ware, J. (1977), 'Physician Conduct and Other Factors that Affect Consumer Satisfaction with Medical Care'. *Journal of Medical Education*, 52: 743–801.

Doyle, W., Crawford, M. A., Laurance, B. M. and Drury, P. (1982), 'Dietary Survey during Pregnancy in a Low Socio-economic Group' *Human Nutrition: Applied Nutrition*, 36A: 95–106.

Draper, P., Best, G. and Dennis, J. (1976), *Health, Money and the National Health Service*, Unit for the Study of Health Policy, Guy's Hospital, London.

Draper, P., Griffiths, J., Dennis, J. and Popay, J. (1980), 'Three Types of Health Education', *British Medical Journal*, 16 August 1980, 493–5.

Drennan, V. (1985), *Working in a Different Way*, Paddington and North Kennington Health Education Unit, London.

Durward, L. (1984), *Poverty in Pregnancy: The Cost of an Adequate Diet for Expectant Mothers*, Maternity Alliance, London.

Ellis, R. (1983), 'The Way to a Man's Heart: Food in the Violent Home' in Murcott, A. (ed), *The Sociology of Food and Eating*, Gower, London.

Entwistle, H. (1971), *Political Education in a Democracy*, Routledge & Kegan Paul, London.

Evening Post (1983), *Seat Belt Saves Lives*: 50, 8 July 1983, Bristol.

Farrant, W. and Russell, J; (1985), *Health Education Council Publications: A Case Study in the Production, Distribution and Use of Health Information*, Health Education Publications Project, University of London Institute of Education, London.

Farrant, W. and Russell, J. (1986), *Beating Heart Disease: A Case Study in the Production of Health Education Council Publications*, Bedford Way Paper, University of London Institute of Education, London.

FEU (1982), *Basic Skills*, FEU, London.

Figlio, K. (1971), 'The Historiography of Scientific Medicine: An Invitation to the Human Sciences', *Comparative Studies in Society and History*, 19: 262–86.

Fisher, B. H. and Cochrane, M. (1982), 'Peckham Health Project, Raising Health Consciousness', *British Medical Journal*, 284: 1843–5, 19 June 1982.

Fleming, D. and Lawrence, M. (1981), 'An Evaluation of Recorded Information about Prevention Measures in 38 Practices', *Journal of the Royal College of General Practitioners*, 31: 615–20.

Foster, A. (1983), Personal communications and 'Hearing Protection and the Role of Health Education' in *Occupational Health*, 35(4): 155–9.

Freudenberg, N. (1978), 'Shaping the Future of Health Education From Behaviour Change to Social Change', *Health Education Monographs*, 6(4).

Friedson, E. (1972), *Profession of Medicine, A Study of the Sociology of Applied Knowledge*, Dodd Mead, New York.

Gatherer, A., Parfitt, J., Porter, E. and Vessey, M. (1979), *Is Health Education Effective?*, HEC, London.

Gill, F. (1985), 'Prevention: The Name of the Game', *Occupational Health*, 137(9): 400–2.

Glass, B. (1943), *Genes and the Man*, Columbia University Press, New York.

GLC Economic Policy Group (1984), *Food For a Great City: GLC Strategy Towards London's Food Sector*. Strategy Document No. 335, GLC, London.

Goel, K. M. *et al.* (1976). 'Florid and Subclinical Rickets among Immigrant Children in Glasgow', *Lancet*, i: 1141–5.

Goel, K. M. *et al.* (1981), 'Reduced Prevalance of Rickets in Asian Children in Glasgow', *Lancet*, ii: 405–7.

Gordon, P. (1983), 'Medicine, Racism and Immigration Control', *Critical Social Policy*, 7: 6–20.

Gough, I. (1979), *Political Economy of the Welfare State*, Macmillan, London.

Graham, H. (1979), 'Prevention and Health: Every Mother's Business, A Comment on Child Health Policies in the 1970s' in *The Sociology of the Family*, Sociological Review Monograph, 28, University of Keele.

Graham, H. (1984), *Women, Health and the Family*, Wheatsheaf Books, London.

Gray, M. and Blythe, M. (1979), 'The Failure of Health Education', in Atkinson, P., Dingwall, R. and Murcott, A. (eds), *Prospects for the National Health Service*, Croom Helm, London: 89–101.

Greater Manchester Food Policy Unit (1984), *A Food Policy in Greater Manchester*, Manchester Polytechnic.

Green S. D. R. *et al.* (1979), 'Surma and blood lead concentrations', *Public Health*, London, 93: 371–6.

Greenwich District Health Authority (1984), *Draft Annual Programme 1984*.

Greenwood, S. (1984), *The Effects of Toxic Substances and Physical Agents on the Reproductive System*, Sheffield TGWU pamphlet.

Greetham, J. (1982), 'Community Development through a Community Health Project' in *Association of Community Workers: Talking Point*, No. 42.

Guillebaud, J. (1983), *The Pill*, Oxford University Press, 2nd Edition, London.

Gulbenkian Foundation (1968), *Community Work and Social Change*, Longman, London.

Hale, A. (1983), 'Is Safety Training Worthwhile?' in *Proceeding of the Annual Conference of the Aston Health and Safety Society*, Birmingham.

Harrington, J. M. (ed.), *Recent Advances in Occupational Health*, 2, Churchill Livingstone, Edinburgh.

Harris, C. (ed.), *The Sociology of the Family: New Directions for Britain*, *Sociological Review Monograph 28*, University of Keele.

Harris, P., Blackmore, E. *et al.* (1978), *Evaluation of Community Work*, London Council of Social Service.

Harrison, P. (1983), *Inside the Inner City: Life Under the Cutting Edge*, Penguin, Harmondsworth.

Hart, C. *Child Care in General Practice*, 2nd edn, Churchill Livingstone, London.

Hawkins, D. F. (ed.) (1982), 'Prepregnancy Counselling in Obstetrics', *Clinics in Obstetrics and Gynaecology*, 9: 12–25.

Haywood, S. C. (1985), 'An Essay in the Government of Health; Griffiths or Status Quo?' *Social Policy and Administration*, 19(1).

Health and Safety Commission (1984), Consultative Document, *Control of Substances Hazardous to Health* HSE, London.

Health and Safety Executive, *Manufacturing Industry Reports 1977–83*, HMSO, London.

Health Education Council (1978), *Annual Report, 1977/78*, HEC, London.

Health Education Council (1979), *Annual Report, 1978/9*, HEC, London.

Health Education Council (1983a), *Programmes for 1983–4, HEC, London.*

Health Education Council (1983b), *Health Education News*, January/February 1983, London.

Health Education Council (1983), *Health Education in the Workplace: A Discussion Document*, Health Education Council, London.

Health Education Council (1984), *Annual Report, 1983–4*, HEC, London.

Health Education Council (1985a), Personal communication.

Health Education Council (1985b), *Health Education Council launches biggest Health Promotion Campaign*, Press Release, HEC, London.

Health Visitors Association/Royal College of Midwives, *Joint Statement on Antenatal Preparation*, 22 June 1982.

Henderson, P. and Thomas, D. (1980), *Skills in Neighbourhood Work*, Allen & Unwin, London.

Henley, A. (1979), *Asian Patients at Hospital and at Home*, Pitman Medical Library, London.

Higgins, J., Deakin, N., Edwards, J. *et al.* (1983), *Government and Urban Poverty*, Basil Blackwell, Oxford.

Hirayama, T. (1981), 'Non-smoking Wives of Heavy Smokers Have a Higher Risk of Lung Cancer', *British Medical Journal*, 282: 183–5, 17 January 1981.

Honigsbaum, F. (1985), 'Reconstruction of General Practice: The Failure of Reform', *British Medical Journal*, 290: 823–6.

Jacobsen, B. (1981), *The Ladykillers: Why Smoking is a Feminist Issue*, Pluto Press, London.

Jamrozik, K. and Fowler, G. (1982), 'Anti-Smoking Education in Oxfordshire General Practices', *Journal of the Royal College of General Practitioners*, 32: 179–83.

Jeffreys, M. and Sachs, H. (1983), *Rethinking General Practice: Dilemmas in Primary Medical Care*, Tavistock, London.

Jenkins, R. (1971), *The Production of Knowledge at the Institute of Race Relations*, Independent Labour Party Publications.

Jewson, N. (1976), 'The Disappearance of the Sick Man from Medical Cosmology 1778–1870', *Sociology*, 10: 225–44.

Johnson, E. (1984), 'Preconceptual Care: A Course for Schoolgirls', *Midwife, Health Visitor and Community Nurse*, April 1984.

Jones, L. (1985), *An Overview of the Health Promotion Function*, Bradford and Airedale Health Education Unit.

Kennedy, I. (1981), *The Unmasking of Medicine*, Allen & Unwin, London.

Kensington, Chelsea and Westminster Health Education Department (1982), unpublished paper given at the BBC, 'Evaluation of Play It Safe!', seminar, London.

Kenner, C. (1985), *No Time for Women*, Pandora, London.

Kerrison, S. (1985), 'Are Your Feet Killing You?' in *Age Well Ideas Pack*, Health Education Council, London.

Khan, V. S. (ed) (1979), *Minority Families in Britain: Support and Stress*, Macmillan, London.

Korsch, B., Gozzi, E. and Francis, V. (1968) 'Gaps in Doctor-Patient Communication: Doctor-Patient Interaction and Patient Satisfaction', *Paediatrics*, 42: 855–71.

Labonte, R. and Penfold, S. (1981), 'Canadian Perspectives in Health Promotion: A Critique', *Health Education*, April 1981: 4–8.

Lawrence, E. (1981), 'White Sociology, Black Struggle', *Multiracial Education*, 9: 3–17.

Lawrence, E. (1982), 'In the Abundance of Water the Fool is Thirsty', in Centre for Contemporary Cultural Studies, *The Empire Strikes Back*, Hutchinson, London.

Lawrence, K. M. *et al.* (1981), 'Double-blind Randomised Controlled Trial of Folate Treatment before Conception to Prevent Recurrence of Neural Tube Defects', *British Medical Journal*, 282: 1509–11.

Lawrence, K. M., Campbell, H. and James, N. E. (1983), 'The Role of Improvement in the Maternal Diet and Preconception Folic Acid Supplementation in the Prevention of Neural Tube Defects' in Dobbing, J. (ed.), *Prevention of Spina Bifida and other Neural Tube Defects*, Academic Press, London.

Lawton, D. (1980), *The Politics of the School Curriculum*, Routledge & Kegan Paul, London.

Leftwich, A. (1983), *Redefining Politics*, Methuen, London.

Legge, T. (1934), *Industrial Maladies*, Oxford University Press, London.

Lee, J. (ed.), *A Guide to School Health Education*, The Health Education Council, London.

Lewontin, R. C. (1972), 'Appointment of Human Diversity', *Evolution Biology*, 6: 381–98.

London-Edinburgh Weekend Return Group (1980), *In and Against the State*, Pluto Press, London.

Lorber, J. (1984), *Women Physicians Careers, Status and Power*, Tavistock, London.

MacIntyre, A. (1973), 'On the Essential Contestability of Some Social Concepts', *Ethics*, 84.

McEwan, J. (1982), 'Health Education at Work' in Ward Gardner, A., *Current Approaches to Occupational Health*, 2, Wright PSG, Bristol.

McEwan, J. (1984), 'Health Education in the Workplace' in Harrington, J. M. (ed.), *Recent Advances in Occupational Health*, 2, Churchill Livingstone, Edinburgh.

McNaught, A. (1985), 'Black and Ethnic Minority Women and the National Health Service', *Radical Community Medicine*, Spring 1985.

McWhinney, I. (1964), *The Early Signs of Illness*, Pitman, London.

Meade, K. and Thorpe, P. (1985), 'Running a Pensioners' Health Course', in *Age Well Ideas Pack*, Health Education Council, London.

Miliband, R. (1969), 'The Process of Legitimation—II', *The State in Capitalist Society*, Weidenfeld & Nicolson, London.

Mitchell, J. (1982), 'Looking After Ourselves: An Individual Approach?', *Royal Society of Health*, 4.

Mitchell, J. (1984), *What is to be done about Illness and Health?* Penguin, Harmondsworth.

Montagu, A. (ed.) (1964), *The Concept of Race*, Collier-Macmillan, Toronto.

Murcott, A. (1982), 'On the Social Significance of the "Cooked Dinner" in South Wales', *Social Science Information*, 21, 4/5: 677–96.

Naidoo, J. (1984), 'Evaluation of Play It Safe! in Bristol', unpublished paper.

National Advisory Committee on Nutrition Education (1983), *A Discussion Paper on Proposals for Nutritional Guidelines for Health Education in Britain*, HEC, London.

Nordenfelt, L. (1983), 'The Concepts of Health and Disease', a paper presented to the Society for Social Medicine, 27th Annual Meeting.

Nutbeam, D. (1984), 'Health Education in the National Health Service: the Differing Perceptions of Community Physicians and Health Education Officers', *Health Education Journal:* 43.

Office of Health Economics (1981), *Accidents in Childhood*, Briefing No. 17, OHE, London.

Ohri, A. *et al.*, *Community Work and Racism*, Routledge & Kegan Paul, London.

O'Keefe, D. (1981), 'Labour in Vain: Truancy, Industry and the School Curriculum', in Flew, A. *et al.* (eds), *The Pied Pipers of Education*, The Social Affairs Unit, London: 29–42.

Parmar, P. (1981), 'Young Asian Women: Critique of the Pathological Approach', *Multiracial education*, 9: 9–29.

Pearson, M. (ed.) (1985) *Racial Equality and Good Practice—Maternity Care*, National Extension College, Cambridge.

Pendleton, D. and Bochner, S. (1980), 'The Communication of Medical Information in General Practice Consultations as a Function of Patients' Social Class', *Social Science and Medicine*, 14a: 664–73.

Pendleton, D., Schofield, T., Tate, P. and Havelock, P. (1984), *The Consultation: An Approach to Learning and Teaching*, Oxford University Press.

Peto, R., letter, *New Statesman*, 10 October 1982.

Pickard, B. (1984), *Eating Well for a Healthy Pregnancy*, Sheldon Press, London.

Player, D. (1984), *Health Promotion—Reality or Illusion?* Paper given to a conference organised by the Regional Health Promotion Group, South East Thames Regional Health Authority.

Price, L. (1985), *The Social Construction of a Disease Category: Coronary Heart Disease and the Invisible Woman*, Paper to the London Medical Sociology Group, 16 October 1985.

Pring, R. (1984), *Personal and Social Education in the Curriculum*, Hodder & Stoughton, London.

Pollock, M. (1982), 'The Care of Immigrant Children' in C. Hart, *Child Care in General Practice*, 2nd edn, Churchill Livingstone, London.

Rack, P. and Rowell, V. R. (1979), 'Health Education Needs of a Minority Ethnic Group', *Jnl. Inst. of Health Education*, 17(4): 3–18.

Rack, P. (1982), *Race, Culture and Mental Disorder*, Tavistock, London.

Radical Health Promotion Collective (1985), *Radical Health Promotion*, No. 1.

RCGP (1981a), *Health and Prevention in Primary Care, Report from General Practice 18*, RCGP, London.

RCGP (1981b), *Prevention of Arterial Disease in General Practice, Report from General Practice 19*, RCGP, London.

RCGP (1981c), *Prevention of Psychiatric Disorders in General Practice, Report from General Practice 20*, RCGP, London.

RCGP (1981d), *Family Planning—An Exercise in Preventive Medicine, Report from General Practice 21*, RCGP, London.

RCGP (1982), *Healthier Children—Thinking Prevention, Report from General Practice 22*, RCGP, London.

RCGP (1983), *Promoting Prevention, Occasional Paper 22*, RCGP, London.

Reid, D. (1982), 'Into the Mainstream', in Lee, J. (ed.), *A Guide to School Health Education*, The Health Education Council, London.

Renwick, J. H. (1982), 'Food and Malformation', *The Practitioner*, 226: 1479–1953.

Roberts, H. (1985), *The Patient Patients: Women and their Doctors*, Pandora, London.

Rodmell, S. and Smart, L. (1982), *Pregnant at Work*, Open University, Milton Keynes.

Rosenthall, H. (1983), 'Neighbourhood Health Projects—Some New Approaches to Health and Community Work in Parts of the United Kingdom', *Community Development Journal*, 18(2).

Ruddock, J. (1983), *The Humanities Curriculum Project: An Introduction*, Centre for Applied Research in Education, Norwich.

Russell, J. (1982), 'Perinatal Mortality: The Current Debate', *Sociology of Health and Illness*, 4: 302–19.

Rutter, M. (1979), *Fifteen Thousand Hours*, Open Books, London.

Schilling, R. S. F. and Hall, S. A. (1973), 'Prevention of Occupational Disease' in R. S. F. Schilling (ed.), *Occupational Health Practice*, Butterworths, London.

Schilling, R. S. F. (ed.), *Occupational Health Practice*, Butterworths, London.

Schools Council (1976), *Health Education in Secondary Schools*, Evans/Methuen, London.

Schools Council (1981), *The New Approach to Social Studies*, Schools Council Publications, London.

Schools Council Health Education Project (1982), *Health Education 13–18*, Introductory Handbook, Forbes, London.

Scott-Samuel, A. (1979), 'The Politics of Health', *Community Medicine*, 1: 123–6

Scott-Samuel, A. (1982), 'Community Development Outreach and Health Association Community Workers', *Talking Point*, 33, March 1982.

Scruton, R. (1983), 'Why Politicians are All Against Real Education', in *The Times*, 4 January 1983.

Scruton, R., Ellis-Jones, A. and O'Keefe, D. (1985), *Education and Indoctrination*, Education Research Centre, Harrow.

Seedhouse, D. (1985), 'The Need for a Philosophy of Health', *Explorations in Medicine*, 1 (2), and forthcoming papers in 2(1) and (2).

Sheffield Health Care Strategy Group (1984), *Food and Health*, Sheffield Conference Report.

Silverstone R. and Williams, A. (1982), *The Role and Educational Needs of Occupational Health Nurses*, Royal College of Nursing, London.

Smith, A. (ed.), *Recent Advances in Community Medicine 3*, Churchill Livingstone, London, pp. 11–37.

Smith, J. (1981), 'The Idea of Health: A Philosophical Inquiry', *Advances in Nursing Science*, 3: 43–50.

Smithells, R. W. *et al.* (1977), 'Maternal Nutrition in Early Pregnancy', *British Journal of Nutrition*, 38: 497–506.

Smithells, R. W. *et al.* (1981), 'Possible Prevention of Neural Tube Defects by Preconception Vitamin Supplementation', *Archives of Diseases of Childhood*, 56: 911–18.

Somerville, G. (1985), *Community Development in Health: Addressing the Confusions,* King's Fund, London.

South-East Thames Regional Health Authority (1984), *Outline Regional Strategy 1985–94.*

Stellman, J. M. and Daum, S. M. (1973), *Work is Dangerous to Your Health,* Vintage, New York.

Stimson, G. and Webb, B. (1975), *Going to See the Doctor,* Routledge & Kegan Paul, London.

Stock, S. (1980), 'The Perils of Second-Hand Smoking', *New Scientist,* 10–13, 2 October 1980.

Stockwell Health Project (1981), *Mawby Brough—A Health Centre for the Community?* Stockwell, London.

Stott, N. and Davis, R. (1979), 'The Exceptional Potential in Each Primary Care Consultation'. *Journal of the Royal College of General Practioners,* 29: 201–5.

Strong, P. M. (1983), 'Three Social Science Approaches to the Concept of Health', a paper presented to the Society for Social Medicine, 27th Annual Meeting.

Sutherland, I. (ed.), *Health Education: Perspectives and Choices,* Allen & Unwin, London.

Szasz, T. and Hollender, M. (1956), 'A Contribution to the Philosophy of Medicine: The Basic Models of the Doctor–Patient Relationship', *Archives of Internal Medicine,* 97: 585–92.

Thompson, J. (1984), 'Prepregnancy Care—Essential For All?' *Health Visitor,* 57: 64.

Tones, K. (1983), 'Health Education and Health Promotion: New Directions', *Journal of the Institution of Health Education,* 21: 121–31.

Tones, K. (1984), *Health Promotion: a new panacea?* Paper presented at the Annual Health Education Officers' seminar, March 1984.

Townsend, P. and Davidson, N. (1982), *Inequalities in Health: The Black Report,* Penguin, Harmondsworth.

Trichopoulos, D. *et al.* (1981), 'Lung Cancer and Passive Smoking', *Int. J. Cancer,* 27(1): 1–4.

Tuckett, D. (1979), 'Choices for Health Education: a Sociological View' in Sutherland, I. (ed.), *Health Education: Perspectives and Choices,* Allen & Unwin, London.

Tuckett, D., Boulton, M., Olson, C. and Williams, A. (1985), *Meetings between Experts: An Approach to Sharing Ideas in Medical Consultations,* Tavistock, London.

Tudor-Hart, H. (1971), 'The Inverse Care Law', *Lancet,* 1: 405–12.

Turner, M. and Gray, J. (eds) (1982), *Implementation of Dietary Guidelines: Obstacles and Opportunities,* British Nutrition Foundation, London.

Ungoed-Thomas, J. R. (1972), *Our School,* Longman, London.

Unit for the Study of Health Policy (1979), *Rethinking Community Medicine,* Guy's Hospital Medical School, London.

Vuori, H. (1980), 'The Medical Model and the Objectives of Health Education', *International Journal of Health Education* 23(1).

Waitzkin, H. and Stoeckle, J. (1972). 'The Communication of Information about Illness', *Advances in Psychosomatic Medicine*, 8: 180–215.

Ward Gardner, *Current Approaches to Occupational Health*, 2, Wright PSG, Bristol.

Watt, A. (1984), 'Community Health Initiatives: Clarifying the Complexities', Paper given at Conference on Community Health Initiatives, King's Fund Centre, 14 June 1984.

Watt, A. (1986), 'Community Health Initiatives and Their Relationship to General Practice: The Views of Advisers and Course Organisers', *Journal of Royal College of General Practitioners*, 36: 72–3.

Watterson, A. E. (1984), 'Occupational Medicine and Medical Ethics', *Journal of Society of Occupational Medicine*, 34(2): 41–5.

Webb, P. (1982), 'Ethnic Health Project 1979/1980', *Royal Society of Health Journal*, 1: 29–34.

Williams, H. and Sibert, J. R. (1983), 'Medicine and the Steering Column', *British Medical Journal*, 286: 1893.

Williams, A. and Boulton, M. (1985), *Concepts of Health Education in General Practice: The Views of Advisers and Course Organisers*, Paper given at Study Day on Health Education in General Practice, King's Fund Centre, London, 5 June 1985.

Willis, P. (1977), *Learning to Labour*, Saxon House, Farnborough.

World Health Organisation (1982), *The Concepts and Principles of Health Promotion*. Summary Report of the Working Group. WHO Regional Office for Europe, Copenhagen.

World Health Organisation (1984), *Health Promotion—A Discussion Document on the Concepts and Principles*, Supplement to Europe News, No. 3, WHO Regional Office for Europe, Copenhagen.

World Health Organisation (1985), 'Health Promotion', *Journal of the Institute of Health Education*, 23, No. 1.

Wood, P. H. and Badley, E. M. (1985), 'The Origins of Ill Health' in Smith, A. (ed.), *Recent Advances in Community Medicine 3*, Churchill Livingstone, London.

Wright, H. (1981), *Swallow It Whole*, New Statesman Report, 4.

Wynn, M. and Wynn, A. (1981), *The Prevention of Handicap of Early Pregnancy Origin*, Foundation for Education and Research in Childbearing, London.

# INDEX

236